17 Reasons Your Company
Is Not Investment Grade
& What To Do About It

17 REAS⚙NS

Your Company Is NOT INVESTMENT GRADE & *What To Do About It*

PRACTICAL ADVICE FROM AN
OWNER & INVESTMENT BANKER

ZANE TARENCE

WITH KATHRYN BOLINSKE

OWN PURPOSE PUBLISHING

The views expressed herein reflect the experience and opinion of the author, Zane Tarence. The material contained in this book could include technical inaccuracies or typographical errors. The author may periodically change the information in this or subsequent versions of this book. All opinions and estimates contained in this book constitute the author's judgment as of the date of publication, are subject to change without notice and are provided in good faith but without legal responsibility.

Information, examples and opinions contained in this book are for educational purposes only. This book is not an offer to sell or buy any securities, is not an offer to provide investment banking services, and does not contain any advice or recommendations related to investment. Similarly, this book does not provide accounting, tax or legal advice and does not provide any estimates of value. The general recommendations made by the author have been made in good faith but may not be applicable or suitable for all companies; company owners must make their own decisions as necessary using their own independent professionals and based upon their specific situations and objectives.

If you have questions about how any of the 17 Reasons affect your company, please contact Founders Advisors at 205.949.2043 or *https://foundersib.com/contact-us/*

For information contact:
Own Purpose Publishing
2400 5th Avenue South, Suite 100
Birmingham, AL 35233
205.949.2043

For information regarding bulk sales, please visit 17-reasons.com.
First Edition
Designed by Gryphon Design
Denver, Colorado

ISBN 978-1-7346732-0-3

Dedication

Dad, I dedicate this book to you. You taught me to value the truth and pursue it regardless of cost. I inherited my love of discussing and teaching concepts that matter from you. You have modeled for me what it is to be a real man, and your "blessing" is one of my greatest treasures.

Table of Contents

Introduction

Had you asked me what buyers were looking for when I sold my first business, I would have told you they seek innovative and patented products perfectly suited for a massive blue ocean of opportunity. Had you asked me the same question after I sold my second company, I might have said that investors can't resist young, bright, talented teams of software entrepreneurs whose software is gaining traction in coveted niche markets.

But two deals cannot tell the whole story, so for the past two decades as an investor and investment banker, I've kept close track of the reasons investors pulled the trigger on deals and reasons they walked away. Although there are occasional outliers, I've focused on tracking the reasons institutional investors highlight as most important to them.

The list of 17 Reasons I share in this book comes from three sources: (1) my experience as a company founder, owner, investor and seller; (2) my observations during the over 80 institutional transactions I've led for owners/founders; and (3) the relationships I've forged with more talented owners, investors, dealmakers and mentors than I can count.

Owning, investing in, selling and representing companies taught me a great deal, but people—talented, motivated and generous people—taught me, by example, *how to create investment-grade companies.*

Founding owners have shown me again and again that they are willing to do what it takes to change and grow—despite the risk. That willingness makes me optimistic that the ideas I share in this book won't die once you turn the last page and that you will take value-creating action.

In the course of bringing a deal to market, I typically pitch the investment thesis we develop for each client to over 100 buyers. Over the past 20 years, many of the most successful and active middle-market investors (both private equity and strategic buyers) have shared their critiques and have answered my questions about the characteristics they value in their acquisition targets, pain they expect their acquisitions to alleviate and opportunities they hope to exploit.

Perhaps most importantly, my mentors have played a huge role in this book. You'll find insights from several of them in these pages, and I am sharing their insights with you in the same way they have mentored me: candidly—sometimes painfully so.

A mentor is a little like a surgeon, parent, spouse or spiritual advisor: In trying to help you, they may temporarily hurt you. A mentor's constructive advice may sting a bit or cut to the bone, but if you take it in and act on it, you will be better: a better owner, CEO, partner, parent and/or person. For as long as it takes you to read this book, I hope you'll consider me to be a mentor.

And I can't help but be candid. If my style is off-putting, this may not be the book for you. If you are looking for the secret to making money or the five simple things you need to do to flip your business, I assure you that this book is not for you. If, however, like me, you prefer the truth to comfort, growth to stagnation and actionable ideas to theoretical concepts, we're going to get along.

If you don't plan to sell all or part of your business or raise capital anytime soon, please don't assume that there's nothing in this book for you. Similarly, if you intend to transition your business to family members or employees, you can't afford to dismiss these 17 Reasons. In the process of creating an investment-grade company, you create a business that's simply better to own and operate and is strong enough to support acquiring and integrating other companies.

Obviously, my definition of "investment grade" is quite different from the one rating agencies use to assign a level of creditworthiness to a corporate or municipal bond. To them "investment grade" indicates a high to medium rating and a relatively low risk of default.

When I refer to investment-grade companies, I mean privately owned companies that generate more cash flow and attract top talent, great customers and willing lenders. Owners of these companies enjoy the peace of mind and confidence that come from knowing they are excellent stewards, who drive enterprise value every day. And if the day comes when these owners choose to purchase or roll up additional companies, they will be able to use the stock of their investment-grade companies as highly valuable currency.

Think of this book as an executive physical for your business: a systematic examination to determine whether you are building enterprise value or just treading water. The shivering executive in the cotton gown, lying vulnerably on that cold metal table, is your business and, by extension, you.

I've been on that examination table. While wearing that ill-fitting gown, I've scanned the room for sharp objects and tried to play it cool. I know from experience that neither the table nor the gown is comfortable, but both allow the unfettered access to every nook and cranny that clinicians need in order to accurately diagnose.

Are you ready to submit your business to that level of scrutiny? If you are, let me make the first cut, I mean, offer the first big chunk of advice:

You will pay a very high price for ignoring the 17 Reasons.

How high? Ignore these Reasons and you will not be able to sell your equity. To anyone. Ignore them and you will destroy value in your business. It may be a slow death, but as "Gil" learned, death is inevitable.

Since the day we'd graduated from Auburn 25 years ago, Gil and I had only run into each other at our fifth reunion. There I learned that he'd created a data security consulting business after retiring as a colonel from the Air Force. When he invited me to lunch recently, I admit it: I put it off. I suspected that he wanted to recruit me to some nonprofit board or to work on a reunion, and I knew I'd have to turn him down. I was swamped.

When I first saw Gil at lunch, I experienced the usual "Who is this old guy?" reaction that happens when the person in front of me looks nothing like the person I remember from years ago. But in Gil's case, I was concerned; at rest, his face was almost a grimace.

After we ordered, I flat out asked, "Gil, is something wrong?"

"Wrong?" Gil stalled. "Not wrong. I'm just tired. I feel as if I've been on the road nonstop since I left the Air Force 10 years ago. The business that I expected to fill me up is draining every drop of energy I have."

"Is there something I can do?" I asked, secretly hoping that I hadn't left myself wide open for becoming the chairman of the next reunion.

"Actually, there is," Gil admitted. "I want to get out—sell to someone who appreciates what I've built and has the energy to keep it going. The fire in my belly is gone."

"Bullet dodged," I thought. Well, I had dodged the reunion-planning bullet, but I would ultimately have to deliver some tough news to Gil.

By the time we finished lunch, Gil had agreed to send me a list of items for my team to analyze (i.e.,

three years of financials, detailed customer data, growth strategy, compensation figures and an organi-
zational chart).

My team and I quickly learned that Gil's business:
• Had been highly profitable for over 10 years.
• Included some high-profile clients on its customer roster.
• Had provided Gil and his team with nice incomes.

So far, so good. But as our 17 Reasons Assessment™[1] continued, we found that Gil's company:
• Lacked recurring revenue.
• Had operating systems, but not scalable ones.
• Depended entirely on its principals—not processes—for sales and marketing. Gil and one of his part-
ners were generating all new business from their personal relationships.

In short, we determined that there was no real transferable (or equity) value in Gil's core business. Gil
had built a nice lifestyle business but had not kept his eye on the goal of building a business that would
have value when he was ready to "hang up the cleats." Since he'd never kept up with the merger and buy-
out activity in his industry, he didn't know what influenced larger firms to purchase niche consultancies
like his. He'd been so focused on his day-to-day operations that he was completely unaware of what it
would take to be exit ready and even where to find the most likely buyers.

Gil's lack of "situational awareness" meant that his firm was not prepared for an exit. As a result, his
company and team were stranded.

But let's imagine that you ignore these Reasons and are still so spectacularly lucky that an investor buys your
company. In that case, there will be some cash, but not nearly the amount you could have made had you paid
attention to the 17 Reasons.

Public companies build their market capitalization by driving the value of their stock. They can check
their stock tickers all day every day to track changes in value. I want you to think of the 17 Reasons as your
stock ticker. As you improve your company's performance related to each of the 17 Reasons, you build an
investment-grade company and increase value for all of your stakeholders, whether you plan to sell your company or simply want to work in a place that's more interesting, profitable and fun.

In almost every chapter, I've used case studies to illustrate various topics. While these studies are based on
past experiences, all of the people, companies and data are completely fictional. At the end of every chapter,
you'll find questions to help you assess your company's performance in each of the 17 Reasons. You will also
find practical suggestions that you can implement immediately or assign to your management team.

Of course, assessing performance begins with asking the hard questions about your own company, but it does
not occur in a vacuum. You must compare your company's performance to your competitors'. What matters
to investors is how you stack up against industry competitors of similar size, not how you compare to all other
companies in your industry and beyond. We have created the 17 Reasons Assessment™ to help you assess your
performance. You can find a summary of the Assessment on page 243 and can access it at *17-reasons.com.*

When you finish this book, you will know how to create an enduring, sustainable enterprise that is worthy of
institutional investment, whether you seek investment or not. An investment-grade company delivers tangible
value to you, your family, team and all stakeholders while you own it and when you leave it. In the process, you

may rediscover the reasons you work as hard as you do in your business. If you know who you are and why you are in business, you "Own on Purpose." You have clarity about your values, and you know what you want to accomplish and how you will do it.

Once you act based on the information in this book—even taking small steps in the right direction—perhaps you will start firing customers who act in a way that is not consistent with how you treat your people. Maybe you will stop apologizing for how much you charge. I know you will sleep better simply because you know who you are and why you are in business. When we trust our core values, when we listen to our guts, and when we deliver on our promises, we not only sleep better, *we are better.*

If you are ready, put on your gown, get on the examination table and let's get started.

You can't go back and change the beginning,
but you can start where you are
and change the ending.

C.S. Lewis, 1898-1963
Author and theologian

Your Company Lacks Recurring Revenue, So Cash Flow Is Unpredictable.

GET CREATIVE AND DISCIPLINED. DEVELOP RECURRING REVENUE STREAMS, AND LEAVE THE ONE-TIME REVENUE EVENTS TO YOUR COMPETITORS.

"At the beginning of this seminar, you said that there's no real significance to the order of your 17 Reasons but that you had to put one Reason at the top of the list. You chose recurring revenue. Why?" That question came from the owner of a manufacturing company who had been silent during my entire four-hour presentation.

Up to that point, I thought I'd lost this guy, so maybe it was enthusiasm or perhaps relief that prompted a response that completely contradicted what I'd said at the start of my presentation. "Predictable revenue is the number one driver of company value and the indispensable element of investment-grade, salable companies," I started. "Quality cash flow streams are the lifeblood of the increasing, enhancing, optimizing, scaling, measuring, organizing, planning and protecting that go into every one of the other 16 Reasons." As long as I was contradicting myself, I decided to bring it home. "Recurring revenue is the optimal form of cash flow, and without it you risk your ability to reap a significant return on a lifetime investment of time, effort and cash." Had there been a microphone in the room, I just might have dropped it.

Investors pay close attention to a company's top-line revenue characteristics as recorded on its income statement. Revenue generated from

The purpose of the 17 Reasons is to show you how to create an enterprise worthy of institutional investment–one that delivers value to you, your family, team and all stakeholders.

one-time sales is NOT the same as revenue that comes from a stream of expected periodic sales. One (or more) high-quality revenue stream is the fuel that powers well-oiled, high-performance, investment-grade companies, and the most attractive characteristic of a revenue stream is that it is recurring

FIG. 1.1 The Revenue Continuum

NOTE: There is a slight, but important, difference between the verbs *reoccur* and *recur*. Revenue streams that reoccur repeat at least one time but not necessarily again. Revenue streams that recur repeat many times.

One-Time Revenue Example: A commercial contractor builds a bridge for a state Department of Transportation.

Reoccurring Revenue Examples:
- Loyal customers buy cars from a favorite dealership. When they replace those cars (and assuming others do not influence their choice of dealership) those customers will likely return and buy another car.
- A manufacturer of bulldozer parts can reasonably predict when customers will need replacement parts based on mean time between failures (MTBF) data and customer usage patterns.

Recurring Revenue Example: A company subscribes to a mission critical Software as a Service (SaaS) application, paying a monthly or annual contracted amount to utilize the application. Because the application is mission critical, recurring revenue is stable and highly predictable.

If you own a project-based services business, are a manufacturer, are a product reseller or operate under another business model that you think does not lend itself to typical forms of recurring revenue (i.e., long-term contracts, consumables and subscriptions), you are not off the recurring revenue hook! Don't skip or dismiss this chapter. I know, based on long experience, that nearly every business has the potential to generate at least one recurring revenue stream. You can use your data to logically recategorize *one-time* revenue as *reoccurring* and to recategorize *reoccurring* revenue as *recurring*. Each upgrade brings with it a higher valuation. Yes, the impact that recurring revenue has on business value varies by industry, business model and market segment, but *the reasons that buyers are willing to pay more for companies with established recurring revenue streams apply across the board*. Those reasons are predictability, risk minimization and growth.

THE REASONS INVESTORS AND OWNERS LOVE RECURRING REVENUE

I talk to institutional investors and strategic buyers all day every day, and one of the first questions both groups ask about buy-side targets is, "What percentage of their revenue is recurring?"

Recurring revenue makes a business more appealing to buyers for five great reasons:

1. It is predictable.
2. It decreases a buyer's risk.
3. It creates value for owners.
4. It is a launchpad for future growth.
5. It has a compounding effect on growth rates.

No wonder buyers love recurring revenue! But so do most owners. Recurring revenue makes cash flow predictable and keeps you from having to start from scratch every year. In short, it adds significant long-term value.

Once you identify the recurring streams of revenue in your company, you can devote your efforts and resources to improving those that are most valuable. You can reallocate time, energy, people and investments to enhancing existing or creating new and better-performing streams. Just as you fire customers who can never be satisfied, so too should you work to phase out unprofitable, small or difficult revenue channels.

Recurring Revenue Is Predictable.

By definition, recurring revenue is predictable. It is revenue that can be reasonably expected to occur at a given time based on historical data or other factors. Predictability enables you, as an owner, to quantify the amount of income you will receive from your customers each month or year. Since future potential buyers can do the same, recurring revenue mitigates the risk of purchasing your company.

Companies with predictable revenue can gauge how many customers will renew their memberships, subscriptions, licenses, contracts, etc., and/or how much they will spend next month or year. Grocery stores offer reward card programs and incentivize their customers to continue to patronize their stores instead of a competitor's. Special discounts, fuel points and other benefits keep customers coming back. Repeat customers create a predictable revenue stream as they spend their reoccurring grocery budget at a grocery store. Companies with strong brands generate predictable revenue by creating repeat customers, and they can use data to prove this (reoccurring) revenue reality.

Recurring revenue is a valuable subset of predictable revenue because it is based on a *contractual arrangement* or payment schedule. For example, Salesforce offers customers its customer relationship management (CRM) product based on a contractual arrangement that requires monthly payments.

Recurring Revenue Decreases A Buyer's Risk.

Sophisticated buyers are risk averse because their world—private company investing—is a dangerous one. Acquiring companies involves the exchange of very large sums of money that can disappear if buyers miscalculate risk. Those losses affect real people (CEOs, corporate development and business unit executives in the case of strategic buyers, or partners in the case of financial buyers) who can lose their jobs, reputations and companies. (For a summary of the characteristics of strategic and other types of buyers, please see Figure 2.2 on page 19.)

One way that buyers minimize risk is to demand that companies illustrate the predictability of revenue and, by proxy, cash flow. These illustrations also help lenders to become more comfortable, which is critical to buyers' Leveraged Buy Out (LBO) models. Buyers then reward sellers with higher enterprise values and better deal structures.

Recurring Revenue Creates Value For Owners.

Reducing a buyer's risk is an important feature of recurring revenue, but there's another more immediate benefit. It creates value for you as a seller. And we're not talking about marginal increases. Recurring revenue creates *significant* increases in value. For example, quality software companies that can demonstrate recurring revenue (SaaS models) average a 5x to 7x TTM (Trailing Twelve Months) *revenue multiple* in today's market. Compare this to a 2x to 3x revenue multiple for software companies that sell one-time license agreements with annual maintenance contracts. Essentially, recurring revenue more than doubles the value of software companies. Obviously, other characteristics of the revenue streams matter (e.g., gross margin, retention rate, size, market share, health and defensibility), but the recurring nature of the revenue is the primary reason investors attribute value.

Recurring Revenue Is A Launchpad for Growth.

In addition to reducing a buyer's risk, predictable streams of revenue, especially ones with strong customer retention rates, will:

1. Facilitate an organization's ability to grow quickly and start each year where it left off (instead of at ground zero).
2. Offer a buyer reliable "pickup" or room to grow.

While you own your company, highly predictable revenue allows you to focus your time and resources on acquiring new customers rather than on maintaining your existing base.

Recurring Revenue Has A Compounding Effect On Growth Rates.

As the following examples will illustrate, the effect that recurring revenue has on growth is almost magical. What other word can describe the fact that if you have recurring sources of revenue and your competitor does not, you can add the same number of new customers (at the same dollar value) as your competitor and your revenues will grow rapidly while your competitor's remain flat? "Compounding" may be the right word for recurring revenue, but "magic" describes its effect perfectly.

RECURRING REVENUE IN ACTION

Predictability, decreased risk, increased value, growth stimulation and the compounding effect are five great results of recurring revenue. Let's see how recurring revenue affected two fictional companies, Johnny Company and Sally, Inc.

Johnny Company

Johnny Applesauce worked exceptionally hard to build and grow Johnny Company, a software company that sells enterprise resource planning (ERP) software to the food processing and distributing industry. Over the past 10 years, he increased the number of customers to 100 companies. In the past 12 months, he onboarded 16 companies that each paid the $250,000 one-time licensing fee and 10 percent installation fee to implement this enterprise software solution.

Johnny Company also provides ongoing maintenance and support services to clients for approximately $1,300 per month. Company engineers occasionally assist clients with specific projects/customizations. Johnny has kept the software up to date while reducing the cost of implementation, which has resulted in an impressive 25 percent net margin. With $5 million in revenue and $1.25 million in net income, there is a strong chance that Johnny can sell Johnny Company. At age 45, Johnny is still young enough to want to take his company to the next level but old and wise enough to want to do so on someone else's dime. He approached us to help find a majority buyout partner/investor.

Sally, Inc.

Sally Salad operates in the same market niche as Johnny Applesauce, and for five years her company,

Sally, Inc., has offered a similarly viable software solution for food processors and distributors. Sally has focused specifically on young companies in the industry, particularly those that have a hard time paying the $250,000 upfront costs associated with Johnny's software. Instead, Sally's team installs, implements and services the software for $5,000 per month. The standard two-year contract term is subject to renewal. Sally, Inc. has a roster of happy customers, and every year it signs up new clients.

Like Johnny Company, Sally Inc. offers consulting and project-based services to customers. Sally and her team have kept expenses low and have a similar 25 percent margin. As a result of sales efforts and hard work, Sally's customer roster includes 75 companies paying $5,000 per month to use Sally's ERP package. This model results in similar annual financial metrics: $4.95 million in revenue per year and $1.24 million in net income. Sally is thinking about the next phase of her life and begins the process of selling her company.

While these companies have many similarities—same industry software solution, financial profile and track record of increasing the number of customers each year—you might be surprised to learn that the valuation for each company is *significantly* different. What differentiates the two? Simply put, it's predictability and quality of revenue.

WE INTERRUPT THIS CHAPTER TO DRIVE HOME A CRITICAL MESSAGE: ALL REVENUE IS NOT EQUAL.

Investors evaluate several characteristics to assess the strength of a revenue stream. Clearly, recurring revenue and the predictability it brings is the foundational value driver, but investors also use five additional metrics:

1. **Provable.** During pre-close due diligence will a third-party auditor find your revenue stream predictions to be as accurate as you claim?
2. **High Margin.** Does the revenue stream contribute positively to gross profit at as high a margin as possible?
3. **Growth.** Is the stream stagnant or growing? Flat revenues warn buyers that there isn't much room left to grow the business or that competitors are gaining.
4. **Sticky.** Is it difficult for customers to replace your service or product and migrate to a competitor? Is the switching cost to choose one of your competitors high? How often do customers use your product or service? Is your product or service a "must have" or a "nice to have"?
5. **Scalable.** Does the revenue stream position you to upsell and deepen the relationships you have with your customers? Does the contribution margin increase as you do more business with a client? (Contribution margin is a product or service price minus all associated variable costs, resulting in the incremental profit earned.) Growing contribution margins demonstrate operating leverage, and that excites buyers/investors.

Many buyers or investors value a company using a sum-of-the-parts method. You may be familiar with this concept as it applies to assigning different values to a company's divisions. The idea as it applies to revenue streams is the same: buyers and investors ascribe different valuations to different revenue streams. For example, let's assume that Johnny and Sally receive offers to buy their companies based on a sum-of-the-parts valuation method.

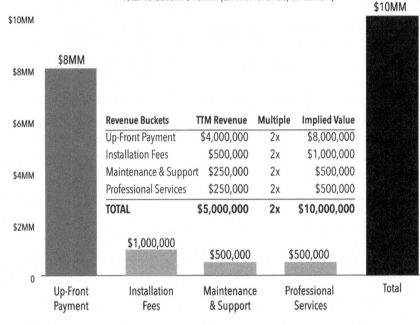

FIG. 1.2 Johnny Company

Total Valuation: $10MM (2x TTM revenue, 8x EBITDA)

Revenue Buckets	TTM Revenue	Multiple	Implied Value
Up-Front Payment	$4,000,000	2x	$8,000,000
Installation Fees	$500,000	2x	$1,000,000
Maintenance & Support	$250,000	2x	$500,000
Professional Services	$250,000	2x	$500,000
TOTAL	**$5,000,000**	**2x**	**$10,000,000**

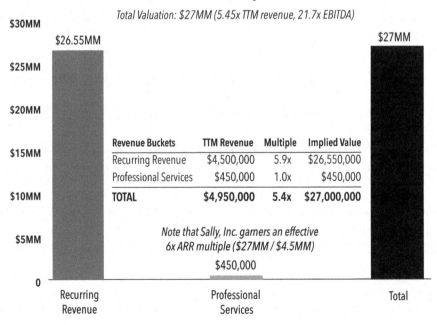

FIG. 1.3 Sally, Inc.

Total Valuation: $27MM (5.45x TTM revenue, 21.7x EBITDA)

Revenue Buckets	TTM Revenue	Multiple	Implied Value
Recurring Revenue	$4,500,000	5.9x	$26,550,000
Professional Services	$450,000	1.0x	$450,000
TOTAL	**$4,950,000**	**5.4x**	**$27,000,000**

*Note that Sally, Inc. garners an effective
6x ARR multiple ($27MM / $4.5MM)*

As Figures 1.2 and 1.3 illustrate, the sum-of-the-parts-based valuation method assigns a drastically higher value to Sally, Inc. than it does to Johnny Company. This difference is due to the revenue model each company uses. Sally's monthly revenue from her customers is predictable ($5,000 per month for at least two years), while Johnny's customers pay the entire cost up front and likely will not need new software for several years. The buyer places a 5.4 revenue multiple on Sally's revenue streams and a 2 multiple on Johnny's revenue. While Johnny Company's support services generate recurring revenue (monthly), that revenue is not contractual; therefore, buyers assign it a 2 multiple. Sally, Inc.'s valuation is considerably higher.

As part of the evaluation of various revenue streams, buyers also assess the likelihood of retaining each stream by assigning it a discount rate, and they judge the strength of the stream based on various characteristics. Revenue sources with stable and predictable streams have a lower discount rate than do project-based streams that require a continual fight for new business.

Thanks to her contracted revenue, if Sally maintains a 98 percent retention rate with customers whose contracts are up for renewal and adds only 10 new customers each year, she can reach over $7 million in revenue by the end of Year 5.

This recurring revenue example highlights two additional factors:

1. Price Elasticity. The assumption is that more people will buy Sally's software because it is initially cheaper than Johnny's. Sally's lower price model theoretically increases the market size, or number of possible customers. Sally, Inc. is positioned to grow faster because Sally expanded the size of her market.

2. Adoption Of New Business Model. Sally's subscription-based model of delivery was only possible because changes in technology, payment methods, distribution channels and customer preferences make software functionality "subscribe-able." Rapid technological changes allow new entrants and increased competition. Sally kept up with market changes and adjusted her business model to protect her competitive position.

A Note About Customer Retention Or Low Churn Rates

The rate of new customer growth is very important, but renewal rates are equally critical to driving enterprise value. A high renewal rate is evidence of low churn. ("Churn" refers to customers rolling off your service or subscription.) At a recent Silicon Y'all event[2], a presenter highlighted the criticality of renewals in any recurring revenue business model and how they reflect the overall health/quality of a company. He argued that renewals are:

1. One of the only metrics that affect growth and profitability.
2. One of the best measures of customer satisfaction. Customers "vote with their wallets," and happier customers are easier to upsell.
3. A strong indicator of product quality and product-market fit.
4. A good indicator of a company's competitive position. For example, if an increasing number of the customers who do not renew their subscriptions or make repeat purchases choose a particular competitor, it could indicate that your value proposition is weakening in the market.
5. Evidence of a moat protecting the company.

In today's market, high retention rates give buyers as much comfort as contracts. Retention is such a strong indicator of health because it demonstrates: (1) how important your product is to your customers, (2) that you stand up well against competitors, and (3) that you have a stellar product-market fit. Buyers typically tell me they can quickly size up a company more from this one metric than from any other indicator.

> The absence of recurring revenue jeopardizes your company's ability to excite investors and support enterprise value, and it signals that your connection to your customers is not as strong as it could be.

Repeat customers create the most basic form of predictable revenue. But what about the retail or service companies that sell more commoditized items? When a gallon of milk at Kroger isn't different than one from Publix, how can these companies be sticky with their customers?

If customers have great experiences at one grocery store and feel valued, they're less likely to incur the tangible and intangible switching costs of leaving the store they view as "theirs." Commodity businesses like these can use rewards programs and other methods of tracking individual consumers to produce powerful data regarding the frequency and size of the repeating revenue. Buyers value these metrics and data, and companies that track customer behavior (in order to identify their most valuable, repeat customers) garner higher valuations than companies that do not track or that track poorly.

Two Traditional Recurring Revenue Models

The most common recurring revenue generating strategies are subscription services and contracts. We'll review those and then move on to other strategies that work for companies that can't offer long-term contracts or subscription services. There are other ways to prove to buyers that you have predictable revenue. You just have to do it in a way that demonstrates that customers consistently come back month after month and year after year. You have to show that you regularly win your customers' budgets for your offering. Better yet, you have to demonstrate that your customers' budgets and the percentage of their budgets that they spend on your product are growing.

Generating Recurring Revenue Via Subscriptions

Customers of product-based companies, distributors, and resellers may only make occasional or one-time purchases, making it difficult to generate predictable revenue. This is why buyers attribute higher value to recurring revenue than they do to repeat customers: They know how difficult it is to generate.

It is important to layer recurring subscription offerings where possible. Examples include:
- Software resellers: Rather than sell one-time licenses, begin offering hosted platforms for a monthly fee.
- Offer subscriptions to industry data that complement your products.
- Introduce customers to partners who offer complementary subscription-based services. In exchange for these referrals, the partners share a portion of the recurring revenue they generate from referred customers.
- Offer complementary consumable products.

Think of your internet service provider (ISP). Every month you receive a bill for services received. Every month you pay that bill because you can't operate your business without those services. I assure you that your ISP can track the longevity of its customers and provide metrics that illustrate average client tenure, what its churn (unsubscribe) rate is, and the average lifetime value of a client. I expect your provider (and others with base tiers of recurring revenue) uses promotional offers, such as $29.99 for the first 12 months or a free widget with enrollment today. Companies like ISPs have successfully established recurring, predictable revenue but continue to miss one major component that even further increases the value that company owners can realize in a transaction: contracts.

As you develop subscription programs or other recurring revenue models, offer multiple price points. Customers love choices, and a tiered approach makes it easier for customers to choose the plan that meets their needs.

Generating Recurring Revenue Via Contracts

Revenue that occurs because of contractual obligations is a better predictor of repeat revenue than is data supporting stickiness or repeat customers. When customers are secured by contracts, buyers can rely on legally binding agreements that obligate those customers to pay a certain amount over a defined time period. Customers may have an option to cancel contracts, but typically only after paying a termination fee or going through an arduous process. Contracts increase the confidence of a potential buyer to create models of future revenue and cash flows, thereby drastically mitigating the risk associated with an acquisition.

A prime example of an industry that has successfully instituted contractually backed recurring revenue is the cellular industry. Typically, customers sign a contract with clear terms and payments due for one or two years. As customers near the end of their contract term, the carrier may offer an opportunity to purchase the latest and greatest phone, sometimes at a discount, but only if that same contract is renewed. This practice enables carriers to keep virtually every customer locked into contracts and to predict (due to the huge repository of longitudinal data, by cohort, related to renewal rates) an extremely high percentage of future revenues.

If you are thinking, "How long should my contracts run?" I hope your next thought is, "As long as possible." That is a good way to think, up to a point. Long-term contracts are great, but customers, in general, don't like them. They accept them in return for your ongoing investment in adding infrastructure (i.e., servers or people) and product updates. It's not a good idea to push the terms beyond the time that it is reasonable for you to recoup your investment.

Unless you are extremely confident that you have priced your products or services correctly or have good reason to question your ability to retain customers without long-term contracts, we rarely advocate pressing your prospects/clients for contracts that exceed three years. Further, your contracts should give you the flexibility to change the price at renewal and give customers the ability to cancel without any more hassle than is absolutely necessary.

If a customer's dislike of "long contracts without a cause" is not reason enough to dissuade you, consider how long-term contracts can be liabilities to a potential buyer.

"Minerva," the owner of an educational technology software business called "MinervEd," asked us to help her consider the possibility of a sale. MinervEd had extremely sticky products, demonstrated clear ROI for its clients, and possessed phenomenal market share in its industry.

After we packaged the business and distributed a confidential information memorandum (CIM), several potential buyers expressed interest in integrating the company's offering into their own software suites. They believed, however, that MinervEd had underpriced its software. They estimated that customers would gladly have paid 20 to 30 percent more, so they were not happy to learn that more than 70 percent of MinervEd's customers had more than 24 months remaining on their contracts. Buyers loved the predictability of the revenue but were handcuffed from maximizing profitability for over two years!

Since most entrepreneurs underprice their products, sophisticated buyers use price increases as a quick value-creation strategy. If you tie customers to long-term contracts, you take that tool away from them.

I know, from experience as both a software entrepreneur and as an investment banker who orchestrates transactions for technology companies, that not all industries have customers who are willing to sign multiyear contracts. For that reason, I do not suggest that you hand three-year contracts to your customers and tell them, "Take it or leave it." Instead, prudently consider the standards and norms in your industry and strategize the best ways to increase the predictability of your revenue streams.

It's Time To Get Creative With Your Recurring Revenue Models.

If subscriptions and contracts just aren't viable recurring revenue strategies in your industry or business, there are others. The goal of each is to achieve—and be able to prove—a high rate of customer retention. Again, if the best you can do is leverage these strategies to move up one link on the value chain from one-time to reoccurring revenue, that is still of significant value.

Brand

One of the most effective ways to increase the predictability of your revenue streams is to deepen your relationship with your customers through your brand power. Brand is typically created around some advantage or differentiation that is "felt and experienced" by your customers in each interaction with your company. Loyal customers continue spending with your company and become brand evangelizers. More on this critical topic in Reason 10.

I once worked with a product company that had such strong customer loyalty that, on average, 40 percent of its customers purchased a new educational product every time it launched one. When this company released a product, customers did not repeat their original decision-making process. Instead, they relied on past positive experiences and quickly purchased the newest product. This consistent customer response to new products enabled the company to reasonably predict sales as it expanded its product mix.

Monthly Maintenance

In traditional project-based services companies, it can be especially difficult to maintain growth when large projects wrap up (because your billable resources are on the bench). To make up for the gaps between these projects, we've seen companies offer discounts for monthly recurring maintenance services or offer discounts to incent customers to prepurchase large blocks of consulting hours.

One of my friends owns a software engineering firm that typically bills its engineers by the hour based on their roles and experience. He understands that his current business model often leads to lumpy utilization of his talent pool and will not drive his exit valuation. Determined to address this lack of recurring revenue, he and his senior management team came up with an idea: under one-year contracts payable on a monthly basis, clients could lock in (at a premium rate) black-belt engineering teams for a minimum number of hours.

The firm launched the offer, and enterprise customers signed up and paid like clockwork. Customers were willing and happy to secure their favorite engineers without fear of losing them to other projects.

The company converted widely variable billing into a smooth stream of recurring revenue, and it continues to promote its "secure your engineering team" offer to all its enterprise customers. If this strategy remains successful, my friend and his management team will likely turn a low-value project-based business into a managed service provider that could trade for twice as much.

Fractional Consulting

Consultants can run into revenue challenges after they complete large client engagements/projects and then find themselves scrambling to find the next gig. One way to avoid these revenue troughs is to offer fractional executive programs payable monthly. Consulting firms can generate recurring revenue by making chief technology officers, chief financial officers, chief research officers, product managers, sales managers and directors of quality assurance available on a fractional basis.

As investment bankers, we are paid success fees when deals close, but in the months before, we do not receive meaningful revenue. To mitigate this lack of recurring revenue, we partnered with a firm to initiate a new program called "Growth As A Service" (GaaS). On a monthly/quarterly basis, we provide young technology companies (those without fully staffed teams) fractional chief financial and marketing officers or corporate development professionals chosen from a deep bench of operational professionals.

Cut-The-Line Memberships

Everyone loves special treatment, and many customers will commit to a subscription to receive it. They value plans or programs that qualify them to cut in line ahead of other customers to secure the products or services that are critically important to them. That special treatment isn't about ego; it's about value that they are willing to pay for.

"Neal" owns a large electrical contracting firm and makes most of his revenue as a specialty subcontractor in large commercial building projects. When business is good, cash flow is great. Since the source of the cash flow is project-based work, however, it is not predictable, and, therefore, not as valuable.

Neal struggles to fully utilize his workforce (much larger than Minerva's) consistently. For Neal, that's especially difficult during down seasons.

In an effort to create a juicy recurring revenue stream and reduce fluctuations in cash flow, Neal recently launched a repair and maintenance business for large commercial customers. At extremely busy times of the year, it can take up to 24 hours to respond to work order requests. Under Neal's premium service plan, customers are guaranteed a response within two hours. This plan effectively moves customers to the front of the line. Neal set up a subscription ($1,000 per month per location) for this service, and his large customers love it. Losing power can cost them thousands of dollars per downtime minute, and they gladly subscribe to receive this guaranteed service level. Revenue from this monthly subscription service goes straight to Neal's bottom line and has grown to over $70,000 per month.

Buyers will value Neal's predictable, highly profitable revenue stream (his subscription-based service) at 10x (or greater) TTM EBITDA value. Had Neal stuck with his traditional contractor model, he could have expected closer to 3x TTM EBITDA. Now that is value creation.

Lease Vs. Buy

Leasing is a tried and true strategy to produce recurring revenue. Look at real estate, automobiles, office equipment or heavy equipment. A lease is a financial engineering strategy designed to create recurring revenue for your business and make your products and services more digestible and acquirable for your customers.

Today creative entrepreneurs are applying the leasing model in new ways to a host of different industries. The technology industry leases software, hosting services and infrastructure services. We not only have SaaS (Software as a Service), but also HaaS (Hardware as a Service), PaaS (Platform as a Service) and IaaS (Infrastructure as a Service). The list goes on and on. This model provides customers with manageable monthly payments and provides business owners with lucrative recurring revenue.

In every case, these services are really just methods to turn a one-time capitalized asset expenditure into an operating lease that customers can expense. Customers often prefer to lease products or services rather than purchase them outright. For example, many firms lease office space versus purchasing a building, to conserve capital, expense the costs, maintain flexibility and maximize their convenience.

Warranty Contracts

Service contracts are common in businesses that provide valuable products or services. The value proposition offers a defined scope of services to program participants if the product they purchase needs to be repaired (e.g., high-end audio/visual equipment) or provides specific services at a certain frequency (e.g., landscape maintenance). The benefits to the customer are obvious: reduced risk, added convenience and peace of mind.

Service contracts can be very profitable and drive a high level of customer satisfaction.

"Abe" was a young residential builder who developed a fantastic reputation in Nashville. One of his strategies was to offer a new home warranty to every one of his clients. (He purchased the policies at a huge discount and resold them to homeowners as a monthly subscription.) If customers bought the monthly insurance plan and anything went wrong during a time period that customers chose (three, five or seven years), Abe performed the necessary repairs after the homeowner paid a small deductible.

We all know that no house is perfect. Things happen. Abe handled every one of those issues without any discussion of who was responsible. He assumed no risk because the home warranty company paid him to do the repairs. Abe's client satisfaction levels were off the chart because he responded quickly to every client request and the home warranty company paid the bills. Abe enjoyed a handsome 200 percent markup on each policy he sold and, at the same time, built a really nice recurring revenue stream.

Can you apply this recurring revenue model to your business?

Service Plans

Many businesses offer products and services that need periodic renewal or upgrades. Rather than approach customers each time they need a product, businesses offer service packages that automatically supply customers with what they are projected to need every month. By monitoring customer use of the product, these businesses proactively provide customers with what they need.

Is this a revenue model you can apply to your business?

Via service plans, your company can earn more predictable/recurring income without devoting time and energy to pressure people to buy again and again. In return for buying on a scheduled basis, your customers don't have to hassle with frequent purchases and they receive a discount. You gain predictability.

Let's say you are a landscape architect. You know that your clients will need a shrub/flower bed refresh every spring (new mulch, seasonal plants, maintenance of irrigation and landscape lighting systems) and leaf removal and winterizing every fall. Instead of quoting projects separately each quarter, you offer a package that covers everything your clients need on an annual basis. To make it even simpler for you and your clients, just bill their credit cards automatically without the complication and costs of manual billing.

WHATEVER YOU DO, TRACK IT!

A few years ago, we worked closely with a New England-based software engineering firm interested in testing the M&A market and exploring its exit options. The company employed over 120 engineers (and 30 other sales and support staff members) and counted numerous Fortune 1000 customers on its client list. Unfortunately, the overwhelming majority of its revenue was project based—the exact opposite of recurring. Once a project was complete, there was little opportunity for either long-term maintenance contracts or other sticky strategies to ensure that the next time a customer had a project they'd return. Our client's initial thesis was that it would be difficult to find a buyer, given the highly relational aspect of business development and revenue.

Thankfully, this company kept meticulous books and customer-level data. It was able to track every penny of revenue earned to a specific customer and division. Using that data, we were able to tell a compelling story: Every one of its top ten customers had not only done business consistently with the company in the past ten years but was doing more business over time. With this exceptionally high retention rate and clockwork-like growth, we were able to negotiate an even more favorable deal for the company than the original offers indicated. The fact pattern clearly proved the revenue streams of this project-based firm were highly predictable and reoccurring.

You might not be able to attract investors or buyers if your company does not have the recurring revenue necessary to create stable and predictable cash flow.

RECOMMENDATIONS

1. **Identify each of your company's revenue streams.**
   - List and describe every revenue center from your income statement (e.g., installation, maintenance, technical support, initial sales, monthly payments, annual contracts).
   - Determine which center produces the most predictable recurring revenue.

2. **Prioritize and rank each of your company's revenue streams.**
   - Is each source of recurring revenue provable, sticky, growing, scalable and contributing positively to gross profit at as high a margin as possible?

3. **Invest resources in your most valuable revenue streams.**
   - Are your most talented people working on your most valuable revenue streams?
   - Do your compensation programs motivate and reward employees to improve the most valuable revenue streams?

4. **Keep meticulous books and customer-level data.** You should be able to track every penny of revenue earned over the history of the customer relationship.

TAKEAWAYS

1. Subscriptions and contracts are the best ways to produce predictable revenue streams but not the only ways.

2. All revenue streams are not equally valuable to you or to a buyer or investor.

3. Knowing which of your revenue streams are the most valuable tells you where to invest your resources to maximize growth and value.

4. Whichever method you use to create predictable revenue, track it meticulously.

Your Company Lacks A Healthy Growth Rate And Sufficient Scale.

GROW FASTER AND BE BIGGER THAN YOUR COMPETITORS.

D o you remember the old joke about the two hikers who stumbled upon a mama grizzly and her cub? One hiker cried out, "Oh no, we are as good as dead! We can't outrun a bear!" As the other hiker sprinted off, he shouted, "Bear? I just have to outrun you."

Outrunning competitors is as critical in bear encounters as it is in size, growth rate and all of the other 16 characteristics of an investment-grade company. It's critical that your company's *growth rate* outpaces *your* competitors' and your industry as a whole. Scale is relative to other competitors as well as your industry. In this chapter, I use the word "size" as an adjective to describe metrics such as a company's revenue, number of employees, etc. Size refers to how "relatively" small, large or somewhere in between a company is based on these metrics.

Topping competitors operating in your segment and growing faster than your market as a whole is what buyers look at when assessing your company's scale and growth rate.

Comparison is the thief of joy.

Theodore Roosevelt

With all due respect to Mr. Roosevelt, constant comparison to one's competitors and one's market is fundamental to building an investment-grade company. Joy is what you feel when, because of your company's scale or growth rate, institutional buyers pay you an outsized valuation.

No Scale? No, Thank You.

The most common reason a prospective buyer responds with a quick "No, thank you" to an invitation to consider acquiring a high-growth company is that company's lack of size.

Many buyers won't bother to dig into the other 16 Reasons because it takes about the same amount of effort, time and resources to buy a $5 million company as it does a $100 million company.

I routinely see buyers spend upwards of $800,000 on third-party diligence (legal, financial, technical, brand, customer satisfaction, etc.) to close one lower middle-market deal (enterprise value between $25 million and $100 million). Add to that the opportunity costs—the time buyers could be spending on other projects—and the bill can be staggering. Bigger companies move the needle for strategic buyers, meet the minimum check size for financial buyers and provide the multiple compounding that hybrid buyers require. (We call portfolio companies of private equity groups "hybrid buyers.")

Size and scale create real advantage and influence valuations as the following chart from GF Data illustrates.[3]

FIG. 2.1 GF Data

Total Enterprise Value (TEV)/EBITDA*

Earnings Before Interest, Taxes, Depreciation and Amortization

TEV	2003-14	2015	2016	2017	2018	YTD 2019	Total	N =
10-25	5.5	5.9	5.8	6.3	5.9	6.2	5.7	1,308
25-50	6.2	6.6	6.4	6.6	6.9	6.9	6.3	983
50-100	6.7	7.8	7.2	8.2	8.9	7.5	7.2	676
100-250	7.3	9.0	8.9	9.1	8.8	9.6	8.1	343
Total	6.1	6.7	6.7	7.3	7.2	7.2	6.4	
N =	2,111	245	237	255	265	197		3,310

Please note that N for 2003 - 2014 incorporates 12 years of activity.

EXCEPTION: Portfolio companies of private equity groups (PEGs), or hybrid buyers, often look to grow via acquisition, and they have access to the capital (both debt and equity) necessary to purchase what they often refer to as "add-ons," "bolt-ons" or "tuck-ins" for their platform companies. If the timing is right and you have a quality company in the enterprise value range of $5 million to $10 million, these PEG platforms can be excellent buyers. They will come downstream to fish for quality smaller companies that accelerate the growth of their existing platform companies.

Growth Rate

Just as scale is a comparison between the size of your company and your competitors', so is growth rate. Merriam-Webster defines rate as a fixed ratio between two things. Instead of a target or set percentage, growth rate is the ratio between your company's growth and your competitors'. That fact became crystal clear between 2008 and 2010.

Back then, a "new normal" growth rate characterized almost every non-countercyclical industry sector. If a company's growth rate was zero, investors considered it to be growing. If a company's margins were holding up and it was not slashing prices while competitors' revenues were decreasing by 20 percent and their margins were shrinking, it was something special. That company could demand—and receive—handsome valuation premiums even in a downturn.

In good industry cycles, don't expect to elicit excitement from buyers if your sales and growth are holding steady or slowing down. Investors/buyers know that healthy organizations are always growing, always improving, always expanding. Healthy things grow: people, plants, families and definitely companies. It is difficult to attract an institutional buyer if your company is a relatively small player in your market sector or has a pedestrian, year-over-year revenue growth rate compared to your competitors.

> If your industry is currently in a down cycle, what matters to buyers is that your company holds its own compared to its competitors. Great companies differentiate themselves even in tough markets.

SCALE AND GROWTH: THE DOUBLE WHAMMY

What I left out of the example of a company that maintains a zero percent growth rate during a period of economic contraction was scale. To attract the interest of a buyer, that company has to be bigger than its competitors. "Franco" learned the hard way about the importance of scale when he put his fast-growing IoT (internet of things) company on the market.

> *Franco's company, Glastonbury Solutions, had a lot going for it. It had earned a great reputation in a white-hot industry and amassed a loyal customer base of well-known companies that depended on its secure, reliable and customized solutions. It had a highly experienced management team, and its products had broad potential application. Its TTM (Trailing Twelve Months) revenue was just over $6 million, and its TTM EBITDA[4] was $1.2 million. Glastonbury's strong patent portfolio gave it multiple, defensible barriers to entry.*
>
> *What more could a buyer want?*
>
> *Franco recognized the potential for a big exit and retained an M&A advisory firm that focused on serving industrial technology firms.*
>
> *The M&A firm fired up a marketing campaign to carefully approach over 80 strategic buyers that it expected would jump at the chance to "bolt on" this young, fast-growing, innovative company. It made introductory calls and sent a one-page, high-level confidential summary to the corporate development professionals within the prospective buyers' organizations. As expected, several recipients signed nondisclosure agreements (NDAs) and the exchange of information began.*
>
> *Due to the strong level of initial interest, Franco could practically taste the exit he had dreamed of. But once buyers really dug in, got beyond the glittering growth numbers and learned about the size and scale of the business, the M&A firm received a steady stream of messages similar to this one:*
>
>> While Glastonbury is an innovative company and appears to have a lot of good momentum in the IoT space, we'll pass. It just doesn't move the needle for us. We target companies that are accretive[5] to our earnings and typically have $15 million and greater in revenue. Do you have any companies in that range? Thanks for thinking of us, and best of luck in your process.
>>
>> John Doe
>> Vice President of Corporate Development
>> XYZ, Inc., A Fortune 1000 Company

How big is big enough? That depends on how your company compares to others in your market segment.

Despite its excellent product and clear growth potential, Glastonbury was simply too small to make a significant impact on a strategic buyer's business and justify the time and effort involved in acquiring and integrating it. While some financial buyers did make marginally attractive verbal indications of interest (IOIs), Franco turned them down. The valuations were way less than he had envisioned.

THE WONDERFUL WORLD OF BUYERS

In this chapter, I've mentioned three types of institutional buyers: strategic, financial and hybrid. Noninstitutional buyers are small competitors, family members, partners, employees, angel investor groups or individuals who purchase companies.

Because the purpose of this book is to help you create an investment-grade company, we limit our discussion to the buyers you want to attract. Those buyers *can and will* pay up for your company.

Institutional Buyers

Both financial and strategic buyers are classified as "institutional" because they are highly sophisticated and experienced entities that take an extremely disciplined approach to buying private companies.

Hybrid buyers are also institutional because they are private-equity-backed platform companies that are looking to add on synergistic smaller companies to their platforms.

What Do Buyers Want?

All buyers want to make money. All buyers hate risk. After that, the acquisition choices they make depend on how they will pay for the companies they acquire and how they will use them to deliver a return on their investments.

Growth rate and scale play a huge role in the choices buyers make, so the balance of this chapter is devoted to a discussion of how each type of buyer views growth, size, risk and return in today's marketplace.

To facilitate this discussion, I've created Figure 2.2. It defines three types of institutional buyers, the rules under which they operate, how each typically uses debt and growth, why size is important to them and how they measure return.

Buyers Are People Too.

Owners often make invalid assumptions about who buyers are and how they behave. I regularly encounter sellers who believe that private equity buyers are control freaks poised to rush in and make sweeping changes to a business and culture. As soon as the wire transfer clears the bank, they fully expect strategic buyers to reorganize the newly acquired business and deep-six its key product offerings. Neither is true in the vast majority of cases.

One way to better understand buyers is to imagine yourself as one. That's a strategy that helped my client "Alanna."

"There's a part of selling that I know isn't going to go well for me," said Alanna. "It's relating to a soulless organization that obsesses over every little detail." Every one of the successful owners at the table nodded in agreement.

The way she said "organization" made me think of the Mafia or Al-Qaeda. The word "soul-less" made me wonder if she'd ever met a PEG partner, but "obsesses" made me think that she had!

FIG. 2.2 Types Of Buyers

	FINANCIAL	STRATEGIC	HYBRID
Types of Buyers	Private equity groups, venture capitalists, family offices, growth equity funds, search funds, buyout funds	Operating companies: public and private	PEG-backed platform companies engaged in a growth-by-acquisition strategy
Operating Criteria and Rules	• Target must meet minimum check size/value threshold. • Fund size may limit the number of companies PEG can manage, i.e., a few larger companies rather than several small ones. • Set holding period.	• Acquisition must integrate successfully and be highly accretive. • Target acquisition must move the needle.	• Must see synergies and ease of integration of cultures, technology, customers, etc. • Target acquisition must significantly accelerate growth of the platform.
Use of Debt in Making Purchase	Typically use debt to the extent feasible.	Most use balance sheet resources and stock.	Typically use debt to the extent feasible.
This buyer uses growth rate to:	• Achieve a 3x cash-on-cash return target more quickly. • Support the detailed financial models it builds to calculate likely return over a 3- to 5-year time horizon. • Decrease the time it takes to hit their ROI target, and drive multiple at exit.	• Calculate post-acquisition return. • Assess the quality of a company's market position, product suite and lifetime value. • Increase its earnings per share.	Expand platform's size or accelerate growth rate (exponentially, if possible) for the next buyer.
Size matters to this buyer because it:	Meets its minimum check size.	• Moves the price of public company stock. • Makes the deal worth all the work and resources it takes to close.	Moves the needle by making a measurable impact on buyer's size and growth metrics.
This buyer estimates ROI by:	Using a financial model.	• How accretive the acquisition is to the value of its stock, or • How well the target facilitates expansion (or speed of expansion) into new markets or product areas, or • Whether the target eliminates competition and/or addresses a weakness.	How well the acquisition will help the buyer accelerate the next exit and drive exit multiples.

I've heard variations on Alanna's comment from many, many owners. Their assumptions are:
- *The PEG they will deal with has a hidden and nefarious agenda.*
- *Buyers obsess over details to test (or torture!) owners.*
- *If owners don't perceive an issue as a huge risk, why should a buyer?*

I get that owners want buyers to relax when it comes to the "small" potential risks of an acquisition. I get that a private equity group or bigger buyer can seem soul-less and clinical as it requests every last detail about your company during diligence. But every buyer I've ever met has had at least one lead individual who had *a lot* at stake. That person's compensation, in large part, is based on the post-integration success of the deal. A financial buyer's compensation is tied to a percentage of the carried interest[6] generated by the investment. Peer approval/recognition is at stake as well; one bad deal can label a person a poor dealmaker. These individuals must meet stringent performance requirements to remain employed and qualify for bonuses, and they put their careers on the line with each acquisition. Usually, a deal is almost as personal to the buyer as it is to the seller.

- Think of all investors as natives of Missouri, the Show-Me State. In God they trust. Everyone else must "Show them the data!"

  Buyers relax (and then only partially) only if sellers can prove that their businesses are growing nicely and have room to grow and scale for many years to come. "Trust me. My business is solid" is a dog that just won't hunt with this group.

- Buyers like to secure their acquisition track records, bonuses and jobs. They know that the risk of losing all three decreases as the size and growth rate of the companies they acquire increases. They assign bigger multiples to larger companies as a reward for reduced risk.

Buyers Can't Resist Great Growth Rates

Growth has a beautiful effect on valuations of both public and private companies. Perhaps that's why it mesmerizes me. Or maybe it's because as a metric, growth says so many positive things about a company: its products, market, talent, scalability and customer loyalty. Sustained growth year over year screams, "This is a special company!" Flatline, or worse, negative growth says, "Something. Is. Not. Right."

A company's post-acquisition growth is the "pickup" that buyers are looking for and can help justify the valuation multiple that they assign to a company. Keep in mind that managers of both PEGs and operational companies are accountable for the continued growth of the acquisitions they recommend and champion. The business case they develop to acquire a company must hold up in order for them to keep their bonuses, and oftentimes, their jobs.

Strategic Buyers

Strategic buyers use growth rate to assess the quality of a company's market position, product suite and lifetime value. They are motivated to *buy* versus *compete* or *build* when they see impressive growth. An acquisition's strong growth rate can often increase the value of a strategic buyer's shares.

Financial Buyers

A company's rate of growth is a critical tool that financial buyers use in their models to estimate post-acquisition return on investment. These buyers depend on growth to support the conclusions they draw (about likely return over a three-to-five-year horizon) from their detailed Discounted Cash Flow (DCF) and Leveraged Buyout (LBO) models. Faster rates decrease the amount of time it takes to hit their ROI targets (often three

The Rule of 40 is a simple rule of thumb that many software companies use to gauge their health. It states that annual growth rate plus profit margin percentage should equal 40 percent or greater.

Example: If your company is growing at 30 percent, it should be generating a profit margin of 10 percent. If it is growing at 40 percent, it could generate a profit of 0 percent and still be considered healthy. In fact, if you're a tech company that still isn't cash flowing and is experiencing a profit margin of -20%, you'll still be viewed favorably if you're growing greater than 60% annually. I'd argue for a Rule of 30 for non-tech companies, but each industry has its nuances. I love the way growth and profitability tie together in a simple rule.

times cash-on-cash during their hold periods) and drive multiples when they sell. Financial buyers are able to stretch beyond their return models when they can plug in impressive growth rates to their financial models.

Hybrid Buyers

Hybrid buyers acquire companies that can make the buyer more valuable through cost or revenue synergies. They look for growing companies so they can accelerate their growth by, for example, expanding cross-selling opportunities. These platform companies use fast-growing "add-ons" to make themselves bigger at a rate they cannot under their own organic steam. Think of a platform as a balloon that inflates as quickly as the CEO and team can blow. When the CEO acquires a fast-growing add-on, she's hooked the balloon up to a compressed air tank. The balloon inflates to maximum size much more quickly, or the platform reaches its exit target valuation within its exit time frame.

Can Cash Flow Outweigh Growth?

Entrepreneurs often ask me (with hope in their hearts), "Which is more important: my company's growth rate or its profitability?" Or they ask, "Haven't you seen situations in which buyers put more stock in stable, predictable profitability than rapid growth?"

My answer is not the clean either/or that most owners want to hear. "It depends" almost always disappoints them. The proof of a company's operating leverage/scale is a strong unit economic model. Yes, I've seen profitability outweigh crazy rapid growth, but the *relationship between growth and operating margins* is what matters to investors. It is this relationship that the Rule of 40 seeks to capture for technology businesses.

Does your company's unit economic model prove that you can grow while maintaining scale and operating leverage? Some buyers in the tech industry don't fret over negative operating margins if they are suppressed due to aggressive marketing spending to attract and onboard highly profitable customers with strong lifetime values. Similarly, depending on an investor's goals, some won't complain about a *slightly* lower growth rate if EBITDA margins are higher than others in your cohort.

I understand from my experience as an owner how difficult it is to combine rapid revenue growth and profit growth in the same annual period. It is like an athlete who has to gain 40 pounds while cutting his 40-yard-dash time. I also understand from my experience as an investment banker observing many, many buyers in action, how they weigh growth in relationship to profitability.

THE PREMIUM BUYERS PAY FOR SIZE AKA REDUCED RISK

Buyers assign higher multiples to larger (same industry) businesses than they do smaller ones because bigger companies are safer investments and enjoy the benefits of scale. Think of a company as a boat. A wave (market externality) capable of capsizing a small boat has no effect on an ocean liner. Larger companies have deeper management teams, so one injured crew member doesn't take the boat out of the race. They sell more products to customers in more industries in more marketplaces. They can obtain debt more easily and at better terms. If buyers find your company large enough to consider, the bigger it is the higher the multiple. As is true with boats: As size increases, risk of capsizing decreases.

Buyers and strategic partners assign value to a company based on their confidence in the performance of various revenue streams into the future. Rather than assessing present value based on trailing numbers, their value assessment depends on their estimates of future cash flow (after risk-adjusting cash flow for a number of factors). Buyers are able to underwrite a larger business' future cash flows with less risk.

EXCEPTION: While size and the relationship between growth and cash flow matter, I've frequently seen large public strategic buyers purchase very small companies ($3 million to $5 million in revenue). But those small companies had something special going on and could check many of the 16 other boxes that make a company investment grade. Typically, they provided their large suitor several of the following valuable items:
- Unique intellectual property, patents, tools or business methods.
- Product or service offerings that radically improved the acquirer's offerings.
- Access to new talent, skills and technology.
- A strong and growing brand in an attractive market.
- Highly trained and scarce human capital.
- Flexibility around new geographies.
- Unique distribution channels.
- A complementary customer base.

As a rule, investors reward owners like "Savannah" who put together company scale and healthy growth.

I met Savannah for coffee early one hot August morning. "Lucy," a friend of Savannah's and former client of mine, set up the meeting.

When we sat down, I noticed that Savannah looked exhausted. I wondered if 7:00 a.m.—the time Lucy had suggested—was one Savannah would have picked. "Zane," she said, "my company is growing faster than gossip in a church parking lot."

As she began to describe a company growth rate that would exhaust any owner, I understood why she looked so tired.

"In the last three years, my company's annual revenue has increased from $3.6 million to over $45 million," she started. "EBITDA exceeds $3.3 million."

Lucy had told me that Savannah's oncology-focused specialty pharmacy was "fast-growing," but these numbers blew me away. So much so that I forgot to impress her with a highly insightful first question and simply asked, "How did that happen?"

"Lots of reasons, really," she answered. "My team and I have concentrated on three initiatives: forging strong relationships with oncologists, providing excellent customer service, and working with drug manufacturers to make pricier drugs more affordable for patients."

"With these growth rates, you have a great formula," I observed. "What else could you ask for?" I asked, only half joking.

"I feel as if I've got a tiger by the tail," Savannah started. "Don't get me wrong. I love what I'm doing,

but I think—no, I know—that without help my team and I can't execute well on the opportunity ahead of us. If I could bring in partner—someone with the expertise the company needs and growth capital that I could really use—that would be ideal."

"Savannah, I know that there are loads of investors out there who would jump at the chance to own a piece of your company," I responded. "But to see what kind of multiples buyers in your industry might pay, I'll need some financials. We'll review those, do some research and you can decide whether to move forward."

When my team conducted the valuation assessment, we found that heavy M&A activity in Savannah's industry supported strong enterprise value/EBITDA multiples. Multiples for smaller companies were between 5x and 6x EBITDA, while the largest private companies traded for up to 12x EBITDA.

When I called Savannah with these estimates and told her that we anticipated good market interest based on her company's size and growth rate, she agreed to begin a competitive auction process.

The response from prospective buyers and strategic partners was as strong as we had anticipated. Buyers, both strategic and financial, recognized that Savannah's company's growth rate could generate a high return on their investment. With over $3 million in EBITDA, her company exceeded the size mandates of many middle-market private equity firms, and the acquisition was large enough to move the needle for all but the largest strategic players in the industry.

The next time Savannah and I met for coffee, it was a cool March morning, six weeks after closing the deal. On that day, Savannah looked both rested and happy. And why not? She'd cashed out 80 percent of her interest in her company to a strategic buyer. Well, technically it was a hybrid buyer: A large private equity group's platform company was consolidating regional specialty pharmacies. The buyer left her management team in place, had a similar culture and vision and had the industry relationships and capital to fuel Savannah's growth strategy.

Size And The Financial Buyer

When acquiring a lower middle-market platform, financial buyers must meet an equity check-size threshold specified in their investment guidelines. Further, fund size may limit the number of operating companies a private equity group can oversee and add value to as active board members. Given those limits, multiple small investments are not an option for funds ranging from $300 million to several billion dollars in size. A $500 million fund with fifteen professionals simply cannot manage fifty $10 million check-size investments/companies. Instead they focus on ten $50 million check-size investments/companies.

A financial buyer's return model is highly correlated to the length of time it will hold an acquired company. Most plan to hold companies for four to six years. During this time, their goal is to professionalize the business and continue to grow it at a healthy pace. This growth enables them to sell the business at the end of the holding period for a higher multiple (because businesses with bigger EBITDA and revenues draw higher EBITDA and revenue multiples from buyers). These two factors (higher EBITDA and revenues) along with some financial engineering can produce handsome returns for the PEG and the original owner(s) that remain with the business and roll equity from the first transaction.

Size And Strategic Buyers

Franco's story on pages 17 and 18 illustrates the fact that strategic buyers love a great growth rate but sometimes just aren't willing to execute small deals.

How Buyers Measure Return

When financial buyers make an acquisition, they are looking for a specific financial return. Since they are buying future earnings, they look at both historical earnings and the projected earnings of the company. Obviously, they don't just accept a seller's earnings projections without a lot of modeling and data to support all the assumptions. But rest assured, financial buyers are looking for evidence of future growth and scalability.

Financial buyers demand growth in revenue as well as in:

- Market share.
- New customer acquisition rate.
- Gross margin percentages.
- EBITDA and EBITDA percentages.

All buyers interpret a plateau in any of these areas as a signal that continued operating cash flow growth is problematic or that macroeconomic factors, increased competitive pressures, or industry cycle or sector performance are unfavorable. This translates to lower valuations and even walking away from the opportunity.

While strategic buyers do not ignore return or size necessary to move their valuation needles, they target companies whose synergies (achieved through eliminating duplicate costs or seizing growth accelerators) make them more valuable. Strategic buyers also value the multiple arbitrage—buying a company for a lower EBITDA multiple than their own multiple due to the acquired company's lack of scale. In doing so, they immediately pick up value in this scenario.

Strategic buyers are hungry for bolt-on acquisitions that add accretive value to their stock or ones that will help them expand (or expand faster) into new markets or product areas, eliminate competition or address a weakness. For example, a strategic buyer may want to acquire your company for its customer list, expand into your geographic market or access your unique technology. Strategic buyers are all about "synergy"—the concept that the value and performance of the two companies combined will be greater than the sum of the individual parts.

Some cost-saving synergies flow straight to the bottom line, including:

- **Product Combinations.** If two companies provided similar products (i.e., an ERP software platform for grocers), the combined entity could sunset one product line over time and sell, support and enhance one tech platform. Single-product focus would generate significant savings and streamline all resources into one great solution.
- **Supply Chain Efficiencies.** If either company has access to better supply chain relationships, together they may be able to secure cost savings.
- **Better Distribution Channels.** The merged firm may save on costs that both companies expensed individually prior to the transaction.
- **Lower Wages.** One merged company does not need two CEOs, CFOs, CTOs and so on across and down through the organizational chart.

Revenue enhancing synergies could include:

- **Complementary Products.** If the individual firms delivered complementary products pre-merger, post-merger they can creatively bundle and price them to produce higher and more profitable sales.
- **Complementary Customers.** Cross-selling new products into additional customer bases can quickly produce higher revenue and profits.

- **Pricing Pressure Release.** When two fierce competitors combine, competitive pressure eases, resulting in margin expansion.

When working with publicly traded companies, strategic buyers want to make acquisitions that move the price of their stock. This requires their acquisitions be of a size large enough to be highly accretive.

Pretend for a moment that you lead the corporate development team of a medium-size public company. Your acquisition-target spending for the upcoming year is $300 million. Given that the cost, energy and resources that go into a $150 million acquisition are not significantly greater than a $10 million acquisition, would you purchase thirty $10 million companies or two in the $150 million range?

Buyers who want to enter your industry niche or geography may decide that it is easier and faster to purchase a company already in that niche than it is to build from scratch the capability the target company already has. (The process of building from scratch is often referred to as greenfielding.)

If your company has ever made an acquisition, you are a strategic buyer. Think back on why you made this acquisition. What synergies did you expect to achieve?

Hybrid buyers are PEG-owned strategics, so they measure return the same way strategic buyers do.

Is Your Scale and Growth Rate Investment Grade?

Would Buyers Take A Second Look?

If you can check the scale and growth boxes, what else do buyers want from you? Well, I can think of 16 other things, but believe me, they'll tell you. I receive emails like the one in Figure 2.3 every day from institutional buyers. (If you're an owner of a private company, I'm sure you receive dozens of similar emails a month as well.) Notice the level of detail the writer provides about her company's desired acquisition.

FIG. 2.3 **Message From Meredith Smith**

From:	Meredith Smith
Sent:	Thursday, March 19th, 2020 11:26 AM
To:	Zane Tarence
Subject:	JMW Associates Outreach
Attachments:	JMW Associates_Overview.pdf

Zane,

The team at JMW Associates continues to actively hunt for an exceptional business to acquire. I wanted to reach out and highlight our initial criteria and attributes as a buyer. Our strike zone includes businesses between $5 million to $50 million in revenue with EBITDA margins greater than 10 percent. We are looking for services businesses focused in B2B, health care, energy and tech-enabled services.

As past operators with significant capital, we are looking for one business to actively operate post-acquisition. We offer a flexible and very compelling solution for business owners seeking liquidity, succession, growth and legacy preservation. Our investor roster is composed of accomplished entrepreneurs, executives and family offices / institutional investors.

I have attached an overview of JMW Associates. Please let us know if you have any opportunities that may fit our investment criteria.

Thanks

How do you know if your company's growth rate is "healthy"?

To determine if your company's growth rate, relative to others in your industry, is above or below average, check with your trade association or reach out to an investment banker who specializes in your industry. Because these professionals are active in these segments of the market and subscribe to proprietary databases that provide detailed market information, they know many of the companies and investors in the space and have a good handle on the growth rate norms.

Note: Fast growth does not always equal healthy growth. A healthy growth rate is supported by a solid company infrastructure and mature systems, and it is not dependent on one or two customers. More on this in the next chapters.

Show me your written growth strategy.

Given the critical importance of growth rates to buyers, I am always amazed—and not in a good way—by the number of owners who do not have written growth strategies for their companies.

First, unless you document a plan, it isn't a plan. There is something powerful and almost prophetic about writing your plans in black and white. Second, laminate your plan. As I once heard leadership author John Maxwell say, "What gets laminated becomes holy." Third, if you do not have a written growth strategy, I'm going to give you (for the price of this book!) an outline and samples of what yours should include.

1. **List no more than three major annual growth strategies.** They might include:
   - Geographic expansion into a new region or internationally.
   - Product or service line expansion.
   - Partnership development.
2. **To each strategy, assign one or more tactical initiatives**. For example, if you
   listed product or service line expansion as a goal, two initiatives might be:
   - Add an analytics module to your software.
   - Add a security practice service line to your consultancy.
   If your strategy is partnership development, initiatives might include:
   - Identify and onboard three new resellers.
   - White label the software to a leader in another applicable industry.
3. **Estimate the amount of investment necessary to achieve each strategy** both
   in personnel hours and hard dollar investments.
4. **Assign a leader on your team to own each strategy.** Doing so demonstrates
   the weight you put on each strategy and that you expect it to be executed.

Once your plan is complete, stick one laminated copy on your wall, bathroom mirror or next to your computer, and give copies to your key team members and stakeholders.

Let's look at two examples of especially well-designed, well-written, one-page growth strategies: one for a software company and one for an ecommerce company.

Software Company Growth Strategy

"Marshall" walked into my office and said, "I think I'm ready to do a deal."

"You've come to the right place," I responded. "But I'm curious. Why now?"

"The market is white hot, and that's a good thing," he explained. "But two very large CRM software companies have just announced that they're entering my space. And that's bad. It could be really bad over

time because of the mountain of resources that they have at their disposal. I've got the lead for now. With the right plan, focus and resources over the next two years, however, they could catch me. The headwinds they'd create for my growth would be brutal."

Marshall's company, Alma Matters, was in the business of helping colleges and universities maintain and build strong relationships with alumni. He'd started his company four years earlier, and it now had over 500 customers.

Marshall's product was working for his customers—many of which were marquee institutions—and provided a strong ROI.

"I see the window closing on my ability to grow rapidly," he lamented.

"Unless," I suggested, "we inject enough capital to create a boatload of additional value for your customers and other stakeholders. Before we can do that," I continued, "you have to document a growth strategy—what you'd do with that capital." I admit it—I started to lecture while Marshall rooted through his messenger bag. "Be clear and concise. Make sure you can measure each strategy. Assign your best people to own the strategies, and hold them and yourself accountable."

"You mean like this?" Marshall asked as he handed me a laminated version of the following chart.

Lecture over. His growth strategy was spot on. I was impressed. Marshall knew exactly what his company needed to do to grow. He just needed the resources to put the pedal to the metal.

FIG. 2.4 **Alma Matters Growth Strategy**

The ideal buyer will have the ability to accelerate Alma Matters' product road map and market penetration.

Launch and Monetize Alma Matters' Analytics Platform	• Capitalize on momentum for "Big Data" solutions to address alumni network tracking and leverage seven-plus years of transactional data housed in Alma Matters' systems. • Provide industry's first quantitative assessment of donor outreach and historical giving. • Expect 25% to 40% upcharge over base annual subscription fee with projected uptake of 40% to 70% over life of contracts and estimated annual revenue potential >$1 million.
Develop Predictive Analytics for Donor Management and Alumni Support	• To compete with larger vendors for higher-dollar RFPs, Alma Matters must deploy analytics to identify potential alumni donors. • Management believes that there is significant pickup and market interest in an offering that provides alerts to college development professionals related to alumni activity.
Expand via Professional Sales Team, Broader Distribution and Acquisitions	• The Alma Matters solution deserves a professional sales team and expanded utilization of marketing automation tools. • To extend Alma Matters' market reach, it can pursue partnerships with software firms and higher education vendors through mutual referral, reseller and license agreements. • Management has identified potential acquisition candidates and communicated directly with one that uses an outdated technology to serve a complementary customer base.

Ecommerce Company Growth Strategy

"Nick" and his wife, "Theresa," had built DCF Furnishings as a value-added distributor and etailer of high-end home remodeling products. Nick handled the product management, tech, and merchandising, while Theresa headed up operations.

Nick's thoughtful growth strategy is a great example of one that follows all the rules:

- *In written form.*
- *One page.*
- *Concise.*
- *Summarizes no more than three initiatives.*
- *All initiatives can be easily measured.*

Nick had taped a full-size version of the following infographic to the wall behind his desk.

FIG. 2.5 DCF Furnishings Growth Strategy

Three-Prong Expansion Strategy

The Company has formulated three strategic initiatives to guide its growth strategy:

1. DCF Furnishings will expand into additional segments focusing on non-seasonal products to smooth out its revenue stream.

2. DCF will investigate other home furnishing segments to seek opportunistic acquisitions that are accretive to earnings within two years and whose product categories can leverage the company's platform and core capabilities.

3. DCF will seek to establish strategic alliances serving as the conduit linking manufacturers needing online distribution with service providers wired into online communities forming large consumer bases.

Segment Expansion	• Expand the product line in furnishings into untapped niches using DCF's systematic and repeatable processes. • Offer private-label substitute for products that require research, have limited seasonality and a ticket price above $500.	
Targeted Acquisitions	• Pursue the following acquisition categories: 1. Vertical product sites that have not reached scale 2. Well trafficked / hype blogs	$50 Million Revenue Company
E-Commerce Platform Outsourcing	• Create strategic alliance program to partner with manufacturers needing online distribution and with service providers that have large captive audiences and "kittable" products. • Develop technical infrastructure and standardized processes to quickly add new alliance partners leveraging DCF's ERP software capabilities.	

Can Your Company Grow More Quickly?

If growing like gangbusters (See Savannah's company on pages 22 to 23.) is currently just not possible but your company has "good bones," you should seriously consider the pros and cons of becoming a buyer yourself.

That's exactly what I recommended to "Linden," the owner of a software company that was strong in most of the 17 Reasons but was not growing at a rate that would knock anyone's socks off. Since his company was squared away and executed well, the foundation was in place for an "add-on" strategy.

Together we created and implemented a disciplined plan to roll up three small SaaS companies in the nonprofit tech space within an 18-month period. Linden became a master at integrating products into his organization and culture and cross-selling newly acquired products/solutions to his company's rapidly growing install base. In only three years, Linden drove his company's valuation from $25 million to $130 million.

> If you are struggling to operate a solid company now, rolling up other companies will just compound your problems.

The Rezoning Effect Or Financial Arbitrage

Linden's acquisition strategy is a great example of the "rezoning effect." A smaller company's EBITDA trades at a higher multiple once it is "rezoned" on to the platform of a larger company. Bankers refer to this as arbitrage.

Imagine you own a nice house "with good bones" in a less-than-desirable neighborhood or in a rural setting far from any city of real size. Suppose that a massive helicopter could lift that house up and drop it (gently, of course) in Malibu, California, or Westchester County, New York.

Now calculate the pickup in value based on a value per square foot. In its original setting that house might be worth $100,000 tops—if you could find a buyer. If it overlooks the Pacific Ocean, is situated next door to Beyoncé and is updated and staged by a professional, that house could sell for high single-digit millions.

This rezoning effect holds true for moving (integrating) a small business "with good bones" into a larger (platform) business that checks all of the 17 Reasons boxes. In Linden's case, the smaller companies' revenue streams became 3.5 times as valuable simply by putting those businesses on a bigger and more professionalized platform. In this case, one of his acquisitions saw its 5x TTM EBITDA acquisition price tag jump to 12x TTM EBITDA once it became part of Linden's company.

Now that's what I call value creation.

Buying Your Way To Scale

Implementing an acquisition strategy to stimulate growth does carry risk because you can easily lose focus on your core business while finding and performing due diligence on new opportunities. Also, integration can be tricky and a resource hog.

Combining and integrating people, cultures, products, customer bases, geographies, etc. takes planning and expertise. So much that I highly recommend that you seek professional advice and hire a buy-side transaction advisor before undertaking it. Look for an experienced advisor who uses a proven buy-side methodology that includes:

1. Executing a comprehensive target and industry search.
2. Creating an approach plan tailored to interest each target.
3. Initiating, managing and maintaining contact with prospective targets.
4. Evaluating potential targets.

5. Facilitating key stakeholder meetings.

6. Securing an executed letter of intent.

7. Conducting due diligence and closing.

8. Advising on integration of the acquisition.

You might not be able to attract investors or buyers if your business is relatively small or is growing more slowly than your competitors' businesses and your market.

RECOMMENDATIONS

1. Obsess over how the scale and growth of your company benchmarks against your rivals and how it compares to the growth rate of your market.

2. Create a formal growth strategy.

List no more than three major growth strategies, assign specific initiatives and people to each goal, estimate necessary resources, hold people accountable and track your progress.

- Do you have a formal/written growth strategy? If so, does your team know about it?
- Have you assigned key team members to each initiative, and are you holding them accountable for progress?

3. Consider implementing an acquisition strategy.

Making acquisitions can produce substantial value IF you orchestrate them properly and IF your company has the good bones to support them.

- Do you have a list of potential companies you'd like to acquire?
- Where could you achieve the "rezoning effect"?
- Have you implemented a formal buy-side process so you don't miss out on solid opportunities?

4. Document, format and laminate your growth strategy.

Then use it. (See Figures 2.4 and 2.5.) Review and update your growth strategy often with your leadership team.

- Is your growth strategy in written form?
- Does it fit on one page?
- Is it laminated?
- Do team members own this strategy and accept accountability for its execution?

5. Become a student of public company growth strategies in your market.

Public companies spend loads of money on consultants and have access to deep market data, insights and trends. If you compete with them, listen to their quarterly earnings calls. Pay attention to their comments about the headwinds and tailwinds they encounter in their efforts to grow! Take notes because those calls are tutorials on how they plan to meet the growth imperatives of their investors.

- Do you know the growth rate of your industry?
- Do you know the growth rate of your competitors?
- How do you compare in size and growth rate to your named competitors?

TAKEAWAYS

1. Solid growth points to forecastable value creation over time.

2. Superior size (scale) and growth rate prove that you are stronger/better than competitors.

3. Buyers award a size premium to larger businesses over comparable smaller ones because larger companies present less risk.

4. Unless a growth strategy is documented, it does not exist.

5. If your company is not experiencing high rates of growth organically but has good bones, consider growth through acquisition.

   Even if you are experiencing nice organic growth, consider making acquisitions that can accelerate that growth rate and "rezone" well into your platform.

REAS⚙N 3

Your Company's Market Does Not Excite Investors.

DON'T JUST SIT THERE: PIVOT, EXTEND YOUR REACH OR ACQUIRE!

Markets that attract investors are those that offer excellent current and long-term profit potential and have strong characteristics that support stable and long-term growth. Entering, operating or remaining in a stagnant, unhealthy or shrinking market is like trying to win a surfing competition in a pond.

. . . neither a stellar team nor a fantastic product will redeem a bad market.[7]

Marc Andreessen, General Partner
Andreessen Horowitz

Think of assessing your market like a surfer picking a wave. Riding great waves, surfers can show off their moves, yet even the greatest surfers in the world can't show off their best stuff on weak waves. For that reason, the best surfers don't always end up in the top spots on the podium. Instead, competitors who caught the best waves collect the glory and the prize money. So it is with entrepreneurs and investors and the markets they operate in. Dynamic markets produce winning entrepreneurs, and unattractive markets make it almost impossible to create significant business value. For investors, the right market (wave) is critical and often determines whether they will even consider investing in a business. I've had many initial calls with prospective buyers that have ended abruptly once I tell them the seller's market segment.

When I use the surfer-and-wave analogy during my 17 Reasons seminars, inevitably an owner rolls her eyes, clears his throat, rustles papers or otherwise signals, "Maybe that's true for management teams that aren't as good as mine. My market may not be on fire, but we're doing just fine, thanks."

That's when I share one of the many stories I can tell about talented entrepreneurs and management teams (usually in the lower middle market) that "did just fine" in tough markets. Only when they went to market in search of an investor did they learn that all the skill and time they'd spent fighting headwinds mattered little to sophisticated buyers. That's when they discovered that few buyers have any interest in buying into difficult markets because they have too many promising targets operating in attractive markets. "Paul's" story is one I often tell owners who are convinced that buyers will reward them (and their teams) for success in a difficult market.

As I pulled into the parking lot of the offices of Paul's third-generation business, the outward signs of success were everywhere: a campus-like environment; modern, well-tended landscaping; curving paths between a modern corporate office and two 20,000-square-foot, state-of-the-art printing plants; a few hundred late-model cars filling the lot; and signage for Paul's company only.

I'd been introduced to Paul a year before my visit, during an event hosted by one of my friends who is a wealth manager. Paul was a young 50-year-old who called me to discuss some strategic plans that he and his family were considering.

On the walk to his office we talked SEC football, but as soon as we were seated, he dove right into his strategic plan.

"Zane," Paul began, "It's been a good ride, but I'm ready to sell the company."

This was not the strategic plan I was expecting, so I waited for details.

"We've done well over the past 25 years. Some years have been better than others, but each year we show a 10 to 15 percent EBITDA margin. My grandfather started this business in 1955 from scratch, and in our best years we've reached over $80 million in revenue."

I wondered to myself how long it had been since the last $80 million year, because headwinds in the printing industry hadn't slowed since 2008. Technology (especially print-on-demand) and the appearance on every corner of small specialty printshops (and large ones like FedEx® Office Print & Ship Centers) capable of printing high-end brochures, laminating menus, creating signage, and even designing professional exhibition booth graphics had significantly changed the market.

There were still plenty of high-volume jobs that required the industrial printing equipment Paul ran in his plants, but these were not high-margin jobs. The workbook and supplemental education product printing demand that had fueled his family's business in the late 80s and 90s had almost evaporated as educational publishers provided ebooks to schools and universities and students printed sections as they needed them. Most students preferred ebook versions due to ebooks' advanced note-taking capabilities and real-time end-of-chapter practice tests.

As gently as I could, I asked Paul how his team was responding to these headwinds, rising postal rates (that made shipment of high-end printed products more expensive) and mounting environmental concerns about printing practices.

"My team is the master of the pivot," Paul assured me. "We've added new list management, emailing and marketing management services to our menu. Unfortunately, our competitors keep margins low, so it is a daily challenge to cover all our overhead," he admitted.

Even though I had not anticipated that Paul's first agenda item would be a sale, I'd looked at the buyer landscape before I made the trip. As expected, I found few active investors in printing companies like Paul's, since institutional buyers were aware of the market's challenges. On the other hand, I found plenty of very active liquidators eager to talk.

In the end, Paul did work with one of these liquidators. From 200 miles away, I watched his company lay off 70 percent of its workforce as part of a systematic liquidation. The liquidator carved out the outsourced marketing business because that market was poised to grow 25 percent for the next four years. The liquidator could position that business unit to sell because of a healthy growth forecast, the fact that customers were willing to pay for outsourced marketing services, and the fact that gross margins were double that of traditional printing.

Investors want to be where the opportunities are, and that's in growing markets. They look first at the markets they want to be in, then at the players in them. Like home buyers, they target a good neighborhood first, and then they find homes in those neighborhoods.

Too often I've told variations of this story that feature skilled entrepreneurs and management teams that failed to create investment-grade companies because they put every ounce of their formidable talent, time and resources into poor or weakening markets. As in Paul's case, their markets were once strong, but they did not shift quickly or radically enough when their markets showed long-term systemic weaknesses. In every case, their efforts cost them when they went looking for investors.

Ironically, I've watched far less talented management teams build thriving companies because they were in the right place (or market) at the right time (during a period of strong growth).

SIGNS THAT YOUR COMPANY MIGHT BE IN AN UNEXCITING MARKET

> You want to dig your well where you have the best chance of finding water with the least amount of digging.

Theodore Levitt, Author and professor
Harvard Business School

Think for a moment about a neighborhood that is thriving in your city: top schools that children walk to; zero crime; easy access to high-end grocery stores, restaurants, and unique retail shops; beautiful parks and running trails; places of worship that bring a sense of peace and purpose; and neighbors who take pride in their homes and landscaping. You know the neighborhood I'm describing. Let me guess what's happening to home values there: They are going up, if not skyrocketing.

Now think about a failing neighborhood, the one that has the same momentum but in the opposite direction. No one is excited to invest in that area, build a dream home or launch a chic new restaurant. Not going to happen!

The same motives drive investors in businesses: They want solid businesses operating in thriving neighborhoods/markets. Is your business thriving in a good market?

Some signs you might be in the wrong market include:

- Organic growth is becoming increasingly difficult.
- Your target customer segment is not doing well because of systemic changes in the industry and may be experiencing stagnant growth, or worse yet, declining rates of growth.
- There is significant margin pressure on your business.
- Key personnel you need to operate your business are scarce.
- A formidable competitor has gained strong traction, and you don't have the resources to compete.
- New technology is pulling your ideal customer to more promising solutions than yours.

Owners who want to build investment-grade companies don't ignore these signs. Instead, they acquire add-on businesses, pivot or extend into exciting markets.

I devote the rest of this chapter to sharing with you the exciting market characteristics that catch and keep the attention of investors.

MARKET CHARACTERISTICS THAT EXCITE INVESTORS

Market Size

Total Addressable Market (TAM) matters. It determines how big you can grow and your chances of building an enduring sustainable enterprise. When it comes to market size, bigger is absolutely better because small markets don't energize investors. Billion-dollar TAMs are the norm in the venture capital community. But size is relative. What may be too small of a market for one type of investor could be perfect for another. As a general rule of thumb, I rarely see any type of institutional investor invest in markets with less than $400 million in TAM.

If you aren't currently operating in a market that large, *that's not a problem if as your business model matures, your product or service appeals to a larger TAM.*

For example, in Mark Zuckerberg's early pitches to venture capitalists, he described Facebook's TAM as college students who were early adopters of technology and wanted to connect with other college students—a small market. Later, Facebook discovered it could expand its TAM to users of any age who wanted to stay better connected to their friends, family and communities. That's a leap into a much larger TAM.

In a similar situation, one of my friends built a nice business providing online giving solutions for a market of an estimated 350,000+ U.S. Protestant churches. Five years in, my buddy put the systems and products in place to rapidly expand his company's TAM to include all types of religious and nonprofit organizations in the U.S. and abroad.

A Few Notes About Size

While a large market is important to investors, a large market with systemic factors working against it over the long term can be problematic. If you are in such a market, you must demonstrate that you understand these trends and have a plan to position your products/services as the market evolves.

If your market is (relatively) small today but forecasters predict rapid growth, investors will check their TAM requirement box. If you can successfully build the case that your product-market fit potential can put you on top of this rapid market growth wave, you are golden.

Doing the work to determine your true market size allows you to set realistic growth goals. It directs your efforts to position your product in the marketplace and provides insight on whether your growth can be sustained via profits or you'll need to raise capital.

Growth Rate & Potential

Ideally, you considered the size and health of your target market before developing your business plan or growth strategy. You must have the ability to serve a market for a good length of time, recouping any marketing expenses and the cost of any product or service modifications.

Obviously, investors prefer markets that are growing, not shrinking, because untapped potential gives investors more opportunity to generate business and expand market share. Well, I thought that it was obvious, but I was wrong—wrong because I see many owners enter or hunker down in markets that are stagnant or shrinking. You would think that they would do more market research (research that is at the fingertips of any undergraduate intern) before investing in a C-minus market. But you would be wrong.

"Pradeep" was a young entrepreneur, but he did not make the mistake that too many of his much older peers make about their markets.

Pradeep had a knack for high-stakes test taking. He'd scored a perfect 36 on the ACT® back in his high school days and a perfect score on the math section of the SAT®. His GMAT™ and GRE® scores were equally impressive.

During graduate school Pradeep developed a bustling tutoring service for students from affluent families that didn't mind investing heavily in their kids' college entrance exam scores. These parents felt that their investment in test prep/tutoring would pay off in scholarships and acceptance letters from top-tier schools.

Over a period of three years, Pradeep perfected his methodologies, practice tests, and test-taking tactics. When he had completed development of his highly interactive, self-paced virtual tutoring system, he asked me to review his plan to raise $3 million to quickly scale his marketing efforts.

As I reviewed his plan and his product, I found that:

- *His online product was impressive and engaging.*
- *The longitudinal data that he'd collected proved that his product helped students increase their ACT® scores dramatically.*
- *His business model was scalable.*
- *He had a built-in distribution system through his relationship with one of the largest associations for school guidance counselors.*
- *He had all the early signs of product-market fit. Word-of-mouth testimonies were producing referrals faster than he could respond to them.*

What moved me from simply sold to hyper-enthusiastic on his plan was his target market. Using data, Pradeep demonstrated that the number of test-prep dollars spent per child in U.S. households making a combined income of over $150,000 was sizable and increasing by 40 percent per year. Analysts projected that this investment would grow at this rate for another five years. International growth rates for test-prep tutoring were expected to outstrip domestic rates.

Pradeep was riding a tremendous market wave—one that, with the continuous efforts of a best-ever management team, he rode to wealth.

Competitive Landscape

The number, size and quality of competitive firms currently serving a particular target market affect a company's ability to enter that market and compete profitably. More competitors mean more headwinds to weather as you work to increase market share and margins.

If you haven't performed a detailed competitor analysis and realistically assessed how your company stacks up, you should. Collect fact sheets about your competitors, build comparison matrices, and ask your team why you win and why you lose sales pitches. Then develop a strategy to improve your win rate. If you implement that strategy and your win rate does not improve, find a new market—preferably one that is underserved or even neglected.

Easily Identifiable Target Customers & Established Distribution Channels

Identifiable targets are easier to find, study and market to. It should be simple to identify who your ideal customer is based on a set of reliable characteristics. Relationships with customers in some market segments, however, require more effort to nurture, build and maintain. These customers just don't run in packs or value community as much as others, so they do not write about the companies that serve them.

It is difficult to market to customers who don't belong to professional associations, attend trade shows, read trade journals, identify as enthusiasts or suffer from a disease or condition. A gardening enthusiast, for example, is much easier to market to than executives that value family vacations. Some markets are much easier to reach, even if Google, Instagram and Facebook provide access to almost any niche market. Ideally, find a target customer that you can market to easily, who wants and needs what you offer and will pay up for it.

Once you identify, describe, and find your ideal customers, you must be able to access them affordably. Affordable access is a whole lot easier when established distribution channels exist to reach and serve these customers.

Market Awareness

You want to *participate* in a market rather than educate it about the problem(s) that only your products or services can solve, because educating a market is brutal and brutally expensive. Contrast that with frictionless marketing: Prospects are eager to buy anything that will solve their pain/issue.

Uneducated prospects do not drive sales regardless of your marketing budget. Eager prospects do. They know what their problem is (one I call the customers' "migraine" or "back pain problem") and what it costs them. Sufferers (customers) will readily pay to relieve pain and will enthusiastically tell others about the cure. An aware market paves the way to our next attractive market characteristic: product-market fit.

Product-Market Fit Potential

The most "attractive market" is the one in which you can achieve a high degree of product-market fit (PMF).

In his essay "The Only Thing That Matters," Marc Andreessen asserts the primacy of the combination of market *and* product. He defines PMF in a simple phrase: "being in a good market with a product that can satisfy that market."[8] PMF fuels rapid growth and expands gross margins, and it is virtually impossible to build a fast-growing, healthy and sustainable business without it. For that reason, achieving it should be at the top of your agenda.

You'll know you've achieved PMF, or hit the strategic nerve of your ideal customers, when your value proposition, pricing, and product or service delivery delights them. You will know when customers sing your company's praises from the mountaintops, in online reviews, on blogs and in user groups. Better than you ever could, they'll tell others how your company has eased their pain or made their lives and businesses much, much better. When your customers become evangelists for your brand, you've achieved PMF.

Customers singing from mountaintops? That sounds a bit like an impossible dream, but it happens. It is not simple to achieve, but passionate teams that never quit experimenting, listening, testing and tweaking make PMF dreams a reality. You and your team might fail repeatedly before you finally realize the power of PMF, but I assure you, the benefits of PMF are well worth any skinned knees and bruised elbows.

Great product-market fit means that buying friction is nonexistent or nearly so. If your customers haven't yet started singing, there are ways to assess whether they are moving toward the mountains:

- The alignment between the core problem customers face and the product you've created to solve that problem is improving.
- The harmony between the problem/need that your customers have and your ability to build and deliver solutions using current resources and technology is on key. Harmony happens when you can deliver at a price point that offers you a superior margin.
- Available distribution channels make it easy for you to reach your customers and deliver your solution.

> The right market is the one that has a HIGH product-market fit.

My friends Scott and Brian have achieved PMF. Their company (*www.scottscheapflights.com*) offers a compelling subscription service to passionate international travelers that turns them into raving fans. Their flight experts and deal-finder engine find flight deals at up to 90 percent of the retail price. Their subscription-based service delights customers, who can explore the world for a fraction of what nonsubscribers would pay. The service subjects each of its recommendations to a rigorous quality evaluation, so customers know that they're receiving an incredible deal. The company's growth rate is off the charts, and customer acquisition costs are practically nonexistent.

Credibility

In an attractive market segment, your company already has—or could easily build—credibility. Conversely, a market is unattractive if you can't get prospective customers to take seriously what you provide. You must be able to develop influence in your market so that other industry leaders will assign weight to your products, services, brand and ideas. If you aren't a thought-leader in your market or don't see a path to become one, you are in the wrong market.

Company Fit & Industry Expertise

Not every company has the right strengths, resources and industry expertise to compete in every market segment. Markets have cultures and personalities that you must take into account when choosing where to focus your company's strategy, money and efforts. Don't underestimate market nuances.

I'm a huge fan of hiring veterans from the industry that you plan to serve (assuming that you are not an expert yourself) because industry knowledge is critical. Bringing industry subject-matter experts (SMEs) on board should help you avoid serious missteps caused by a lack of target market understanding. Had "Jackson" done so, he could have saved himself from an epic fail.

Before the entrepreneurial bug bit Jackson, he'd led the product development department for one of the top providers of professional education to financial professionals. Over the years, he had designed dozens of continuing education (CE) courses that had achieved massive distribution among U.S. accounting firms. He understood his CPA target market, its needs, and how to meet those needs.

In his late 30s, Jackson decided to launch his own online company to focus on creating and distributing professional development courses to teachers. He knew that the K-12 professional development market *was a $6 billion market and was growing nicely. Jackson sensed that there was a major opportunity for a company that could bring his innovative brand of online training courses to this burgeoning market.*

Only after investing over $350,000 from his savings and a home equity line of credit and raising another $750,000 from friends and family did he discover a tragic reality. Professional development in the K-12 market was drastically different from the continuing education market for financial professionals.

Jackson learned that to gain traction in the K-12 market you needed endorsements from top researchers and stacks of studies that demonstrated the efficacy of your courses. Under the best of circumstances school districts were painfully slow to adopt new training materials and preferred the highly researched, older, less flashy courses.

Under the next rock he turned over, Jackson found that four states (California, Texas, Florida and New York) set the standard for what the other 46 states purchased. If you didn't win in those four states, you didn't win anywhere. Jackson had either limited or no inroads into these states. He didn't have the contacts or the capital to engage the lobbyists that could make a case for his courses.

Jackson had been so dazzled by the size of the market that he'd overlooked what it took to achieve acceptance, much less distribution, in it. His innovative product line couldn't overcome the barriers to this market.

Had Jackson recruited a subject-matter expert for his team, he might have succeeded. As it was, he lost his business and his savings.

Profit Potential/Gross Margin Profile Of The Market

Gross margins, which represent sales minus the cost of goods sold, are the best indicator of solid, long-term unit economics. High-margin businesses have more available cash to fund growth and expansion, so markets that can provide high gross margins for its participants are alluring.

As we discussed in Reason 1, investors will pay a premium for businesses with higher margins because all revenue is not created equal. How profitable it will be to work in a specific market depends on the industry and types of companies involved.

> Every market is unique, and without deep industry understanding and expertise, navigating a market successfully can be problematic.

Mature markets tend to suppress the gross margins of their suppliers, but higher profit margins are possible in nascent, fast-growing markets because the products offered are new and competition is low.[9] It's possible to have a low realized profit margin while you are blitzing after market share, but you can show nice potential to expand that margin over time. Hint: Focus on serving highly profitable businesses and industries in growing markets. Designing a high gross margin business model (which means you must operate in a market that supports that model) makes your chances of success greater and the rewards of success even greater. Low opportunity profit margin market segments do not support the building of valuable enterprises. Find a better neighborhood/market in which to build your dream home/business.

Differentiation: The Power Of Niche Markets

"If you're not thinking market segments, you're not thinking."

Theodore Levitt

A niche market is a subset of a larger market, characterized by its unique quantifiable and serviceable needs. Large, general markets have many incumbents, most of whom can't focus their resources on smaller markets and simultaneously meet their growth goals. Often niche markets are fast growers, and the companies that serve them well can generate outsized growth/results because specialized competitors have not overrun them.

Investing in market research always provides a healthy ROI.

"Malcolm" owned a successful high-end fitness center in the Dallas area. Over 400 loyal members—mostly 30-something professionals—paid dues of $200 per month to work out using Malcolm's unique blend of interval cardio workouts and Olympic powerlifting.

Malcolm's dream was to expand his concept to other areas of Dallas and beyond using a franchise model. As he considered the idea, several oil industry executives who worked out at his facility suggested what they thought would be a more attractive concept and said they'd be willing to fund it.

Their concept was a gym that catered to the serious high-school athletes, college athletes and competitive weekend warriors who participated in CrossFit® and Tough Mudder® events. To these potential investors, the demand in large cities for facilities committed to the elite athlete seemed evident. Commitment would make those athletes loyal members and lower the risk of attrition compared to the typical (i.e., non-elite) gym member.

As a former running back for the University of Texas, Malcolm loved the idea of enhancing performance for elite athletes. He was prepared to pivot from his current model and eager to attack this market segment.

The group of angel investors (deep-pocketed but new to private company investing) was ready to fund a rapid expansion of this new concept.

In preparing for his meeting with his interested investors, Malcolm prepared a business plan. He asked one of his current gym members (Pete, a private equity pro) to review that plan. When the member asked about market research, Malcolm admitted that he'd used anecdotal data. Pete challenged Malcolm to go deeper in his market research. "Hire a local MBA student to do some research," Pete advised. "Only a rookie investor accepts anecdotes as evidence."

Malcolm took Pete's advice and hired a local MBA student to do some research on his new target market. The student's research revealed that:

- *Elite athletes are the most demanding of all gym members. They require more expensive equipment, spend more time in the gym (which limits member capacity), and are not as loyal as more casual athletes.*
- *Elite athletes are not as likely as non-elite-athletes to recommend their gyms to others.*

This market research proved that Malcolm's current model was the correct one, and it saved Malcolm and his investors from making a HUGE mistake. The findings told Malcolm that his current model was the one to expand, since he had begun to see signs of an amazing product-market fit.

When Malcolm presented his plan to the oilmen funders, they understood that the market research had proved that their desire for elite gyms was flawed. Instead, they used that research as a reason to fund Malcolm's current model. Today Malcolm has seven gyms in the Dallas-Fort Worth market, and he is looking to expand into two other major markets.

If you can identify what makes a market segment unique (or how customers in that segment respond differently than other customers to products and services), you have a valuable angle to better communicate your value proposition effectively. This insight positions you to customize your products/services offerings to this market niche and beat competitors.

Finding The Right Market

Validate The Market Before Diving In.

I've watched too many entrepreneurs (like Jackson, who tried unsuccessfully to enter the K-12 professional development market) make the fatal error of diving or pivoting into, or acquiring, a business in an unfamiliar market without validating it first.

A Market Validation Plan (MVP)[10] documents how you will engage your target market to determine whether the market:

1. Sees a need for your product.
2. Likes the product or product concept.
3. Is willing to buy the product at a price that supports healthy gross margins.

An MVP involves using a series of interviews to test a product concept against a potential target. By asking thoughtful questions and engaging with potential customers, you can validate whether your product solves a real need, who your potential customers are, where they hang out, and ultimately whether there's a viable market for your product.

Have you completed an MVP that confirms the *ideal market* for your products and services? The better understanding you have of your target market, the better probability of a high product-market fit.

Acquire Your Way Into An Attractive Market.

If at this point in the chapter you suspect that your market doesn't qualify as exciting, much less attractive, in the eyes of investors—perhaps because it is showing signs of decline—take action before your business loses significant value.

Maybe you have taken action. You've studied several potential pivots into new markets, and the market validation results are soft. What now?

Identify hot adjacent markets that you understand and have the unique requirements to thrive in. Then go look for the right company to purchase. As we discussed in the previous chapter, acquisitions accelerate growth but they can also position you in a better market. Large public companies employ this value-creation strategy every day:

- The Coca-Cola Company purchases a fast-growing kombucha brand because of the brand's early leadership in this burgeoning market.

- Microsoft purchases an innovative Xbox gaming headset company to ensure it has a stake in this lucrative and growing gaming accessory market.
- Amazon purchases a leader in a fast-growing durable equipment home health care category to leverage its world-class distribution systems.

Small private companies with limited resources execute acquisition strategies even more often than the big hitters. If you haven't yet tested the acquisition waters, you might be surprised at how many companies, operating in fantastic markets, can be acquired efficiently and affordably. Think about all the baby boomers who are eager to sell their businesses and retire. Or consider all the owners who are ready to exit because of issues like divorce, failing health, aging parents, partner disputes or burnout. And don't forget about the many owners who can't scale their companies and are actively looking for someone with the ability, energy and capital to take on the opportunity.

Surf's Up!

The bottom line is that you must ask yourself on a regular basis whether your target market would excite an investor. Here's your checklist:

- Sizable TAM (or a niche market with all the following characteristics).
- Healthy growth rate and potential for future growth.
- Favorable competitive landscape.
- Easily identifiable customers and established distribution channels.
- Customers who are aware of their need for your product or service.
- Great potential for positive product fit.
- Credibility in the marketplace.
- Synchronistic company fit and resources.
- Favorable profit and gross margin potential.

If your market doesn't have these characteristics and you want your company to be investment grade, you can't just sit on your surfboard and hope the pond you're in will provide a great wave.

Pivot radically, extend your reach thoughtfully and dramatically, or acquire your way into a great market, because if you aren't riding a great wave, your company will lose enterprise value.

Investors love big waves. Find yours.

You might not be able to attract investors or buyers if the market your company operates in is unattractive, insignificant, or has slow or no growth.

RECOMMENDATIONS

1. **If your market is no longer as vibrant as it once was and/or it shows signs of long-term systemic weakness, you and your management team must shift quickly—and perhaps radically—into a new market.** You can't build an investment-grade company by working harder.
   - Do you suspect that your market is a nonstarter for investors?
   Ask an investment banker who works with companies in your industry about buyer activity.

2. Know the facts about your current market.
- Define and quantify your addressable market.
- Survey, study and profile your customers.
  - Who are they? (age, demographic)
  - How do they use your product or service?
  - Why do they choose to use your product or service?
  - What would cause them to switch to another product or service?
- Perform a detailed competitor analysis and be realistic about how you stack up. You should have fact sheets on all your major competitors that include information about why you win and why you lose against each. The analysis should also include whether competitors are getting better or worse at meeting customer needs.
- If you are losing more than you are winning against competitors, can you execute a strategy that allows you to win more and become stronger?

3. Test a new market to assess whether it has the characteristics that attract investors *before* you choose to enter it.
- Would adjacent product or service lines appeal to a broader market?
  As an example, my firm broadened its service line to include fractional CFO services. In the private-company space we serve, not only do fractional CFO services act as a funnel of opportunities for our M&A practice, there's a broader market for them than for our core M&A transaction services.
  - Would adjacent product or service lines appeal to a more attractive niche market?
  For example, a company that specializes in on-premise estimating software for commercial specialty contractors could acquire a SaaS compliance-software package for the HVAC specialty contractor segment. The HVAC contractor segment is one of the healthiest specialty contractor niches and shows no signs of slowing.
- Would substantially expanding your geographic footprint increase your market TAM and, therefore, make your market more exciting for investors?
- Commission a Market Validation Plan.

4. Before you develop an adjacent service or product, expand your geographic footprint, or acquire a company in another market, ask questions.
- What is the growth rate and potential of this market?
- How numerous, what size and how adept are the firms already in this market?
- Are consumers in this market easily identifiable? Do they want and need the product or service you would offer, and are they willing to pay for it?
- Are customers in your target market aware that they need what you offer?
- Can you create a compelling product-market fit in a given market? (If not, you aren't going to grow.)
- Can you access customers in this market affordably? Do they attend trade shows, use industry consultants, and/or belong to trade associations?
- Will the influencers in the industry listen to you? How easy is it to grow and maintain credibility with this market? If you have already established credibility, can you build on it in a new market? How?
- Does your company have the right strengths and resources to compete in this segment? Is your company's culture consistent with this market segment's traits and attributes?

- Will this market support a high-gross-margin business model?
- Is this market so unique that you can customize your product or service offerings to it and beat competitors?
- If you are considering a niche market, have specialized competitors already dominated it? (If not and you can serve the market well, you can generate outsized growth/results.)

TAKEAWAYS

1. **Buyers want to be in markets that have excellent current and long-term profit potential and strong characteristics that support stable and long-term growth.**

2. **There is a direct correlation between the attractiveness and growth potential of your target market and buyer/investor interest.**

3. **If you can't beat competitors in your market consistently and improve your win rate, find a new market.**

4. **It is easier to pivot into an adjacent market than to pivot into a completely different one.**

5. **There is no greater accelerator of growth than product-market fit (PMF).**

    Slugging away when PMF is not present is miserable to live through and painful to observe.

6. **Focus on serving highly profitable businesses and industries in growing markets.**

7. **Be constantly on the lookout for synergistic add-on acquisition opportunities that could better position your company in highly attractive markets.**

    Before entering an attractive market, execute a Market Validation Plan to assess its viability.

REASON 4

Your Company Does Not Have Dominant Market Share.

IF YOU AREN'T THE BIGGEST FISH IN YOUR POND, FIND AND DOMINATE A NEW POND.

L et's be realistic. Not all of us can grow our companies to the size necessary to attract high caliber investors or buyers. That's why it's a very good thing that there's another way for us to get their attention and receive premium valuations for our companies. The owner of a small ($6 million in annual revenues) technology services company shows us all how it's done.

A few years ago, an email appeared in my inbox from "Blake," the owner/operator of "Bright Lights Tech" (BLT), a New York City-based IT outsourcing company. He wanted to pick my brain about raising capital to buy out one of his partners.

Before I picked up the phone to ask Blake a few questions that would help me determine if there might be some capital options in the market, I poured myself a glass of sweet tea. Sweet tea in the Deep South is more like syrup than tea, so I prefer mine diluted and over crushed ice.

Six months earlier, I'd learned that playing the stereotypical southerner against Blake's New York City bluster was a lot of fun. At a conference, we'd been paired up in a negotiation skills exercise and had won the "Odd Couple Award." I guess my drawl and his Brooklynese impressed our colleagues. Or maybe it was my smooth delivery punctuated by his, "You gotta problem with dat?"

"Zane, it's been awhile!" Blake started. "How's life in the slow lane?"

"Not much doin' down here," I said—drawing out every syllable to maximum length. "How's life in the Big Apple?" I couldn't resist. I knew Blake flinched a little every time he heard that phrase.

"Living the good life, Zane. Except for this puny issue with my partner."

"The cubes in my tea are starting to melt, so for now, let's skip the 'puny issue' and tell me where you are financially," I said.

"No time for the niceties, huh Zane?" Blake asked. "We sure don't want your tea to get watery." (Little did he know that "watery" was how I preferred my tea. I could tell he was enjoying this.) "We're just shy of $10 million in annual revenues with an EBITDA margin of around 17 percent. We're pushing 24 percent annual growth. You know, we do things quickly up here."

"I'm impressed," I responded. "That's a nice clip for an outsourcing company of your size. Challenge is, you may be just a little small to attract the interest of growth equity or buyout firms in this space. They typically want a minimum of $2 million in TTM EBITDA to meet their minimum check size."

"Check size, schmeck size. Listen, Zane, I've got some good stuff going on up here."

"I've got a few minutes left on these ice cubes so tell me about it," I offered.

In those few minutes, I had become increasingly impressed. Blake had his company squared away. He knew his business and had built a loyal team of highly competent and certification-decorated engineers. BLT's offerings were legitimate, and he described a highly systematized service delivery model.

My tea went untouched as Blake kept talking. It was when I squeezed in my questions about his target market, geography and any niche specialization that the conversation got really interesting.

Blake told me that BLT operated only in "The City" and in one vertical niche. "Tight geography, vertical niche," I interjected. "Tell me more."

"We target the K-12 market exclusively by offering to outsource their tech infrastructures. Busy school districts need to focus on teaching, not fooling with the latest security updates from Microsoft. All our customers are charter schools, so we're, by a long shot, the No. 1 outsourcing company in the NYC market."

"Define 'long shot,'" I requested.

"We've locked down over 45 percent of the market, and our biggest competitor is a fifth of our size" he replied.

Forty-five percent market share is a special and substantial barrier to entry.

"Whattaya think?" Blake asked. "And try to make your long story short. I gotta train to catch."

"Well," I started out deliberately slowly, "on paper BLT is too small to attract institutional capital, but …" As tempted as I was to drag out my explanation, I was too excited. "With your market share/penetration, the opportunity is real. I think we can attract strategic buyers and growth capital providers."

"Well I'll be!" said Blake. "You got to the point in time for me to make it home for dinner! Have your folks call me, and I'll send whatever you need to put something together for these money guys."

When we subsequently contacted the companies on our prospective buyer list, several strategic buyers and growth capital providers indicated interest in Blake's niche customer base. The strategic buyers had lots of complementary technology products to sell to charter schools—a market that wasn't going away. These buyers saw that BLT's model, offerings and specialized tool kits were scalable and could be quickly replicated in other large U.S. cities with growing charter school populations.

BLT's market domination meant that his sub-$10 million, "local" company had a huge market opportunity to grow into a "national" company.

To illustrate BLT's current control of the charter school market and show the regional markets it could expand into we created Figure 4.1.

FIG. 4.1 Niche Focus: BLT

Vertical Market Focus

Charter schools are generally well-funded and rely on technology and communication systems.

Recent surveys indicate that "vertical-market MSPs* seem to be the most profitable, most highly-valued MSPs."

BLT's focus on an underserved vertical gives it targeted segment expertise and an advantage in a competitive bidding process. BLT further leverages its resources by contacting respected consulting centers of influence within the education community.

A Managed Service Provider (MSP) manages (remotely) its customers' infrastructures or the software that its customers provide to their users.

Niche Vertical Focus: Building Franchise Value

BLT has captured 57 of the 211 charter schools in its target.

Regional Market Segments

Vertical Market	Estimated Quantity	Detailed Breakdown
Charter Schools	211	· NYC: 211
Private Schools	603	· NYC: 165 · LI: 200 Religious: 238
Public Schools	2,200	· NYC: 1,700 · LI: 500

Blake's investor willingly paid a market multiple (8.5x TTM EBITDA) that far exceeded the norm (4.5x to 5.5x TTM) for general outsourcing companies, primarily because Blake's company was the dominant player in a very hot niche. Without BLT's level of niche penetration, I would argue that it would have been next to impossible to find any institutional buyers who would want a general tech services company of this size in the NYC market.

Blake's buyer planned to use BLT to enter other charter school markets and then pivot into private schools, public schools and even higher education. BLT's success in dominating the NYC market gave strong indication that it would have success in other large cities with thriving charter school movements. The buyer included geographic expansion in its growth plan and would exploit a host of cross-selling opportunities.

By focusing exclusively on a narrow niche, Blake was able to position his "small company" as a "large fish in a small pond" and produce a premium valuation for BLT.

Stand Out From The Herd.

When strategic buyers go hunting for an acquisition, they first decide where they're going to hunt (based on their growth strategies), and then they go after the big game. They aren't interested in starting from scratch (greenfielding), because it takes years to raise a champion. Once they pick the market to enter, they pursue the No.1 player in that market.

Financial buyers aren't much different. Their objective is the same: They want the biggest player in the market. This is where they get the value and the growth accelerators they're after. Small deals don't appear on their acquisition criteria screens, because they just don't move the needle.

In either case, you want your company to stand out from the crowd and garner attention from buyers.

When strategic buyers decide to pursue a new market, geography or product line, they prefer to purchase "ready-made" enterprises. Greenfielding is just too time consuming. Time is money, and collapsing time frames is critical to their growth strategies. Starting up an internal new product team or focusing a marketing team on educating new markets is too slow. Time is precious and, therefore, valuable. For this reason, positioning your company as the leader in your chosen niche is exceptionally valuable when strategic buyers come looking.

If You Can't Be The Biggest, Be The Fastest.

Rapid growth garners lots of attention, so it is one of the best ways to catch the eye of strategic buyers and investors, who just can't help but be curious about how companies manage to capture market share quickly and distance themselves from competitors. Rapid growth also attracts the attention of larger and more resourced competitors, so you'd better be prepared to protect your territory—think barrier to entry or competitive advantage—because you'll need everything you've got to defend against their attempts to take over your market and destroy your business.

Getting noticed requires commanding a *good chunk* of your market niche. "Good chunk" may not be a technical term but it is broad enough to cover every situation. A good chunk in your market is the size that it takes to get noticed. A good chunk is the quality that makes you the prettiest girl at the dance. It's having more market share than your competitors and expanding on that percentage every quarter. A good chunk is what makes you stand out *relative* to the crowd you're standing in. Or, as we said in Reason 2, it means running from a bear faster than your hiking buddy can.

Go Niche Or Go Home.

Unless you're John Doerr (venture capitalist and former presidential advisor), being the smartest guy in the room at the reunion of your Harvard MBA class is a tall order. But being the smartest at your grade school reunion? That's doable.

Standing out in a smaller crowd (as BLT did) is possibly the smartest strategy small companies can use to drive value and make noise among buyers/investors. If your company is small today but you have big aspirations for it, "Go niche or go home."

Dominating A Niche Cuts Through The Noise.

When you customize a solution and create a product/services road map that is compelling to your target market, you can streamline your marketing messaging and tell the perfect story. You know which trade shows to attend, which lists to purchase, which influential clients to pursue, etc.

As my friend David Gray, former CEO of Daxko (a firm that dominated the software provider space for YMCAs), says, "You should be hyper-focused on your niche and suck every bit of oxygen out of it before you start looking elsewhere."

Customers And Prospects Love Niche Dominators.

Everyone—clients included—likes to think they are special and different. Clients absolutely love it when we make it our passion to meet their specific requirements and refuse to "dumb down" our products for the broader marketplace.

Dominating A Niche Creates A More Persuasive Value Proposition.

The niche domination strategy of one of my clients, "Bones Billing," was to focus on large orthopedic practices. Instead of offering revenue cycle billing services to physicians in multiple specialties, "Bones Billing" focused on the unique set of needs/challenges of 100 orthopedic practices.

Bones spoke the language of its niche. It understood what makes orthopedic practices unique and could highlight how it better met their needs and challenges. It made a compelling case that competitors who offered more generic services simply could not make.

Dominating A Niche Makes You The Expert.

Who doesn't want to do business with the expert that speaks your language?

On the way to the recycling bin one Saturday, I picked out one of those neighborhood circulars. The cover listed a few articles, one by a local physical therapist. The tagline said something like "Catering to high-performance athletes." No mention of "mature" or "aging" athletes.

I admit it. The tagline appealed to my ego. The article? Even more so. Without ever using the "M" or "A" words, the author discussed the issues that athletes—along a continuum of ages—experience in a variety of high-performance movements (e.g., CrossFit®, tennis and basketball). As I read, I felt connected because the author understood my goal: to continue to be relevant on the court and in the gym as I age. (Don't laugh. Competitive relevance is still a need of mine).

The author wasn't offering a cookie-cutter plan. His services were specialized and designed "just for me." My competitive nerve had been activated, and I called him.

Each market and submarket has nuances, vocabularies and peculiarities. Differentiate yourself by mastering these, and you'll outshine your "generalist" competitors. Narrow the focus, and you'll increase the speed at which you become a thought leader.

How To Position Your Company To Dominate

There is a straightforward process that companies—one-day investment-grade companies—use to dominate their markets. The steps in that process are:

Step 1. Define your total addressable market and serviceable addressable market.

Step 2. Tier the market.

Step 3. Choose your niche.

Step 4. Maintain constant communication with your niche market.

Step 5. Invest in your market segment.

Step 6. Make market share your North Star.

Step 7. Perform iterative competitive analysis.

Step 8. Thoughtfully expand your market focus to the next adjacent tier and return to Step 1.

Step 1. Define Your Total Addressable Market And Serviceable Addressable Market.

Defining total addressable market (TAM) and serviceable addressable market (SAM) and profiling the customers in each take research and attention to detail. (SAM is the portion of the TAM that can best be served by a company's existing core competencies, comparative advantages and geographic reach.) Defining these markets also requires the input of stakeholders and an objective advisor because as we push each day to make meaningful strides in our target markets, it is easy to tell ourselves that we are just on the uphill climb to the summit. Objective advisors can tell us whether we are climbing or just wearing ourselves out pedaling around a cul-de-sac.

Perseverance is a key character trait in leaders and winners, and I'm a HUGE fan of people who do not quit. But perseverance can blind the toughest entrepreneurs to the signals that we are climbing the wrong market hill—or no hill at all. Luckily, advisors (e.g., attorneys, bankers and CPAs) and stakeholders often have better vantage points on the races we're running. Those stakeholders include:

- Customers.
- The prospects who say "No."
- Partners.
- Employees/key team members.

If you take the time to listen to these advisors and stakeholders and are open to their observations, you may find that market pivots are sometimes the right strategy.

Carefully defining your TAM and SAM focuses your efforts and resources appropriately. One reality that I've witnessed time and time again in both my career and life is **"Over time, focus on the right actions ALWAYS creates significant value."** If writing that sentence a second time would drive home the truth of the point, I would. Do me a favor. Read it again.

Step 2. Tier the Market.

The owner of Bones Billing did his homework before he picked his niche. He researched and documented the nuances of geography (e.g., large city vs. small city practice), insurance reimbursement processes and rates, practice size, and coding practices. Tiering the market involves going deep and examining each layer (submarket) and the unique characteristics of the layers.

Step 3. Choose Your Niche.

Once you've done your research, identify where you can move the needle. You do that by contracting your target market size/scope to the point where you can register on the radar as a player. (Radars only pick up the top three players.) Quickly establish yourself and "suck all the oxygen out" of that smaller market before you incrementally broaden your focus.

Let's look again at Bones Billing. Its options were to target orthopedic practices:

- In 15 southern states and establish a presence in 5 percent of the practices in each.
- In five states (Mississippi, Alabama, Tennessee, Georgia and Louisiana) and establish a presence in 17 percent of the practices in each.
- In Tennessee and establish a presence in 69 percent of the practices there.
- In the metropolitan areas of Memphis, Nashville and Knoxville and establish a presence in 80 percent of the practices in the metropolitan areas of each of those cities.

Focus also increases gross margins because a tighter geography lowers delivery costs.

When the board of a national or regional medical services powerhouse decides to market its services to orthopedic practices in the South and looks for a company that gives it access, Bones Billing will jump off the target list in flashing neon lights. Bones Billing provides a beachhead (i.e., proven systems and processes) and a head start for expansion into the market that the prospective buyer wants to crack.

> If you chase two rabbits, you won't catch either one.

Step 4. Maintain Constant Communication With Your Niche Market.

Initiating an ongoing conversation with your customers provides valuable insight into your business. Many software platforms facilitate this conversation through feedback from your sales force, customer service call records, online chat sessions, social media and survey forms.

Step 5. Invest In Your Market Segment.

Once you've chosen your segment, focus your growth initiatives on customers in that segment. Go to the trade shows they attend. Read what they read. Do everything you can think of to build your credibility with them. Over time, your company will gain traction and influence as a thought-leader. As it does, buyers and investors will begin to take notice as well.

> As owners, it is tempting to flit from niche to niche rather than commit to one market segment. Resist the temptation and do what creates value, not what is easy. Focus and once you dominate your niche, move out into other markets.

Step 6. Make Market Share Your North Star.

If your company invests in activities that don't improve its market share, stop. Orient your company and all of its resources toward increasing market share. Create a pie chart that shows your company systematically eating more of your market's pie, and hang it above your desk. Obsess over winning in your defined market.

Step 7. Perform Iterative Competitive Analysis.

To dominate your target market, you must understand your strengths and weaknesses and those of your competitors. Why do they win with your target market, and why do you?

You must have the answers to those questions before you can design strategies to provide differentiated value over your competition. Those strategies should:

1. Exploit competitors' weaknesses (as you would a competitor's weak backhand in tennis).
2. Muffle the impact of their strengths by improving in areas where you can close the gap.

Maintaining market dominance takes daily commitment, as every day your competitors commit to undermine your leadership position. Your job is to continually improve compared to your competitors—especially the strongest ones. They are the ones who drive you to improve and innovate.

> Your competitor got better today. Did you?

Step 8. Thoughtfully Expand Your Market Focus To The Next Adjacent Tier And Return To Step 1.

Only after you demonstrate the ability to dominate your initial (narrow) market can you build a credible growth model. That growth model/plan should highlight how you will systematically expand your market opportunity as you demonstrate success in progressively larger markets.

Investors love disciplined execution based on increasing levels of success. That's why I cringe when entrepreneurs say they are going national, or worse, international before they have demonstrated market share growth (i.e., validated product fit) and real traction in a small, targeted segment of their TAM (i.e., SAM).

FIG. 4.2 Bones Billing Company

Step 1	Define Your Total and Serviceable Addressable Markets.	Quantify the U.S. market opportunity for physician practice billing services.
Step 2	Tier The Market.	Determine which practice specialties are the "best market." Use trade association data to categorize practices into small, medium and large.
Step 3	Choose Your Niche.	Decide which type of physician practice (e.g., pediatric, family, orthopedic) to target. Choose initial geographic focus. For example, within a100-mile radius of capital city, one major U.S. designated market area (DMA), etc. Don't allow customer demand to make the decision for you.
Step 4	Maintain Constant Communication With Your Niche Market.	Have ongoing conversations with orthopedic practice managers and doctors. Ask what they most value in doing business with you, and act on what you learn. Ask customers how your company compares to your competitors.
Step 5	Invest In Your Market Segment.	Become a hungry student of your market segment. Hire subject matter experts (e.g., former practice managers for large orthopedic practices) who have worked in this space their entire careers. Interview orthopedic surgeons/practice owners. Go to trade shows and ask questions.
Step 6	Make Market Share Your North Star.	Document the market share you own, the one you want and your plan to grow your share.
Step 7	Perform Iterative Competitive Analysis.	Continually study the best teachers—your best competitors. Study adjacent market competitors, and adopt best practices that could fit your niche.
Step 8	Thoughtfully Expand Your Market Focus To The Next Adjacent Tier And Return To Step 1.	Once you control 10% to 15% of your chosen market, consider whether to open in a new market in a nearby city or DMA to maintain your orthopedic practice focus or add a new medical specialty in your geography.

Great product-market fit results in rapid market share growth and proves that you are ready to expand into another market. If customers love your product/service and can't help but talk to others about your company, stand back. Growth can be explosive.

Figure 4.2 illustrates how the eight-step process that I've just described would apply to Bones Billing. As you read it, think about how the process applies to your company.

A STORY OF MARKET SHARE DOMINATION

Blake's company, BLT, (See pages 47 to 49.) was a great example of a small company leveraging its significant market share in its market niche to attract the attention of very large buyers. In our next example, we see how another "small" company with $3.9 million in annual recurring revenue (ARR) used detailed customer segmentation to demonstrate its leadership in niche sectors of a larger market.

Every member of "BankRite's" management team knew what motivated bank executives and that compliance with state and federal regulations kept them up at night. Using that understanding, they built an offering carefully crafted to help bankers sleep better.

BankRite offered community banks a novel data service via monthly subscriptions of $500 to $650—depending on the size of the bank. (Note the recurring revenue business model.)

Within three years of the initial rollout, BankRite had over 586 subscriber banks. Management attributed its success to: (1) the right product, (2) a persuasive story about its product solution, and (3) conveying its story consistently to the right people.

With market domination in place, BankRite set out to systematically segment its market and become the dominant player in each segment. Figure 4.3 on the following page summarizes the results of BankRite's research, and its share of each segment after three years.

As you can see, BankRite collected information about the total U.S. community bank market (its TAM) and segmented that market into three asset size categories (small, medium and large). It knew the number of possible customers in each segment and into which category its customers fit. Once it established its footprint in the large community banking segment, it moved into each smaller segment until it achieved traction in all three. In contrast to Bones Billing, BankRite had customers in every state demonstrating its sophistication or ability to operate in compliance with 50 different sets of state regulations.

It's worth noting that Figure 4.3 isn't something my team cooked up as a marketing piece. Unlike Blake at BLT, BankRite's management team wasn't out looking for an investor. It had been contacted by a senior vice president of corporate strategy from "Bank Behemoth," an international public company that provided core banking software. It had been trying to break into the U.S. banking market unsuccessfully for years when this executive stumbled upon one of BankRite's quarterly newsletters.

The more research this executive did on BankRite, the more drawn in he was. When he contacted BankRite, its management team called me to discuss possible responses.

BankRite's market segmentation chart was a central feature of the carefully packaged response that we prepared. One look at it and Bank Behemoth was hooked. It had to have BankRite.

The market valuation that Bank Behemoth ultimately assigned to the acquisition of BankRite proved just how compelling this story of market share across the three U.S.-community-bank segments really was.

FIG. 4.3 Niche Focus: BankRite

Sizable Presence in Community Bank Market

Primary Target: community banks under $8B in assets

U.S. TAM: 5,200 institutions – Average asset size: $200MM

Customer Base: 550+ (≈11% of market share) Average asset size: $45MM

Total Customer Assets: $220B (more than 15% of the $1.2T in total market assets)

BankRite serves banks in all segments, but has strong presence in the large bank segment:
   · 320 members
   · ≈20% share of the market segment
   · ≈60% of BankRite's customer base

The community bank market offers ample growth, and BankRite is well-positioned and on the right growth trajectory to further expand its footprint.

Estimated Market Size

U.S. Community Bank Market Breakdown	Prospect Universe	Market Share by Segment	Total Asset Size by Segment	BankRite Customers by Segment	BankRite Market Share by Segment	BankRite Total Asset Size by Segment
Small Community Banks <$100MM in assets	1,500	28.9%	$65B	70	4.7%	$3B
Medium Community Banks $100MM-$200MM in assets	2,100	40.4%	$285B	190	9.1%	$17B
Large Community Banks >$200MM in assets	1,600	30.7%	$850B	320	20.0%	$200B
TOTAL	5,200	100.0%	$1.2T	580	33.8%	$220B

**You might not be able to attract investors or buyers
if your market share is practically invisible.**

RECOMMENDATIONS

1. Position your company to dominate in eight steps.

    Step 1. Define your total and serviceable addressable markets.

- Do you have a current (within the last three years) market study?
- If not, you could contract a local professor or business school student to assist you with an assessment.

    Step 2. Tier the market.

- How do you define small, medium and large customers?
- Can you tier your market by geography?
- What determines size (e.g., revenue, number of employees, number of locations)? Trade associations can provide appropriate categorization metrics.

    Step 3. Choose your niche.

- How easily can you systematically move from one tier of the market to the next larger or adjacent one?
- Will you focus on a particular type of customer or on a particular geographic area?
- Are you thinking the way strategic buyers think when they execute a roll-up strategy?

    Step 4. Maintain constant communication with your niche market.

- Do you ask customers what they most value about doing business with you?
- Do you know where you fall short of your competitors in your customers' eyes?
- Do you act on what your customers tell you?

    Step 5. Invest in your market segment.

- Do you read the publications your customers do?
- Hire a subject-matter expert to educate you on the detailed requirements of your target market.
- Do you know everything there is to know about your existing and prospective customers? If not,

    Step 6. Make market share your North Star.

    Have you documented (via a graph on your office wall or whiteboard) the market share you own and your strategy to conquer a bigger share?

    Step 7. Perform iterative competitive analysis.

- Do you study the competitors in your current market (and those in the market you wish to move into) and have a strategy to take market share from this?
- Do you maintain a competitive matrix with unbiased ratings that compare you to your competitors around the key buying requirements of your market?

    Step 8. Thoughtfully expand your market focus to the next adjacent tier, and return to Step 1.

2. If you can't be the biggest fish in a big pond, find a smaller pond where you can be the big fish.
(See BankRite on pages 55 to 56 and Bright Lights Tech on pages 47 to 49.) For example, if you discover you're the No. 4 commercial security firm in the Chicago market, decrease your target market radius to a few Chicagoland ZIP codes until you break into one of the top two spots. Once you do so, broaden your geographic radius and work to take one of the top two spots in that broader market. When you've accomplished that, broaden your geographic radius again.

3. Design your growth strategy to gain control of your market niche.

Document and invest in growth initiatives designed to acquire greater market share. If BankRite's management team had chosen to expand into banking accounting software, that move would have done nothing to increase its share in its compliance niche market. Your investments in growth must align with the market you are trying to win.

- Is your growth strategy focused on activities that move the needle in the niche (or core) market that you seek to dominate? For example, have you improved your Net Promoter Score®* or built barriers that matter? Have you concentrated efforts on high-margin revenue streams?
- Have you attached market share goals to each growth strategy?

4. Describe your core/niche market in your executive summary.

Include a succinct description of your current target niche market share (and how you plan to grow it) and your present and projected share of it.

5. Track your share of the market at least annually.

Use industry and trade association data and government research reports (e.g., information from the U.S. Small Business Administration and Census Bureau). Purchase segment information from information technology research companies such as Gartner, Inc., International Data Corporation, IBISWorld and 451 Research.

TAKEAWAYS

1. In today's noisy market you must stand out to get sales traction.

A dominate-the-niche strategy attracts notice more quickly than attempting to take a bite out of a larger market.

2. The riches are in the niches.

The "gold" is in the niches and mining them shows the world that you are a "player" in the space.

3. Buyers pay big for No. 1, so there's real differentiated value in being No. 1 in the market you serve. If your company is not No. 1 in its defined market, you need to demonstrate that it is gaining ground on the competitor who is.

4. Grow strategically from your core.

Don't go after growth in markets far beyond your boundaries or capabilities.

---

* Fred Reichheld (a partner at Bain & Company) first introduced this metric in an article in the *Harvard Business Review* in 2003. Reichheld, Bain & Company and Satmatrix have converted a metric into a management system.

Your Company Does Not Have What It Takes To Scale.

EVALUATE, IMPROVE, DELEGATE, AUTOMATE AND DOCUMENT YOUR SYSTEMS.

Horse racing is a metaphor that I like to use when discussing buyers/investors and the qualities they want in companies they seek to acquire. Buyers and investors are the bettors in the M&A marketplace. They put their money on quality managers (jockeys) with great track records, who run top-notch systems (thoroughbred horses) that dominate a quality market niche (the inside rail).

In June of 2013, a six-year-old mare, Downtown Hottie, came from behind to finish ahead of the nearest horse by almost a full length. She was first in the sixth race of the day at Belmont Park, but she didn't win. She was disqualified because she'd lost her jockey right out of the gate. I tell that story because in this chapter I'm going to add to our horse racing metaphor and seemingly contradict it. I'm going to suggest that we talk about how to make your company attractive to a bettor/buyer *even if you lose critical employees.*

Beyond the initial shock of losing key talent and obvious challenge of quickly hiring replacements, how critically would your business be impacted?

- Would these losses be a temporary setback or a critical blow?
- Could new salespeople quickly adopt your CRM system and seamlessly continue with prospects no matter where the prospects are in the sales cycle?
- Is your code so well documented that a new lead developer could make sense of your software products and quickly become productive?
- By day five could customer service personnel answer frequently asked questions about your services or products?
- Could a newly hired finance/accounting group know which key performance indicators (KPIs) you track and how to calculate them?
- Could your implementation team onboard new customers successfully?

If you answer, "Oh, give me a break. Of course not!" your company lacks the repeatable, documented, scalable processes that investment-grade companies have in place.

Systems Defined

If you think of your organization as a system, rather than as a collection of people, the system or operation exists no matter who is working for you. Or, think of your business as a franchisor: The operations manual that you hand to franchisees should enable them to quickly, and so completely, replicate your processes and procedures, that they create carbon copies of your company.

In an article in the Southwest Airlines magazine, company chairman and CEO, Gary C. Kelly, summarized the beauty (and value) of Southwest's systems in just three sentences. "Look outside your window when you land and watch the sequence of events that takes place as we unload your bags, provision the aircraft, refuel, deplane, load another set of bags, and welcome onboard a new plane full of Customers. It's fascinating—much like watching your favorite sports team brilliantly execute a play on the field. You can quickly gain an appreciation for why the Team concept is so important, not only to what we do but also to how we do it."[11]

Every company has systems. They may be great like the one Kelly describes. They may be ad hoc, mediocre or substandard, but every company has a way to produce and deliver its service or product.

In fact, all businesses have three types of systems or processes. In his book "High Performance Through Business Process Management: Strategy Execution in a Digital World,"[12] Mathias Kirchmer defines three broad types of processes:

Type 1: Operational processes that focus on properly executing the operational tasks of an organization. Employees use these processes to "get things done."

Type 2: Management processes ensure that the operational processes are conducted appropriately. These processes equip managers to "ensure efficient and effective work processes."

Type 3: Governance processes ensure that an entity is operating in full compliance with necessary legal regulations, guidelines and shareholder expectations. Using these processes executives bring the company into compliance with all "rules and guidelines for business success."

Usually, a company's core processes are operational (Type 1), but not always. In any type of financial business, the governance processes (Type 3) are critical. Let them slide, and regulators will close the doors.

Characteristics Of Investment-Grade Systems

In investment-grade companies, all three types of systems are:

- Proven, reliable and successful. They enable a business to repeatedly deliver on the promises it makes to customers: to provide consistent, valuable products or services. Essentially, they are a business's "best practices."
- Documented clearly and concisely rather than held in the brains of individual team members. Documentation reduces costs, increases efficiencies, and helps employees to avoid significant mistakes.
- Not orphans. They are the cherished adopted "children" of named, responsible employees who are accountable for ensuring that they run smoothly and are continuously improved. These employees are consumed with improving and differentiating them.

- Overseen by CEOs who continually ask, "How can we do more and better with less?" If the answer is to outsource less critical processes to other service providers, they do it.
- If scalable, the proof buyers require that a company has growth potential and that its success is not—nor will it be—solely dependent on key employees.

Taken together, these systems make up the operations of your company.

Checklists

One type of system documentation that can guide the way in which your company operates is a checklist.

In *The Checklist Manifesto: How To Get Things Right*,[13] Atul Gawande shows how checklists can help us (and our organizations) execute critical processes more consistently, efficiently and accurately. Our companies' operations are so complex that it is naïve to think we can train/educate people to be experts in all of them. Crystallizing our core processes into checklists increases the probability of stellar execution.

In addition to documenting core processes, checklists are a great way to:

- Keep your team from forgetting or putting off routine, but mandatory, tasks.
- Save time by preventing costly errors that can occur when employees skip basic steps in a process.
- Drive your team toward action in an organized and satisfying way. (There's nothing like checking items off a list!)
- Give your team the freedom to focus on higher-level, value-add tasks because they know that the mandatory tasks are handled.
- Onboard and train employees more efficiently and collapse the time frames for them to become productive.
- Make process improvement easier to implement and track.
- Protect your organization from litigation and defend it should litigation occur.

Checklists are not the only way to manage, sort, prioritize and remember massive amounts of complex information. Other forms of documentation include training manuals for new employees and detailed road maps for creating and delivering a company's primary products or services. I recommend that you put key documentation into simple wikis that your employees can access from their computers and mobile devices.

Choose whatever documentation technique works best for your company, but no matter what you do, do not allow employees to keep information in their heads only as "Nina" did.

Several years ago, we met Nina, the owner of "nITch," an IT consulting company, when she set up a meeting to talk about exiting her business. nITch was experiencing strong growth due to its excellent brand and its reputation for quality advice and software engineering excellence. At first glance, the company appeared to present an attractive opportunity for many of the buyers we work with, but deeper diligence indicated that the company's success and brand relied primarily on the individual expertise and methods of a handful of its top consultants.

My team sent Nina our standard information request, and I highlighted the section on process documentation. We planned to showcase Nina's competitive advantage: an onboarding process that quickly ushered new consultants into billable client work.

Two days later, Nina called me. "Sorry, Zane," she said. "I'm not really sure what you're looking for."

"It's no big deal," I assured her. "We want to show prospective buyers how incredibly efficient you are in onboarding talent and equipping them to quickly become productive/billable. To do that, just send me what your people have developed to deliver consulting services. You know—the methodology documents, design guides, questionnaires, work-product templates, etc."

The silence that followed my list extended long enough for me to wonder if I'd lost the connection.
"Nina?" I asked.

"Oh, I'm here," she responded. "I don't think I have what you're looking for. I've never asked my people to put anything in writing."

This time the silence was from my end. No documentation for the delivery of consulting services? "I see," I finally said.

"I can tell you're stunned, Zane," Nina said. "But my six senior consultants have been doing this type of work successfully for over 20 years! They are hands-on leaders who have closely mentored their teams. Each of them has their personalized approaches to delivering value to their clients. Can't we explain that to buyers?"

"But none of them has documented any of their methods?" I asked.

"No. In the everyday push to get good work out the door, I never asked them to," Nina responded.

Nina's employees had all the critical processes/methods in their heads. I know they were senior and highly experienced, but how did nITch deliver *any* consistency across its service line?

If any of the six employees left nITch, their expertise would leave with them. If that happened, buyers would legitimately wonder about Nina's ability to attract new talent. Given her company's unique service offerings, there were very few individuals anywhere who could match her employees' level of knowledge. This talent scarcity, coupled with the absence of service delivery system documentation, made the likelihood of maintaining the company's growth trajectory difficult for a buyer, if not impossible. nITch's systems were not scalable, and that made nITch unattractive to buyers.

> Video is a great way to document processes. Ask your best practitioners to capture short video "how-to snippets."

Ultimately, we recommended to Nina that, prior to pursuing an exit, she devote resources to thoroughly documenting methodologies and assembling in-depth training materials.

Documenting systems would enable nITch to hire less-experienced consultants who could deliver a "wow" customer experience/solution quickly. With documented systems, a potential buyer would be less concerned about its ability to continue to grow the company following an acquisition.

DOCUMENT SYSTEMS. DON'T MUMMIFY THEM.

When formally documenting a process, it is tempting to (try to) capture every detail, set it in stone, make it non-revisable, and do it all ourselves. Instead, conduct meetings with those responsible for each business function. Invite input and participation in the creation of a very high-level outline of the key system. At that point, delegate (to an employee or group of your "best and brightest" employees) the task of documenting the best practices for that specific area. Act on their recommendations, and reward them for their participation.

As the documentation process continues, prompt employees to continually tweak (or overhaul, if necessary) the documentation to improve the business's processes. Checklists, workflows and other forms of documentation should be constantly evolving.

While several employees may contribute to the documentation, assign only one "owner" to each system document. That owner has ultimate responsibility for collecting and reviewing other employees' feedback and making any necessary revisions.

Meet "Ginny" a process documentation genie.

After completing her degree in software engineering, Ginny went to work as an application developer for a Fortune 500 company. She lasted about five years before she felt an "entrepreneurial itch." Now the owner of a successful software business, Ginny was as devoted to documenting her company's processes as she'd been to the complex ERP systems/software in her first job.

That's the only explanation I had for the detailed, yet constantly updated, checklists for multiple processes that linked together seamlessly and produced excellent and predictable outcomes for her customers in higher education. Ginny also used documents and checklists to train her people, "cement" the way she did business, and deliver on her company's promises.

Figure 5.1 on the following page is an example of just one of Ginny's company's documented processes: Product Implementation.

"I can't imagine the number of hours you must have spent on these," I marveled when she showed me just three examples of processes she had documented. "Even with your background, these must have taken months to create."

Ginny burst into one of her signature laughs that had a way of lifting a person's day. "Yes, I guess they took months to create, but not months of my time. I farmed them out."

"These have your fingerprints all over them," I objected. "I just can't believe—"

"Oh, believe it," she assured me. "I assigned each process to a key person on my team. I gave them an outline of the level of detail I wanted and a list of elements to include. I also gave them a design guide to ensure a consistent look and feel. I told them that their names would be on the final product and that they'd be responsible for revising it no less than once each year. Then I let them go."

Ginny skipped over the quicksand I'd seen too many owners sink into when they tried to personally build, perfect and execute process documentation and improvement. Ginny intuitively, or through experience, understood that these are tasks to delegate as soon as practical.

That doesn't mean that Ginny delegated her role of overseeing the ongoing development of process documentation. She made sure that all 100 or so process artifacts were consistent in look and level of detail. She actually read the annual (and usually more frequent) updates and gave rewards for automation and continuous process improvement.

As a result, her company's repeatable, definable, and constantly improving processes consistently delivered "wow" outcomes for its customers. These systems could be monitored, measured and improved. Most importantly, the processes were investment grade, meaning they were scalable by an investor. That made them tremendously valuable.

For the most part, Ginny's customers were unaware of these processes, but the consistent—even expected—performance that they produced gave her customers good feelings about their choice of software provider. Compare this customer experience to its opposite: a business that delivers using ad hoc processes that change on a dime. One day the business delivers. The next day, for no reason that's apparent to the customer, product or service delivery fails.

FIG. 5.1 Process Documentation

Our Implementation Process consists of: Discovery, Data Integration, Training & Launch, and the Client Success Program. The typical implementation will take 6-12 weeks and will vary based on client preparedness and project scope. A Client Success Manager (CSM) is assigned and will guide customers through implementation and beyond.

DISCOVERY	DATA INTEGRATION	TRAINING & LAUNCH	CLIENT SUCCESS PROGRAM
· Assemble implementation team · Overviews of product · Needs Assessment · Data integration planning · Plan implementation time line · Set goals	· Build Data import file · Automated import setup · Single-Sign-On setup · Data integrity tests · Configure settings, permissions and user roles	· Train key staff members · Train other users for specific interfaces and common-use cases · Configure settings and data in production site · Go Live	· Transition to Client Success Program · Post-launch review · Resolve any current issues · Review goals and product expectations with client and key users

1-2 weeks ⟶ *2-4 weeks* ⟶ *3-6 weeks* ⟶ *Ongoing*

DISCOVERY	CLIENT RESOURCES
· Fill out and return Client Needs Assessments · Review project expectations, implementation process and team roles · Establish a project plan, roles and responsibilities · Initial call with Implementation IT and Project Manager to discuss scope · Define Implementation team on site and begin to set timeline and expectations of Go Live and training dates · Provide overview of all company associates to be involved with the client	· Project Manager · IT Project Manager · Executive Sponsor

DATA INTEGRATION	CLIENT RESOURCES
· With Implementation Team decide what data to include based on anticipated use case(s) · Set up training environment and begin importing data · Set up automated uploads in training site and begin to test · Set up logins and begin to test in training environment · Set up Roles, Permissions, Locations, Services and Reasons in application for various user groups	· Project Manager · IT Project Manager · Implementation Team

TRAINING & LAUNCH	CLIENT RESOURCES
· Revisit needs assessment to build users' training platform · Set up training dates and times for on-site visit (if applicable) and webinar training · During the tail end of training, begin to work with the IT Project Manager to import data to the production environment · Set up all predetermined Roles, Permissions, Locations, Services and Reasons in production environment · Configure card swipe for kiosk functionality · Resolve outstanding issues and Go Live	· Project Manager · IT Project Manager · Implementation Team

CLIENT SUCCESS PROGRAM	CLIENT RESOURCES
· Plan follow-up discussion for two months after Go Live date · Record and review any issues found since Go Live date · Review goals and expectations to ensure all were met · Transition to Client Success Program · Set up regular meetings with CSM to discuss usage patterns and review any issues	· Project Manager · Executive Sponsor

Throughout the implementation process and beyond, there will be ongoing Project Management meetings. During these meetings, internal personnel will meet with their CSM to discuss challenges, goals, issues, data needs, and any questions and concerns.

THE FOUR CRITICAL SYSTEMS

In most businesses, there are four major systems or processes that you must document because they are crucial to scalability (a topic we'll discuss in a moment):

1. Sales and Marketing.
2. Product or Service Implementation Process.
3. Employee Onboarding and Retention.
4. Finance and Administration.

According to Gino Wickman, founder of EOS Worldwide and author of *Traction: Get A Grip On Your Business*, the time you spend systemizing processes in these four areas is time well spent because doing so enables:

- Employees to "master the basics more quickly."[14]
- Owners and managers to "spend far less time making sure the basic blocking and tackling is being done well (or cleaning up messes when it isn't)."[15]
- Your company to "spend more time with your best customers, creating creative, unusual, memorable experiences. You can spend more time connecting with your best employees, making sure they feel valued and appreciated."[16]

> I highly recommend that you share your detailed, documented process flows with your clients and prospects. Leverage them in sales calls and client review sessions. Viewers will be highly impressed, and this level of process excellence will differentiate your company from its competitors.

System 1: Sales And Marketing

A sales and marketing system that is scalable documents a company's processes and procedures for finding prospects (lead generation) and closing sales (lead conversion). You can read more about the characteristics of investment-grade sales and marketing systems in Reason 8.

System 2: Product Or Service Implementation Process

We've all got systems to deliver our products or services, but those systems are not scalable unless they:

- Are documented in detail.
- Include clear workflow-based procedures that guide employees.
- Include documented processes to initiate and complete continuous improvement cycles.

System 3: Employee Onboarding And Retention

New employee training consumes valuable time from existing employees' job functions. Scalable employee onboarding systems are made up of clear job descriptions, efficient processes, and procedures that quickly educate new employees on the organization, their roles within it, and core processes that differentiate a company from its competitors.

While only your people can provide training on your "secret sauce" systems, it makes sense to outsource (think online tutorials) specific training functions related to regulatory compliance or to broadly applicable skills such as the ability to use important software tools (e.g., Microsoft® Office products).

System 4: Finance And Administration

Accurately recording how your company spends and makes money is paramount to your survival, decision-making and future value. Accounting systems should be based on standardized processes and preferably be GAAP compliant. Rigorously managing your forecasts and cash flow is an absolute requirement of a professionalized business. See Reason 13 for more detail.

In my first company, Virtual Learning Technologies, I stuck this sticky note to my computer monitor to remind me of the essential importance of financial processes.

One example of a critical accounting process is a scalable collection system that provides timelines, procedures and communication templates for pursuing overdue collections and identifies dispute resolution processes for seriously delinquent accounts. These software systems/solutions also schedule opportunities to create new ways to increase the velocity of incoming cash.

No cash.
No business.

THE BENEFITS OF SYSTEMS TO OWNERS, EMPLOYEES AND INVESTORS

I also heard Gino Wickman say something about the combination of systems and humans that I'll never forget, "Systemize the predictable so you can humanize the exceptional."[17]

The Value Of Systems To Owners

High-quality systems in the hands of a talented and dedicated team of employees create nearly self-sustaining, high-performing engines rather than *jobs* that require constant time, work and attention. Engines demand less time and energy from their owners than jobs do, so they give owners more time to focus on business growth or spend in nonbusiness activities.

Unless you teach and motivate your team to create and constantly improve your company's processes, you'll forever be a prisoner to your business. To create an investment-grade company, you must shift the responsibility for getting things done from your shoulders to the solid systems and processes that enable your business to deliver on its promise to the marketplace.

Since 2007, Nick Saban has been at the helm of one of America's greatest college football dynasties: the Alabama Crimson Tide. As an Auburn Tiger, it is REALLY TOUGH for me to say, but I give credit where it is due: "The Process" that Saban created and executes produced national championships in five of nine seasons.

The Process is predicated on a relentless focus on every detail involved in executing each play in the Tide's playbook. It begins with recruiting the right talent and creating the right culture. It also involves all the planning and preparation necessary to execute each play. Winning is "simply" a series of one flawless play after another. The team that executes the most flawless offensive and defensive plays wins.

Coach Saban explained The Process this way, "We decided to use the approach that we're not going to focus on the outcome. We were just going to focus on the process of what it took to play the best football you could play, which was to focus on that particular play as if it had a history and life of its own."[18]

Saban's system—a methodical, efficient approach to organizational management—has evolved thanks to a constant analysis loop of what works and what does not, and a ruthless willingness to embrace new methods when necessary. Saban isn't afraid to tweak and adjust The Process as needed.

The Value Of Systems To Employees

Well-documented systems make employees' jobs easier and increase efficiencies in producing the desired business outcomes. Ad hoc delivery systems hurt morale and drain the organization. Good systems allow employees (and, by extension, the business) to create more value in a shorter amount of time. Strong systems also foster teamwork. When everyone understands the playbook, coordination and efficiency generate energy.

The Value Of Systems To Buyers

Documented operational systems reduce a buyer's risk. They prove that a company's success is not, nor will it be, dependent on its key employees. When institutional knowledge is in the hands of only certain employees, scalability isn't possible.

If buyers were satisfied simply by the existence of documented systems, this chapter would end here. Unfortunately, they aren't.

SCALABLE SYSTEMS

Buyers want scalable systems—systems that efficiently and effectively deliver products or services to the market—because scalable systems are critical to growth that takes the form of future increases in (and high margin) cash flows.

For a moment, think of your company's systems (or operations) as golf clubs. If the clubs are well-engineered, whether they are in your hands or in the hands of the guy who just won The Masters, they work. No offense, but they will absolutely work better for the guy wearing the green jacket. Same goes for operations: If they are designed well and work for your company, they will work as well, or better, for a sophisticated buyer with more resources.

Building systems that equip your company to deliver on its promises to the marketplace—*and are scalable*—involves:

1. Documenting the internal high-value processes (at a minimum) that are critical to your company. High-value processes are those that are core to your competitive advantage. You may need to outsource the processes that do not differentiate your company from its competitors.
2. Maintaining and motivating a team of talented employees who are dedicated to implementing, improving and taking ownership of those systems.
3. Being (or becoming) an owner capable of trusting the people and systems enough to delegate responsibility. Delegating may include outsourcing functions that can be performed better and more cost effectively externally.

If you've documented your best systems, have a team dedicated to implementing and improving them, and trust your systems and employees to run your company without your constant interference, congratulations! Your systems are almost investment grade!

Investment-Grade Companies Use Automation To Leverage The Power Of Their Systems.

Once your processes are documented and well-tested, automate them. Quality software applications are everywhere, but it isn't a given that owners implement them in ways that truly enhance a company's core processes. Automation can help your company do what it does in a better, faster and cheaper way and collect actionable data for improvement initiatives. But better, faster and cheaper happens only if the processes you automate are strong and proven. Automating dysfunctional processes just helps your company achieve chaos better and faster.

Investment-Grade Companies Are Chock-Full Of Scalable Employees.

For an organization to be scalable, its employees (who are responsible for scalable systems) must be scalable as well. They must love the goal of incremental improvement. Like you, they must always be asking, "How do we do more with less and do it better for the customers and markets we serve?" When you hire, screen for the intellectually curious: people who love learning, improvement and growth in themselves and in the systems that drive their lives.

Investment-grade companies also have "scalable" owners leading them. As the CEO of a supply-chain software company once told me, "I'm an efficiency nerd. I constantly obsess over how to push myself and my team to find methods and tools to *do our business better.*"

YOU KNOW A COMPANY IS SCALABLE WHEN...

Scalability is one of the most important factors that buyers and investors look for in a business, because they demand the growth that scalability creates.

So, when investors hunt for their holy grail—a scalable company—what signs tell them that they may have found it?

- Gross margin that improves as a company grows
- Operating margin that improves as a company grows
- Minimal workforce (i.e., people efficient) as compared to industry cohorts
- Inexpensive product distribution
- Strong product-market fit
- High rate of customer retention
- Large TAM and SAM

Gross Margin Improves As A Company Grows

We calculate gross margin by subtracting the direct costs of producing or delivering a product or service from the revenue earned from selling it. Gross margin is just the direct percentage of profit in the sale price. In accounting, gross margin refers to sales minus cost of goods sold.

The following (modified) income statement is for a specialty manufacturing company. As represented, gross profit is the preliminary measure of profitability before operating profit and net income.

FIG. 5.2 Income Statement

Revenue	$10,000,000
Cost of Goods Sold	< $5,000,000>
Gross Profit	$5,000,000
Operating Expenses	< $2,500,000>
Operating Profit	$2,500,000
Interest	< $500,000>
Taxes	< $500,000>
Net Income	$1,500,000

Gross margin is important because it reflects the core profitability of a company before overhead costs, and it illustrates the financial success of a product or service.

Operating Margin Improves As A Company Grows.

Operating margin is that portion of a company's revenue that is left over after both costs of goods sold and operating expenses are considered. In accounting terms, it is the ratio of general overhead and related expenses

> Businesses that scale are businesses with operating leverage. Put simply, if you add operating costs (sales, marketing, administrators, R&D, etc.) at the same rate you grow revenue, then your business does not scale. Alternatively, if additional revenue requires relatively smaller and smaller additions to operating costs, then congratulations... your business scales!"[19]
>
> Alex Taussig
> Venture Capitalist, Partner
> Lightspeed Venture Partners

that are not directly attributable to any particular product or service provided to customers (e.g., certain employee payroll and benefits, corporate office rent, utilities, marketing, and IT systems) to revenue.

If a business is scalable, we can predict with reasonable certainty the point at which the business will achieve a certain level of profitability. Even companies that are not yet profitable (or are break-even) *but are scalable* excite buyers because scalability increases the likelihood of future profit and growth. "RapidScale," a SaaS company whose owners I met with several years ago, illustrates that point and one more: It is never too early to begin building scalability into the foundation of your company.

> If your systems are scalable, as your company sells more products or services, its gross and operating margins expand.

When I met "Greg" and "Luke" at a Vistage® event in Central Florida, their company (RapidScale) had only been operating for 24 months. Given how new they were to ownership, I was surprised that they'd carved out time to attend my presentation on "The 17 Reasons You May Not Be Able To Sell Your Equity In Your Family-Owned Business."

After the meeting ended, they invited me for dinner at a nearby restaurant. There, they told me that they'd developed a software-as-a-service product for transportation and logistics companies.

"We've got a great client list of over 100 customers and $4.25 million in annual recurring revenue," boasted Luke. It's hard to fault a guy for taking pride in some seriously impressive numbers. I followed up with a few questions and learned that the two had invested heavily in their team and several initial iterations of their product.

"Our net income is currently in the red," added Greg. *"We're running at negative $900,000, but at this point, we've worked out all the product bugs."*

"We anticipate only minor updates for the foreseeable future," Luke said. *"With the employees we've got now, the only new hires we'll make in the next few years are customer service reps to handle increasing call volume."*

"And," Greg reminded him, *"some occasional additions to the engineering team."*

With their negative net income, I knew I'd be buying the dinner this time, but if what they were telling me about their operations was correct, this might be the last time the meal would be on me.

As the time for my flight back to Birmingham drew nearer, I still wasn't clear about what these two wanted so I asked. Luke took the lead, "After listening to your talk, we know we've done a lot of things right to this point, but—"

Greg finished the thought, "We wonder if there's a way for you to tell if we're on the right track."

I suggested that my team of analysts take a look at all their numbers and create the type of projected income statement that we would produce for prospective buyers if we were taking RapidScale to market. The new owners readily agreed, and I grabbed an Uber to the airport.

When I met with my team the next morning, my inbox had several messages from Greg, all containing financial data. I explained the task to one of my senior analysts and one of our newest associates. They came up with the following estimates on Figure 5.3.

FIG. 5.3 RapidScale Pro Forma

	Year 1A	Year 2P	Year 3P	Year 4P	Year 5P
Revenue	**$4,250,000**	**$5,525,000**	**$7,182,500**	**$9,337,250**	**$12,138,425**
Growth	N/A	30%	30%	30%	30%
Less: Cost of Goods Sold	$850,000	$1,105,000	$1,436,500	$1,867,450	$2,427,685
Gross Profit	**$3,400,000**	**$4,420,000**	**$5,476,000**	**$7,469,800**	**$9,710,740**
Gross Margin	80%	80%	80%	80%	80%
Less: Operating Expenses	$4,300,000	$4,600,000	$4,800,000	$4,950,000	$5,050,000
OpEx as a % of Revenue	*101%*	*83%*	*67%*	*53%*	*42%*
Net Income	**($900,000)**	**($180,000)**	**$946,000**	**$2,519,800**	**$4,660,740**
Net Margin	*(21%)*	*(3%)*	*13%*	*27%*	*38%*

As you can see, while RapidScale would lose money in Years 1 and 2, it had (as long as it could maintain its gross margin) the proper infrastructure in place to reach profitability in Year 3. In Years 4 and 5, profit margins continue to widen due to the effect of scalability.

This ability to rapidly increase profitability (measured in both dollars and margin) demonstrates why buyers are willing to pay up for scalable companies, even while the companies are still losing money.

On the day we agreed to present our findings, storms across the Southeast made our Skype connection choppy. Rather than go through the numbers line-by-line, I decided to jump right to the analysis that I thought the two owners were after.

"Let's assume a buyer purchases RapidScale at the end of Year 2. And let's say that it pays $27.6 million, or 5x revenue. If it sells RapidScale at the end of Year 5 at 8x revenue (or roughly $96 million), its return could top a 4x cash-on-cash return, given the normal use of debt we see in these types of transactions. The exit multiple would most likely be a higher revenue multiple than 5x because of the size premium upon exit. Larger companies sell for larger multiples."

"Let me make sure I heard you right," said Greg. "A return of over 4 times its money in three years?"

"Assuming that your revenues continue to increase and your operational costs increase MUCH more slowly (as is true in SaaS models), yes," I replied. "Guys, you chose the right business model: SaaS is scalable. Looks like you're buying me dinner in Year 3!"

Minimal Workforce Compared To Industry Cohort

When you create the right foundation (i.e., deliver the right product or service using documented, automated, scalable systems), you minimize the number of employees needed to operate the business and satisfy clients. For example, if your plumbing services company can generate 20 percent more contribution margin per master plumber than your competitors, you have a demonstrated scale advantage. Your systems, training, processes, and competitive advantages make you more financially efficient than your cohort.

Inexpensive Product Distribution

Scalable businesses have more frictionless distribution systems than others in their cohort. For example, customers can purchase software with a click of a button from a hosted cloud service: no phone calls, invoices, lengthy installation or delivery fees. Compare that to a furniture manufacturer's distribution model and the associated costs/overhead.

Strong Product–Market Fit

A highly scalable business typically sells a product or service that the market actively promotes through glowing word-of-mouth reviews. Market excitement reduces the customer acquisition cost (CAC) and keeps it lower than competitors'. Market excitement also reduces the need to spend big on sales and marketing.

High Rate Of Customer Retention

Scalable businesses have sticky customers. If you begin each year with a wonderful base of clients and revenue, every new customer improves your margin because your loyal client base covers your fixed costs.

Large Serviceable Addressable Market (SAM)

Scalable companies sell products in big TAMs and are well-positioned in Serviceable Available Markets to deliver their goods and services. If a low market-size ceiling limits your potential growth, institutional investors will never consider your company to be scalable.

YOUR ROLE IN BUILDING A SCALABLE COMPANY

Let's assume that you have documented your company's systems and have attracted a talented and dedicated team to execute them. Can you trust the systems and people enough to step back?

Systems and people who constantly improve the delivery of your company's products and services create business value. Once you test and trust your key employees and effective systems enough to delegate the ownership of key tasks to those capable employees, you've found the holy grail: scalability.

Delegate. It May Save You.

I give a pass—a very temporary pass—to owners in the early stages of a business. They enjoy a short period of time when they can be hands-on in every aspect of their companies.

As your business grows, however, you either learn to delegate or you give up family, friends, exercise and leisure time, as well as a good portion of your sanity. Owners who cannot delegate limit the growth potential of their businesses. They are slaves to their businesses and singlehandedly reduce business value in the eyes of potential investors. Owners who can't learn to delegate destroy the potential to sell their businesses at any price.

> If your systems are documented well and you don't have confidence in your key employees' abilities to perform, look in the mirror. Do you have an issue with delegating?

Outsource

Owners should have a deep understanding of their businesses' value proposition, customers, competition and market position. With that understanding, owners can analyze every aspect of their operations with an eye toward potentially outsourcing the functions (key processes) that can be performed by third parties at a lower cost and/or higher quality. Manage your company's process portfolio like a wealth manager overseeing an investment portfolio. Outsource commodity processes and invest heavily in the ones that differentiate your company and drive its value.

Need examples? In finance, consider a fractional CFO, accountant or treasurer. Consider these areas of your company: customer service, HR/payroll, logistics and training. For each one ask yourself, "Does this process contribute to differentiating my company from its competitors?" If not, and the process can be performed by a third party at an equal or lower cost with acceptable (or even higher) quality, outsource it!

Great Systems + Great People = Value Creation

If we once again compare creating an investment-grade company to a horse race, we note that buyers bet on great jockeys first, then on good horses. In other words, investors want quality managers running top-notch systems.

Of course, there's more to picking a winner than knowing jockeys and horses. As we learned in Reason 4, investors also look for the ability of horse and rider to control the position on the inside rail—or dominate a quality market niche.

Great systems and people are key, but it is sometimes easy to focus on one and ignore the other. "Elliott" illustrates how easy it is for owners to depend on employees instead of systems.

I live for the days when owners who are at the top of their games walk into my office to talk about finding an investor. The day Elliott sat down across the desk from me was one of those days. His health care technology company was profitable and growing at the rate of 50 percent per year. Several large health care companies and private equity groups had let him know that they might be interested in entering the booming industry niche that his company dominated.

As my team and I examined Elliott's options, we ticked off all the boxes:

- *Elliott's company was riding a strong tailwind.*
- *All of Elliott's stakeholders were on board to take the company to the next level, and they had the documented growth strategy to do it.*
- *The transaction timing was ideal, as all "the right" ingredients were present: strong business performance, plenty of owner energy in the tank, significant market share still up for grabs, and favorable capital markets.*

In preparing for a confidential auction process, we collected information about each member of Elliott's management team. We learned that his key people had been together for nearly a decade and had built the company from scratch. One of those people was Yuri, Elliott's chief information officer.

When we asked Elliott who could best help us prepare introductory information about the company's information processes, he told us that Yuri was "the man." "He built the systems from the ground up."

In the weeks that followed, we found Yuri to be a very capable guy, but he was always in a rush. We joked that his rush-rush attitude probably served him well on the high-level amateur hockey team he played for.

We soon learned—from the early buyer's due diligence—that Yuri was indeed "the man." Over 10 years, Yuri had patched together and kept a tight grip on a system of databases, software and processes. While the system was functional, no one but Yuri understood its architecture, and only he was capable of modifying the software and numerous databases.

We were completely wrong about Yuri rushing because he was an elite hockey player. Yuri rushed because, day in and day out, he had a huge (and constant) backlog of modification requests on his desk.

When the buyer's questions started arriving in batches, we knew that it was struggling to decipher Elliott's (really Yuri's) systems. The buyer questioned many aspects of the systems.

- *Had Yuri shared responsibility for them with members of his department?*
- *Where was the process documentation?*
- *Who else knew how to install and modify the systems?*
- *What back-up systems were in place?*

Yuri had built the systems from the ground up. He took so much ownership of his work, however, that the build-from-the-ground-up philosophy that had made Elliott's company successful was going to make it difficult to close the sale.

We knew that the buyer was in a tough spot. If Yuri skated into the wrong end of a bone-rattling body check and a concussion took him out of action, a vast amount of institutional knowledge would be unavailable for who knows how long. The buyer, however, was more concerned about what would happen if Yuri simply decided not to play for a new owner's team.

I'm glad that the buyer called me to say that it would not negotiate further until Elliott fixed the problem. I was able to convey to Elliott that the buyer was handing him a get-out-of-jail-free card.

Most buyers would have withdrawn their offers. In addition, most buyers would not have waited patiently for the three months that it took for Elliott and Yuri to address the issue. But most buyers didn't want Elliott's customer list quite as much as this one did.

Elliott was a successful owner, and he understood the value of recruiting and retaining great talent. What Elliott didn't realize (but I hope you do) was that buyers/investors viewed what he considered to be an operational glitch or idiosyncrasy as a single point of failure.

In the process of growing a thriving business, Elliott forgot that great people are only one block in the construction of great processes, and that great systems (that are documented) are a key element of investment-grade companies. Elliott forgot that systems (horses) are scalable and people (jockeys) are not.

As you improve your company's scalability you will enjoy your business more, because scalability increases cash flow and brings more freedom and fun immediately! Over time, scalability drives enterprise value.

You might not be able to attract investors or buyers if your business does not have repeatable, definable and scalable processes.

RECOMMENDATIONS

1. **Document key/proprietary and differentiating processes into standard operating procedures because well-documented systems are essential to scale.**
   - Does the documentation you have in place today allow new employees to easily learn and master your processes?
   - If not, which systems are not documented?
   - Does your team continually iterate your documentation—aka your highly valuable organizational assets?

2. View your organization as a system (a portfolio of integrated/related processes), rather than simply a collection of people.

- Would your company run well regardless of the experience level or tenure of your employees?
- Are your people cross-trained on important company processes?
- Would your company suffer if one of your key employees retired or left?

3. Recruit scalable employees that can grow within your organization.

Are your people coachable, intellectually curious and lifelong learners? If not, your company is not scalable.

4. Constantly look for opportunities to turn your valuable organizational processes into checklists.

- Have you identified the core processes that differentiate your business?
- Have you built training modules for each core process?
- Have you made the investment to capture these processes in a checklist?

5. Leverage your best systems using automation.

- Do you constantly look for opportunities to automate your core processes and workflows?

6. Look at your business from a buyer's perspective.

- Is it scalable? Would the systems you have documented to date give a buyer confidence in your company's ability to continue to grow following an acquisition?
- How do your company's margins compare to your competitors' and to the industry in general?

7. Focus on two key margins: gross and operating.

- If demand for your products and services suddenly increased, could your existing systems respond quickly?
- As your company grows, will your margins expand or contract?

8. Constantly improve your systems.

Are you and your employees continually improving your most valuable systems? These likely include:

- Sales and Marketing
- Product or Service Implementation Process
- Employee Onboarding and Retention
- Finance and Administration

9. Delegate meaningful responsibility to key employees.

- How are your employees involved in documenting and improving systems?
- How do you incent employees to invest in your systems?

10. Outsource the business functions that can be performed more effectively and cheaply by others.

What noncore processes or functions can you outsource?

TAKEAWAYS

1. Scalable systems are the holy grail that allows revenue to grow at a faster rate than growth in infrastructure and other expenses.

2. If your operations are more ad hoc than documented and repeatable, you'll struggle to scale.

If your company has mission-critical know-how that's undocumented, you'll never scale.

3. **Documented systems build teamwork and motivate employees, but they don't rely on the owner or individual employees.**

4. **Automate a poor process/workflow and create a disaster.**

   Automate a well-oiled and engineered process and reap an outsized ROI.

5. **Scalability reduces an investor's risk because it:**
   - Demonstrates that a company (even if temporarily losing money) has growth potential in the form of future increases in operating cash flows.
   - Creates operating leverage that proves a path to profitability.
   - Proves that mid-level management is capable of running the business in the owner's absence.

6. **To create a scalable company, you must:**
   - Understand which of your processes drive the most value for the company.
   - Protect process assets, oversee continual improvement and innovation, and (whenever possible) automate.
   - Delegate ownership and implementation of systems to employees.
   - Evaluate which commodity functions vendors can more effectively perform, and outsource them.

7. **If you don't teach, motivate and reward your team for owning and improving your company's processes, you'll forever be a slave to your business.**

   You will also fail the investment-grade company test.

Your Culture Does Not Attract Or Keep The Best People.

SURROUND YOURSELF WITH STRONG PLAYERS WHO FUNCTION WELL AND CAN MANAGE GREAT SYSTEMS.

#obvious

Doing talent management well makes a huge difference for all companies and all organizations: A difference in performance and a difference to buyers and investors.

#question

Then why do so many companies and leaders recruit, hire and retain talent so poorly?

There's a common notion among entrepreneurs that, after closing, buyers want to send in an army to operate/grow the businesses they've just purchased.

Just because a notion is common doesn't make it true.

Buyers dream about buying companies that come with "no assembly required." They want to better equip the troops you've already got on the ground, not replace them with new personnel. They want your management team—one that already intimately understands your markets, people, processes, customers and competitors—to grow the business for them just as they've grown it for you.

People + Systems

Contrast Elliott's experience from the previous chapter with "Jill's."

Several years before I went looking for Jill, I had helped the owners of a Memphis-based mobile app company sell to a publicly traded company that I'll call "AR." Months after closing, AR called to ask if I could find another company "just like the last one." This Silicon Valley firm was seeking a successful company with a talented team of developers that would stick around. In Silicon Valley, firms were constantly poaching AR's employees. Not so its employees in Memphis.

When I introduced myself to Jill, the owner of a company that fit AR's wish list perfectly, she was politely receptive but downplayed her path from software developer to owner. "I had no master plan," Jill explained. "I just wanted to work in a company with a culture I enjoyed."

For a woman with no "master plan," Jill did all the right things. She surrounded herself with great talent, hired to her weaknesses, delegated deliberately, and developed incentives to reward employees for creating systems and other activities that grew her company in the short- and long-term. To Jill, that meant rewarding managers for bringing in new clients, cross-training other employees, deepening relationships with existing clients, and improving the performance of the processes they used.

"Honestly, Zane," Jill said, "I'm finally realizing my vision. I really don't have any interest in becoming a cog in a bigger wheel."

"I get it. Autonomy is what she values," I thought to myself. I then asked her, "What if a buyer offered you and your team complete autonomy? And, what if that buyer could back up that promise by letting you talk to other owners whose companies it had purchased? Would you be interested?"

Jill was interested, and she did talk to other owners who had sold to AR.

When Jill went into negotiations, at the top of her must-have list were autonomy for herself and her team, and additional resources necessary to serve both her company's existing clients and AR's clients. At the top of AR's must-have list were three-year employment agreements with all members of Jill's management team.

Jill's managers happily signed those agreements because they were linked to stay bonuses that guaranteed them 80 percent of their annual salaries at the end of that three-year period. They also gained access to a more lucrative benefits package.

Both Elliott and Jill had recruited top talent, but only Jill had paired great jockeys (top employees) with great horses (sustainable systems). She had motivated her employees to create systems that could run without them.

Recruiting Talent

A 30-Second Checkup

Think of your friends and peers who own companies or hold high-level management positions. How many of their companies would thrive, much less survive, if they were to hand over the reins to the team below them on their organizational charts? Now, bring the exercise closer to home: Could your company survive and prosper without you? In your absence, could your team, culture and processes deliver on your company's promises?

I ask because I assume that creating an investment-grade company is the reason you picked up this book. I ask because I know that investment-grade companies do not depend upon any one person or even a handful of key people.

Egos Can Be Dangerous.

You may think great buyers/investors are interested in companies that have only one star on a team of average players. They aren't. They want a healthy organization and culture made up of competent and engaged team members at every level.

"If you are the smartest person in the room, you are in the wrong room." I didn't create this maxim, but I wish I had. Great leaders surround themselves with the best possible teams available. They assess all the roles within their company and put the best talent—relative to their industries and the geographies they operate in—into those roles. They understand that the right personnel make ALL the difference.

A great example of the type of leader I'm talking about is "Tyler," the owner of a commercial landscaping business in Orange County, California. While conducting a seminar for his leadership team, I learned that one of the primary reasons for his company's outsized success was that work crew leaders were a cut above the competition. Sure, Tyler paid crew leaders 15 percent more than his competitors paid their employees (and he provided better benefits), but Tyler's work crews delivered a substantially higher level of customer satisfaction. His company's Net Promoter Score® (NPS®) was 22 points higher than the industry average. (See Reason 12 for a detailed discussion of NPS®.) In addition, Tyler's crews were 20 percent more efficient than the industry average. Employee talent translated into more growth, higher net profit margins, and a competitive advantage in its marketplace. Better employees equal better companies every time.

The Owner's Role In Recruiting And Retaining Talent

You will attract talent that stays with your company only if you are the type of leader people aspire to follow and emulate. The culture—and, therefore, the attractiveness of your company, business unit or department—begins and ends with you.

I recently attended a summit at which growth equity fund owners reviewed a study they had commissioned titled "The Top Common Attributes of CEOs of High-Performing Middle Market Companies." I was struck, but not surprised, by the top three characteristics on the list.

1. Coachability and Self-Awareness
2. Intellectual Curiosity
3. Emotional IQ

Do you have these traits? The study indicated that CEOs who do can build lasting cultures by recruiting and retaining the best talent.

The Right Mix: Highfliers And Plodders

I've told you to hire highfliers. Now I'm going to tell you that not everyone you hire must be of that quality. The trick is to put your highfliers in positions to lead innovation and create processes. Once systems are in place, "plodders" (solid players that are not as creative or talented or are not able to devote all their energy to their jobs) can execute, monitor and improve these systems.

If this sounds harsh, think of any sports team. Everyone on that team knows who plays first string and who relieves those players. Everyone has a role to play, but not all are cut out for leadership. Many don't have the makings of a highflier but are still very good at their specific roles.

When I was at IBM, rather than move its sales superstars up into management roles, the company often promoted them to work with its biggest clients. IBM knew that great salespeople did not always make great managers. In other words, IBM found meaningful advancing roles for the people it wanted to keep. You can too.

From personal experience, I know that my people and our culture are the keys to beating the competition. Putting people first sounds unselfish, but it isn't. It is what's best for your bottom line. If you take care of your people, they will take care of your customers. Delighted customers equal exceptional businesses.

Recruiting Is Worth Obsessing About.

Not that I know any personally, but I've heard that there are a few die-hard football fans here in the South who lose sleep over which five-star high-school senior defensive lineman will stuff the run two years from now at their chosen colleges. I do personally know many owners of investment-grade companies who obsess about finding, hiring and retaining the best-of-the-best employees. I hope you are one of those owners.

The amount of effort that you should devote to recruiting the best players for your company rivals that of college coaches. They are always on the lookout for talent. They know the skills required for each position they're looking to fill, and these "job descriptions" aren't static. Winning coaches tweak these descriptions as their teams develop.

If you know what talents each slot on your organizational chart requires, you can constantly be on the lookout for the right person to fill each slot. "Constantly" means considering whether a great waiter, concierge, coach or personal trainer you encounter could become your next great customer service rep or salesperson. "Constantly" means hanging on to resumes that catch your attention, even when you aren't hiring for that position.

Pretend for a moment that "Lionel," one of your best software developers, is hired away by a competing firm. Lionel had completed 55 percent of a key module for a core product that you expected to open up a completely new channel for your sales team. Now you must fill Lionel's position as quickly as possible to get your product to market before your competition does.

You spring into action. Your chief talent officer posts the opening on all the online job boards possible and immediately contacts a recruiting firm to begin drumming up candidates. Within a month, your headhunter identifies a dozen candidates, and you personally interview the most promising four. You make an offer, and the candidate accepts and gives her current employer two weeks' notice. On day one, your new employee is excited to dive in and expects to complete the module two months to the day after your first developer gave notice. Your new employee does work diligently, but, because of the two-month hiatus, your competitor beats you to the market and your module never gets the traction you planned.

Now consider a different scenario. Imagine that when Lionel gives you his two-weeks' notice, you look within the company to see whom you can promote into the open position. Usually this strategy works for you, since you make it a practice to hire from within and cross-train employees, but the technical skills required for the module are just a little outside the scope of your other employees' expertise. You also make it a practice to constantly scout top talent, so you remember a resume you received several months earlier. You pull it out and it all comes back to you: This developer had indicated that she would love to work for your company and seems to be a great fit for your culture.

You call her and set up a 30-minute meeting for the next day at a local coffee shop. Five minutes into that meeting, you whip out your company's executive summary (See Reason 15.) and deftly articulate your company's story and your vision so well that she can't help but see where she fits in the future of the company. You leave that meeting confident that you are both interested. Your HR manager makes an offer, and the developer accepts and starts only three days after Lionel leaves. She completes the module on schedule. You bring it to market before your competitors, and your sales rise 30 percent in the first year alone.

There is never a wrong time to look for and recruit top talent. Even when you do not have openings, you can be on alert for A-players. Identifying A-players before you need them gives you a huge competitive advantage when you do.

Owners who can quickly add depth can exploit opportunities that less well-positioned competitors cannot. With a full bench of great talent, no one employee has outsized influence on company success or can leverage his or her value to damage the company. These owners also better position themselves when dealing with a controlling team member that would like to exercise leverage over them.

> Recruiting never stops, and there must be synergy among everything related to talent (e.g., policies, compensation, development opportunities and culture).

If you are poised to replace departing employees quickly, you can deliver projects on time, keep clients happy, and leave your growth projections intact. But let me say it again: Retaining A-players is a much better strategy. How much time, money and other valuable resources could we save if we kept our talent on our team? How much stronger would our culture be if our top talent couldn't imagine looking for greener grass with other employers?

The Role Of Contractors

In your constant search for the best talent, don't overlook talented independent contractors when legally appropriate. I know of many companies that have built wonderful cultures in which contractors feel like W-2 employees and are just as loyal and committed to the company's success.

You have access to freelancers on websites such as *upwork.com, freelancer.com, guru.com* and *elance.com.* Access to cheaper and portable health insurance policies and a wide choice of shared office space facilities has made freelancing attractive to more and more workers. These workers want flexibility to fit their lifestyles, whether that means taking care of children, helping aging parents, or pursuing other interests they care about.

Great Teams = Happy Owners

Hiring the best people as soon as you can afford them can be a life changer for owners. With the right team in place, you can spend less time at work. There's no need to micromanage great teams, because they get it right the first time.

"Gus," the owner of a value-added distribution company, describes how he views the huge investment he has made in his employees.

> "I busted my backside for 30 years finding the perfect people for my management team. Sure, if I had a cheaper team, I could make more money, but I'm making enough. The price I pay for knowing that my team will take care of my customers and make decisions that benefit the company in the long run is well worth it. Because of them, I get to do what I want when I want. That may mean going to my son's baseball games, picking up something for dinner on those days when my wife is working late, or playing tennis on a weekday."

Like Gus, you can enjoy immediate benefits from hiring the right team—but you may have to "bust your backside" to do it.

Who's Right For You?

A few years back, I had the opportunity to sit in on a two-day summit hosted by a private equity group for the 60+ CEOs of its portfolio companies. The topic was hiring and retaining talent. While all of these CEOs knew that hiring the right people was important, they wondered if anyone had financially quantified how hiring the *right* person compared to hiring the *wrong* one?

The meeting leader cited a load of statistics that stunned every CEO in the room, yet not one disagreed. Figure 6.1 summarizes the main points.

FIG. 6.1 A-Players & Mis-Hires

	A PLAYERS	MIS-HIRES
Productivity	3x to 5x more than mis-hires	Negatively affect productivity and morale
Effect on Top and Bottom Lines	Increase both	Decrease bottom line by: • 14x salary for those making <$100k • 28x salary for those making between $100k and $250k • 27x base compensation for an executive • 15x base compensation for a manager • U.S. Dept. of Labor estimates that the average cost of bad hiring decisions is 30% of earnings.
Team Engagement	High	Low
Relationships with Customers	Deep	Shallow, if any
Management Level	Minimal need for supervision allows owners to spend less time at work.	Need supervision

The dollar amounts that this seminar leader presented were so dramatic that I wanted to find more recent figures and include them in this book.

Mis-Hire Costs

• 30 percent of first year's earnings — U.S. Department of Labor, 2003 (according to *HR.com*)[20]

• 50 percent to several hundred percent of the person's salary in the case of supervisory, technical and management personnel — Society for Human Resource Management.[21]

• Cost of a single bad hire—$50,000+ according to 27 percent of employers surveyed in 2013.[22]

The high cost of mis-hires does not mean that mis-hiring is rare. In fact, hiring managers said that 20 percent of their new employees were mis-hires.[23]

For a more personal assessment of the cost of mis-hires, I asked a respected co-founder of a highly successful software consultancy company to summarize her hiring philosophy.

This owner's actions reflect the fact that A-players are three to five times more productive, so they immediately impact both top and bottom lines. The right hires engage quickly and participate actively in corporate culture. They contribute to a company's high retention and employee satisfaction rates.

I can relate to missing the ball when hiring for key positions. I am haunted, seriously shamed and almost embarrassed by how easily I can rattle off the many fails in my hiring history over the past 20 years. "How was I SO wrong in this hire?" is a question I've asked myself too many times. Is my talent/fit judgment (or lack of it!) a fatal flaw of my management skills?

Mis-hire statistics and talking to my peers about their hiring fails put my hiring history as the CEO of several software companies into perspective, but neither gave me permission to throw up my hands and accept my 50 percent hit rate. Instead, they: (1) motivate me to improve in this skill, and to improve I must be willing to seek help in hiring from professional recruiters, industrial psychologists and other team members, and (2) make me realize that few mistakes are more costly than hiring the wrong candidate (or putting the right person in the wrong seat). As a result, I've invested time and money in recruiting the right people to play roles on my company's high-performing teams.

> After three months with a new employee, I'm either all in or all out. If all in, I want them to stay for the long term, and I present them with a three- to five-year plan. If all out, I fire them. I've found that if I delay doing the latter, I regret not having fired them sooner because new hires affect the bottom line and suck valuable time from current employees.

A Word About Millennials

Millennials—that group of people born sometime between the early 1980s and mid-90s—have been (unfairly in my experience) dubbed the "Me Generation." We're told that they don't want to start at the bottom or work hard, and that they only want "meaningful" and well-paying jobs.

I try to avoid generalizations, but if I expect to successfully attract and retain employees from this cohort, I've got to know what they value. A trusted advisor gave me the first part of the answer: "Money is important to millennials, but it is not the only thing."

To dive deeper, I asked a millennial owner of a successful digital publishing company for her take on millennials and members of Generation X (those born between the mid-1960s and early 1980s). "We want to feel like we are a part of something bigger. That can mean families, hobbies, work teams, companies and communities."

> High-performing teams are execution-oriented. Dysfunctional teams talk a lot about past successes. High-performing teams are restless and would rather do than talk. They live and die by the question "What have I done for you lately?"

> I noticed that the dynamic range between what an average person could accomplish and what the best person could accomplish was 50 or 100 to 1. Given that, you're well advised to go after the cream of the cream...
>
> A small team of A+ players can run circles around a giant team of B and C players.
>
> Steve Jobs
> Co-founder and
> former CEO of Apple

> Once you cross age 45, spend 60 percent of your time with people half your age or you will lose your sense of reality. If you do not, expect someone to eat your lunch.
>
> Sanjay Singh, Ph.D.
> CEO, Omega Realty

I also asked a millennial sitting on the other side of the closing table—an investor—and his response supported "money not being the only thing." He includes "balanced lives" in his criteria for evaluating possible investments. As he said, "A balanced life is one of our company's core values, so it isn't too surprising that we look for and take it seriously in our investments."

Once we identify great talent, we have to attract and retain it. Those who succeed offer their employees more than money. They provide them the opportunity to live balanced lives and be part of something bigger.

ATTRACTING TOP TALENT

Recruiting is a whole lot easier when the majority of the talented people you want accept offers to join your team. We know that candidates accept offers when they expect to fit into a firm's culture. As the leader of your company, you create that culture—one that attracts the brightest and best or one that doesn't offer what your competitors do. But what exactly is culture?

Company culture shapes the workday experience of every employee and stakeholder, yet culture is easier to experience and recognize than it is to explain. Culture emerges from a company's leadership, mission, values, mood, expectations, hiring choices and even office design. Culture shapes direction and affects whether people like their jobs or value their company. Company culture attracts top talent, retains great employees, and ensures that people are always operating at peak performance.

Culture

Culture, like brand, is a hot topic that is hard to define because so much is about feelings. As my friend David Gray defines it, "Culture is the atmosphere you create with your team and coworkers. It is the environment inside and outside of the company. That environment sets the tone for the interactions among people."

I suggest that you think about culture by asking and answering two questions:

1. What makes employees happy?
2. What are competitors and customers not doing? (Or what can they not replicate?)

As an employer, you want to be able to say, "We aren't like other companies," and for that to be absolutely true.

As I see it, culture means you know who you are as a person, an employer and as a company. You have taken time to articulate your values, and you live and make decisions according to those values every day and in every situation. I believe that this type of integrity or culture attracts and retains A-players.

> Great companies that attract the attention of institutional buyers are a product of good and talented people, leadership with solid values and vision, and a strong culture. Owners who focus on building their companies' culture are not only better positioned to attract and retain talent, but they also substantially increase the enterprise value of their companies.
>
> Duane P. Donner
> Founder and CEO
> Founders Advisors

> Until I came to IBM, I probably would have told you that culture was just one among several important elements in any organization's makeup and success—along with vision, strategy, marketing, financials, and the like...
>
> I came to see, in my time at IBM, that culture isn't just one aspect of the game, it is the game. In the end, an organization is nothing more than the collective capacity of its people to create value.
>
> Louis V. Gerstner Jr.
> Former CEO of IBM

You can't be on-again, off-again about your values: It's a full-time thing. For example, my firm says it values families. For that reason, unlike our Wall Street peers, we don't expect (or reward) employees to consistently work 85-hour weeks. Instead, we developed and put in place the processes and tools that enable us to do our jobs in 60 to 65 hours. Of course, there are weeks when the demands of a deal can push us above 65 hours, but we don't want that to be (nor is it) the norm. Having margins for other things besides work is important to our culture/values.

I'm convinced that over 75 percent of a company's culture is determined during the hiring process. Hiring people that fit who you are as an organization will perpetuate an enduring and healthy culture. *You don't train your culture; you hire it.*

Specific Strategies To Attract And Retain Talent

Experts differ, of course, on which workplace features best position employers to attract and retain top-tier talent. On the next page, Figure 6.2 lists eight features that leading private equity investors consistently identify, and that I've seen make a real difference in an organization's ability to attract talent.

Allow me to share quick stories about just three of the eight features: workplace wellness, corporate mission, and learning and development.

Workplace Wellness

Not long ago, I visited a boutique management consulting firm in South Florida that employed around 20 very bright, Ivy-league-educated process reengineering consultants. These gifted analysts spent long hours in their bullpen of cubicles, pumping out beautiful financial models and process workflows.

Near that bullpen was a break room—more like a fresh market—that was fully stocked with trail mix, nuts, fresh fruit and the team's favorite: protein bars. Alongside the healthy snacks was the coolest assortment of juices, designer waters and kombucha that I'd seen this side of a natural foods store.

The contrast between old-timey cubicles and the new-age snack bar was striking enough that I asked the CEO, "What does all this cost you?"

"Glenn" smiled and explained, "This room costs $2,900 per month to stock. Best investment I've ever made."

As we talked, employees ran in, grabbed one or two items, and disappeared. When we were alone, I asked him, "How did you come up with this?"

Employee expectations vary, and you simply can't be all things to all people. Once you know who you are, recruit and keep the people whose expectations fit your culture. If it is vibrant, your culture will cast off the employees who aren't a good fit. The easy part is finding people with a baseline skill set. Harder is finding the person who will work well with other employees and has a passion for what they do.

FIG. 6.2 Workplace Features & Strategies

WORKPLACE FEATURES	STRATEGY
Learning & Development	Provide opportunities to expand beyond basic competencies and job description.
Workplace Flexibility	Develop policies that address when, where and how a person participates in an organization.
Employment Stability	Create secure environment that fosters engagement.
Benefits & Compensation	Update constantly to adapt to marketplace.
Corporate Mission	Create and adhere to a strong mission as a foundation for a meaningful work environment.
Career Enhancement	Commit to upward mobility of employees.
Workplace Wellness	Implement organizational policies that support healthy behavior.
Respect & Involvement	Flatten the top-down, hierarchical models.

Glenn laughed, "I'm a steak and potatoes guy, and I'm rarely in here. I don't do much snacking since I'm usually taking clients out for lunch. Turns out that my people are championship-level grazers."

As employees continued to stream in and out of the room, I continued, "Grazers? At $2,900 per month, couldn't you have brought in catered lunches several times per week?"

"Maybe, but that's not what they wanted," Glenn explained. He told me that before setting up the break room, he'd surveyed his team. Members indicated that wellness was a huge value, but their biggest challenge to eating healthy was the long hours they worked. "We're too small to justify a chef, and my people are here sometimes before dawn and often long after dusk, so always-available, healthy snacks made more sense."

"What's your return on your $34,800 per year?" I asked.

Glenn hesitated, "That's hard to say. If I'd given every one of them a 10 percent bonus, I honestly don't think they'd have appreciated it as much as they have this break room. And recruits would never see the 10 percent raises, but they consistently comment on how 'cool' this room is when they come in for interviews. I don't know, Zane. How do you quantify the happiness of highly productive millennial employees?"

Good question, but here's what I know: Glenn's response showed his appreciation of his team's desire to live healthy lives. In return, his company reaped huge morale and happiness dividends.

Corporate Mission

One financial professional services company that I worked with included community service/giving back in its list of values. As evidence of that value, for every three years of employment, it offered them one week of paid time (beyond normal vacation time) and $5,000 to participate in any local, regional or international service project of the employee's choosing. Many employees—especially millennials—took advantage of this benefit to travel across the globe to participate in mission or volunteer projects they connected with. The fact that the company supported each employee's unique service passion—rather than recruiting them for the CEO's pet project—personalized the corporate mission while creating a shared vision.

Learning and Development

Learning and development takes many forms (tuition credits, technical conferences, industry certifications, lunch and learns, etc.), but there's another area that CEOs often overlook. When an employee is successful in one area but wants to work in another area, provide incentive and let them run. One owner told me about one of his crackerjack database architects who wanted to work on the front end of the application and hone his user experience (UX) skills. This owner let him make the move, and this architect became the creator of an award-winning app.

Fire Early. Fire Well.

We have all made hiring mistakes, and most of us struggle when a new team member does not meet our expectations. As entrepreneurs, we want everyone on our teams to win and thrive, and we place great value on learning and cooperation. At the same time, our businesses are not ministries. We operate in fiercely competitive environments, and our organizations thrive or flounder based on the quality of our people.

As leaders, we have to fix hiring mistakes—fast. Is it fair to expect excellence from some team members and not others? Is it fair to keep a person on your team who cannot perform at the same level as those around them?

Firing a nonperformer demonstrates to your performing employees that you value how hard and how well they work. Performing team members are the first to spot a nonperformer, but they have no power to fire. Only you can do what it takes to maintain the standard of excellence that you talk so much about.

I've seen plenty of nonperforming employees "wake up" after being fired. Suddenly they become tuned in to their strengths and weaknesses and often move to roles or opportunities better aligned to their strengths. I can't tell you how many successful owners and C-suite executives have told me that getting fired was the best thing that ever happened to them.

Leaders who are serious about a culture of excellence fire the employees who do not pull their weight. This is really an act of love to all the stakeholders. We owe that much to our performers. In addition to the effect firing a nonperformer has internally, it maintains your company's external reputation as an elite group of achievers.

What Buyers Really Want

As a rule, PEGs are not interested in running the day-to-day operations of your company. They want to advise and help fund growth so that your company will operate as autonomously and profitably as possible. If a PEG has to focus on everyday operations of a portfolio company, it bought the wrong company. Running companies distracts from their primary mission of acquiring solid companies that will provide healthy returns on their investment.

Strategic buyers looking to add technology or functionality to their existing operations also prefer acqui-hires. Team members of the companies these buyers roll up generally have key industry relationships, deep segment knowledge, and specialized functional experience that compound the actual value of the business.

Both types of buyers want high-performing team members who understand their roles and execute brilliantly. Hire top talent and pair it with repeatable systems, and you've just increased the franchise value of your company.

Owners (like Jill) who cross-train their employees and promote from within create next-person-up cultures that enable businesses to continue running smoothly if the owner or any other key employee leaves. Jill and Gus created collaborative cultures that they and their employees liked to work in, but their efforts also prevented any one employee from exacting a ransom when negotiating a raise or from holding up a sale in return for a "special bonus."

RETAINING TALENT

Once you have created a culture that attracts the best jockeys (the brightest employees) to train and ride the best horses (repeatable, scalable systems), how do you keep them?

I believe that if you address all 17 Reasons, and thus create an investment-grade company, by definition you have created a company where people are valued, know their work has meaning, understand where the company is going, and have the very real possibility of enjoying a bright future working for a larger company. Creating an investment-grade company goes a long way to keeping employees—as long as you are the leader.

Will creating an investment-grade company keep employees on board, however, once you find a buyer or investor? Since both buyers and investors hate risk, how can you assure them that your brightest stars will stay with the company when you no longer own it?

The Stay Bonus

A stay bonus is a proven and powerful tool to keep employees on board during and after an acquisition—better than issuing stock or stock options. When crafted properly and put in writing, a stay bonus motivates employees to stay with a company throughout and after a sale. (Putting a stay bonus in writing eliminates any fuzzy promises and is a strong motivator to drive up enterprise value.) You can offer stay bonuses to employees who will be involved in a buyer's due diligence, as well as to those whom buyers want to remain with the company post-close. "Seth" ran with that recommendation and persuaded his buyer to pay his key employee the bonus.

Seth, the owner of an industrial technology company, and several of his key employees who had equity positions wanted to take some of their chips off the table. They asked us to help them recapitalize with a private equity group. Seth's COO had only been a key employee for several years and had no equity in the company.

When the PEG offered Seth $45 million, Seth had no stay bonus in place with his COO, but he did have a company that this PEG really, really wanted. When sellers have this kind of leverage, it's possible to persuade the buyer to pay the stay bonus.

We argued that the PEG should offer and pay Seth's COO a stay bonus of $600,000: $300,000 payable six months after closing and $300,000 payable one year after closing. We pointed out that Seth's COO would not only play a vital role in the due diligence necessary to get the deal closed, but also in the company's post-capitalization success. In paying a stay bonus, the PEG would motivate Seth's COO to work hard to close the deal and stay on board after closing to execute the growth strategy. The PEG agreed.

If Seth's buyer had not been so eager to buy his company, Seth would have paid the COO's stay bonus from his sale proceeds—assuming the COO had been willing to stay. If the COO had refused, Seth's buyer would have lowered the purchase price by far more than $600,000.

How you calculate the amount of a bonus depends on the size of the transaction and the criticality of the employees involved. As a (very!) general rule of thumb, bonuses range from 50 percent to 300 percent of an employee's annual salary. These bonuses can be payable at once or in installments, perhaps midway through the sale process, at closing, and again after a certain amount of time post-closing.

> The enterprise value that owners lose if employees are not tied to the company is generally significantly greater than the cost of the stay bonus.

Retaining Millennials

For most of us, millennials make up the majority of our brightest rising stars. Retaining them is the best way I know to build a dynasty. Yes, we can (and do) make professional hires, but compared to growing our own talent, lateral hires are risky. We all face the challenge of recruiting and retaining talented millennials. My firm included.

In the early years, our firm hired summer interns. One of the partners would take the intern to lunch then hand them off to their "mentor"—one of our senior team members. At the end of the summer, we might remember to ask if the intern was "a keeper."

That ad hoc program changed once we began to compete with large and boutique investment banks for the best and brightest college seniors and MBA students. Today our carefully orchestrated intern program includes two weeks of orientation, weekly training sessions centered around our company's processes for both sell-side and buy-side M&A, and multiple mentor meetings before we test their mettle with mean-ingful work.

We also—finally—initiated employee cross-training. We'd long known that employee cross-training made sense both for us and our employees, but, frankly, it wasn't near the top of our to-do list. That changed once millennials told us that cross-training was one way they felt part of something bigger than themselves.

The millennials then showed us that cross-training was only one element of being part of "something bigger." When one of my stars took several weeks off to adopt a child, his fellow cross-trained team members stepped up and filled his shoes. Every one of them worked even longer hours in his absence, but I never heard one complaint. Ever. Later, when one went on a mission trip and another took time off to grieve his father's death, the response was the same: "Go. Don't call us. If we need you, we'll call you." Those members of the so-called "Me Generation" willingly made tangible sacrifices to help others take part in life-affirming "something bigger" activities.

I still smile as I think about how these employees' actions were a tangible example of the culture that my partners and I worked so intentionally to create. This culture was (and still is) real, and it adds substantial value to our firm, clients and quality of our work.

Conclusion

Your company is only investment-grade if you have surrounded yourself with strong individuals who function well together and are completely capable of managing the repeatable, scalable processes and systems that make your company successful.

You might not be able to attract investors or buyers if you can't easily find, hire and retain A+ talent.

RECOMMENDATIONS

1. Create an organizational chart.

Your organizational chart is a critical visual tool to help you identify the skills necessary to fill important organizational gaps. Even if you must insert your own name in most of the boxes (because yours is still a young organization), describe each position as fully as possible so you know exactly the skills and qualities an A-player will bring to each role.

2. Always look for talent to feed the beast.

Not only should you constantly be on the lookout for talent, so should everyone else in your company. Create a one-page summary of the reasons A-players would want to work for your company. Everyone wants to be part of something growing and exciting. Your job is to make sure people know that your company is both.

3. Be a leader.

As the CEO, your job is to ruthlessly and constantly evaluate your team. If you've clearly defined both processes and your people's role in those processes, that assessment should be clear. Processes point out failures. You know that nothing sucks the life out of a high-performing team faster than carrying the weight of a nonperformer. Firing quickly shows your producing employees how much you value them, and it's the right thing to do for your company and for the nonperforming employee.

4. Don't underestimate the value of culture.

Great leaders strive to make their companies great places to work, and they think constantly about how well their culture stacks up against their competitors'.

Regular management retreats for your leadership team provide an invaluable opportunity to devote time away from daily demands to refocus on your organization's missions, goals, strategies and health. Organizations that practice this discipline are overwhelmingly more successful because clarity, personal bonding and renewed focus on what really matters are incredibly valuable.

These retreats don't have to cost a fortune. I've seen small companies that rent modest lodges at nearby state parks hold retreats that are just as effective as those offered by companies that can afford to travel to high-end ski resorts.

5. Keep your winners.

Mentor your star performers. Tie them to your company with employment agreements, profit sharing plans and stay bonuses. Listen to what motivates them. Keep your compensation packages competitive.

Identify your rising stars, show them the path to success, and provide them with opportunities to grow, and you will build a dynasty. Recognize that your best performers are ten times (rather than two times) as productive as average employees.

6. **Create loyal alumni.**

If we recruit entrepreneurial people, they won't stay with us forever. And that's a good thing. You want to be the type of company that holds its employees with open hands. If you truly care about employees and their careers, when they do leave you for that "can't-miss opportunity," handle their departure in a way that creates a loyal alum. Their testimony to recruits about how you supported them in their career is invaluable. If they find that the grass is not greener on the other side of your fence, you will be at the top of their lists to receive their "Can I come back home?" call.

7. **Be willing to change while you stay true to your values.**

You have to adapt your culture—in ways that are consistent with your values—to changes in your workforce. One of my clients who operated a tech firm with over 300 employees told me, "As the average age of our employees rose from 25 to 30 (and was inching toward 35), our fundamental respect for employees did not change, but the ways we demonstrated it did."

8. **Think about your buyer.**

If your key employees are not willing to stay on board post acquisition—at least through a transition period—you will lose transferable value. The best time to tie them to your company with stay bonuses is before there's a buyer in the mix.

TAKEAWAYS

1. **Buyers bet on quality managers first—quality managers running top-notch systems.**

2. **Investment-grade companies don't depend on only one person.**

3. **Always be on the lookout for talent. Your competitors are.**

4. **Great teams running repeatable, scalable processes make your life easier and increase enterprise value.**

5. **Hiring mistakes happen, and only you can fix them.**

Firing underperformers is best for your company, your performing employees, and even the person you fire.

6. **Culture matters to your employees—especially millennials—and to buyers.**

Create a culture that is consistent with who you are as a person, as an employer, and as a company. Once you articulate your values, they should play out in every decision and policy you make.

7. **The enterprise value that you will lose if you fail to tie employees to your company is generally significantly greater than the cost of the employee's stay bonus.**

8. **Talent is the great multiplier. Invest deeply in finding, recruiting and retaining talent.**

9. **Your culture is a strategic asset. Define it, reinforce it, and defend it.**

REAS♥n

Your Company's Competitive Advantages Do Not Protect And Grow Its Market Share.

INVEST IN YOUR DIFFERENTIATED PROCESSES, AND DIVEST YOUR COMMODITY PROCESSES.

I think of a company's competitive advantage as the "secret sauce" that makes it difficult for competitors (ones you know about and those you don't) to replace or replicate your product or service or the way you deliver it.

Michael Porter, Harvard Business School professor and father of modern competitive strategy theory, puts it a little more formally:

> Competitive advantage grows fundamentally out of value a firm is able to create for its buyers that exceeds the firm's cost of creating it. Value is what buyers are willing to pay, and superior value stems from offering lower prices than competitors for equivalent benefits or providing unique benefits that more than offset a higher price.[24]

If Professor Porter used my secret sauce analogy, he might tell you that competitive advantages come in two flavors:

Flavor 1. Differentiation—doing something differently (related to a product, marketing practice, or any activity in the firm's value chain)

Flavor 2. Low Cost—doing something more economically than one's competitors

In his exhaustive study of the topic, Professor Porter makes two additional points about competitive advantage that owners too often overlook. First, he advises that "Potential sources of competitive advantage are everywhere in a firm."[25] Absolutely. In fact, I can think of 16 sources of competitive advantages. (See the list of the 17 Reasons in the Table of Contents.)

Porter also highlights the issue of sustainability. He says, "The fundamental basis of above-average performance in the long run is sustainable competitive advantage."[26] Given the blistering pace of change in the world, I'd argue that very, very few competitive advantages are permanent. For that reason, our job as owners is to constantly ask the hard questions to uncover our competitive advantages, and then to devote our resources to expand and deepen the moats that protect our companies.

But before we look at those hard questions (how to determine if an advantage exists and then how best to use resources to create, sustain or develop new ones), let's do what we always do: examine why investment-grade companies must have at least one—and preferably more—competitive advantage.

INVESTORS AND COMPETITIVE ADVANTAGES

I'd guess that it's pretty clear to you that I'm not a professor or a theoretician. As I do with all the 17 Reasons, I view competitive advantage from the perspective of an entrepreneur, investor and M&A advisor. I know that buyers look for competitive advantages in the companies they acquire, because competitive advantages diminish the risk that another industry player will swoop in, storm the castle, and destroy all the value you've worked for. In more technical terms, competitive advantages reduce the threats to future cash flow and give investors a scalable foundation from which to grow.

But that's not just my opinion.

In his 2008 letter to Berkshire Hathaway's shareholders, Warren Buffett wrote about having four goals, the second of which was "widening the 'moats' around our operating businesses that give them durable competitive advantages."[27] He also said, "A truly great business must have an enduring 'moat' that protects excellent returns on invested capital. The dynamics of capitalism guarantee that competitors will repeatedly assault any business 'castle' that is earning high returns."[28]

Several years ago a buddy called me from Berkshire Hathaway's annual shareholder meeting in Omaha. He was so excited to share what he had just witnessed at the end of a full day of portfolio reports. Opening the floor to questions, Warren Buffett and Charlie Munger fielded one from the owner of a family business. "Guys, you two have been talking about the value and criticality of defensible moats all day. I operate a third-generation family business. How do you suggest that I create a defensible moat for my business?"

Warren glanced over at Charlie, leaned over to his desk microphone, and said, "Damn if I know how to build one. That's the reason I buy companies that already have them."

Investors also know that doing or having something different or special gives you a unique value proposition, so it is fundamental to capturing additional market share. As more prospective customers find out about

Buyers look for companies that have effective moats already in place, because they understand the time and effort it takes to build them. Investors appreciate the role moats play in maintaining and growing predictable revenue streams. For those reasons, buyers pay more for companies with meaningful, sustainable barriers. Not sometimes. All of the time. Companies without meaningful, sustainable barriers are typically not even salable.

that competitive advantage, your company has the potential to grab additional market share. Yes, you can (and should) invest in sales activities to educate as many prospective customers as possible, but a robust competitive advantage beats a skilled sales force every time. Together, however, the combination is unstoppable.

Investors are big fans of secret sauces and get really excited over an assortment of them. They just can't get enough of the methods or systems your company uses to produce something better or more inexpensively than competitors. They know that your competitive advantage is the reason your customers choose your product or service repeatedly over their other choices.

THERE'S MORE THAN ONE WAY TO MAKE A SECRET SAUCE.

The ingredients for your company's secret sauce may be cheaper inputs, better inventory management, or better distribution channels. Or it may be your company's culture or IP.

In my daughter's case, however, her secret sauce was her height.

If I introduced you to my daughter Ellie and told you that several collegiate women's basketball recruiters had pursued her as a junior in high school, you'd likely write me off as just another exaggerating, if not delusional, father. You'd notice that Ellie is 5'1", not 6'1".

I'd explain that when she's in the classic defensive position, Ellie's hands and face are squarely centered in her opponent's dribble zone. Her low center of gravity perfectly positions her to frustrate the players she guards and makes her more defensively disruptive than taller players.

You might be skeptical until I tell you that Ellie not only led her conference in steals, but team statistics showed that her number of steals per game dramatically reduced the average score of her team's opponents.

Notice several points here:

1. My daughter's competitive advantage was in an area one might not expect: She was a small player in a game where height is deemed the ultimate advantage. Turns out her lower center of gravity lined up with the height of the opponent's dribble perfectly.

2. We could prove the impact my daughter had on the scoring ability of her competitors through objective data.

3. Ellie's advantage was sustainable. She had stopped growing, and because the height of the average basketball player is not likely to decrease, she would continue to play an integral role in her team's ability to win.

Ellie's competitive advantage was her stature. Sure, like every effective player she practiced hard, studied the game, and was well-coached. But all that being equal, her height gave her an edge and contributed to her team's W/L record.

What differentiates your product or service from that of competitors who also work hard, study the game, and are well-coached? Why do your customers buy from you (a win) or buy from a competitor (a loss)? Do you even ask yourself these questions?

Your company's competitive advantage is the reason your customers are your customers, and it is the reason they are loyal (buy from you again and again). Your competitive advantage is also the reason your prospective customers are attracted to your product or service in a sea of choices.

Ellie's coaches played her because she neutralized the other team's top shooting guards and had a direct effect on the score. Customers choose your product, service or process because it benefits them more than the product, service or process of your competitors. They "like" it more for some reason. Your job is to figure out what your customers' reason is. What is their "why" for buying from you? Once you answer this question, you can invest more in that "why" and assign your most talented team members to own and focus on that "why."

Sounds Simple, Right?

Winning consistently over competitors—in collegiate basketball or the fast-paced world of business—is only possible when a team has at least one solid competitive advantage. That's why digging deep to discover yours, measuring its value, and intentionally investing in it are so critical to your company's success.

But where do you start? Let's begin with a quick review of the most common sources of competitive advantage in private companies.

Common Competitive Advantages In Private Companies

People

- Customer-first minded
- Smart and technically excellent
- Experienced in industry
- Shared focus on results

Product/Service Innovation

- Engineering and design
- Utility
- Cost advantages
- Continuous improvement cycle

Client Relationships

- All aspects of services truly add value for clients.
- More responsive than competitors
- 100 percent referenceable client base

Culture

- Customer service focused
- Results oriented
- Values knowledge sharing, teamwork, professionalism and open communication
- Accepts and welcomes the challenges associated with change
- One vision. One team.
- Healthy. According to Patrick Lencioni (in his classic book *The Five Dysfunctions of a Team: A Leadership Fable*), "healthy" means trust, no fear of conflict, strong commitment, positive accountability and focused on results.

While people, product or service innovation, client relationships and culture are often sources for competitive advantages, Michael Porter argues that *every aspect of operations* can generate them. Perhaps your company has a vertically integrated supply chain, proprietary technology, slick user interface, an efficient global delivery model, compelling marketing material, or an incredibly easy-to-do-business-with contracting model. Maybe your company's processes are more efficient than your competitors' or your relationships with suppliers are closer. Maybe your location lowers your costs compared to competitors. But whatever it is, secret sauce makes you stand out from the crowd and makes it hard to compete against you. In other words, your secret sauce gives you a barrier to entry.

One of my partners, John Sinders has been involved in the energy industry for years as a lawyer, banker, investment banker and executive. He notes that the industry has changed a lot over the years but strong barriers are no less important to investors. See what he says about secret sauce in today's energy industry in the box on the right.

> Today's investors are much more cautious. To garner investment in the current energy market, you need proprietary technology; returns that align with the capital life of assets; assets and services that truly increase efficiency; lower costs; and increased safety. It is imperative that you can demonstrate your company's operational differentiators with data.
>
> John Sinders
> Managing Director
> Founders Advisors

IDENTIFYING YOUR COMPANY'S COMPETITIVE ADVANTAGE

To identify your company's secret sauce, you have to ask your customers and prospects why they choose your product or service over your competition's. Then listen carefully to the answers.

Don't assume that you know why a customer chooses to do business with you. Presupposition in this category can cost you dearly. Owners of investment-grade companies are truth seekers because they want to win and continuously improve.

Also, don't limit yourself to asking customers the hard questions. Seek input from your front-line teams: sales and customer service reps. They hear positive and negative (highly constructive) feedback firsthand. They talk to customers every day, and unless they can persuade prospects that something about your product or service better meets a prospect's needs, your people don't make the sale, don't earn their bonuses, and can't purchase that much-needed family vacation.

If you aren't sitting down on a regular basis with your salespeople, customer support staff and customers to ask them questions, really listen to their answers, and leverage their feedback into improvements, you aren't leading. You are reacting.

Once you have answers to your questions, you must test each answer to see if you truly have a competitive advantage. Remember Ellie? Her coach suspected that Ellie's height had something to do with her success guarding defenders, so he tested it. He put in another guard (one with similar hand speed, attitude and hustle but 4" taller) and looked at the statistics.

I'm suggesting that you do something similar. To determine if what you think might be a competitive advantage truly is, perform A/B testing, examine the data, then see how they stack up against yourself and your competitors.

Your mother, pastor, rabbi or priest probably told you that comparing yourself to others is not a healthy exercise. I get it, but when it comes to your company and every one of the 17 Reasons, I'm telling you the exact opposite: Compare yourself to your industry competitors and strive to outrank them! Keep track of your competitors' margins and financial and operating metrics. When you consistently outperform your cohort, you drive value. Investors/buyers will notice and come knocking.

THE PERILS OF RUNNING A MOAT-FREE COMPANY

If you can live a happy life while oblivious to the fact that your competitors are constantly prowling about looking for ways to crawl, swim, blast or rocket over your weak or nonexistent moat, you scare me as a leader.

You must be mindful that opponents can come from land, sea and sky, armed with a host of dangerous weapons. We have worked too hard to allow our competitors to hand our heads to us on silver platters.

And those are just the competitors we know about. Most moat-violators aren't the competitors we imagine holding those platters. Also prowling around your moat are:

1. New competitors that today are only in planning mode.
2. Suppliers with bargaining power.
3. Large customers with purchasing power.
4. Competitors who copy simple processes, making it easy for customers to substitute your products for theirs.
5. Employees who long to be entrepreneurs.

These would-be plunderers have numerous weapons in their arsenals. Some come armed with better or more innovative customer service processes. Others locate your Achilles heel and engineer their product or service to take you down with one well-placed shot. Greater financial firepower can propel any one of these thieves over your moat and into your castle almost before you realize what has happened.

Cash buys better people, tools, technology, consulting services and brand awareness. In short, the combatant with the most money/resources usually wins. Proper capitalization is the ultimate competitive offensive and defensive weapon.

> If you aren't asking customers why they buy and then really listening to their answers, you are likely making flawed assumptions, definitely squandering precious data, blindly making investment decisions, and ultimately jeopardizing your ability to extend or discover your competitive advantage.

FIG. 7.1 **SWOT Analysis**

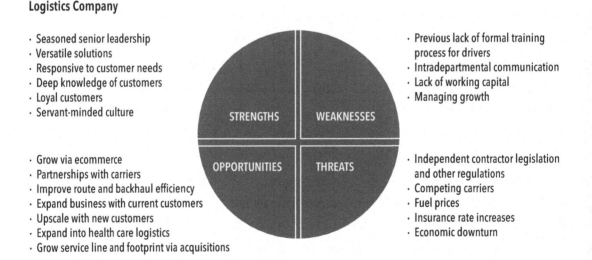

Logistics Company

STRENGTHS
- Seasoned senior leadership
- Versatile solutions
- Responsive to customer needs
- Deep knowledge of customers
- Loyal customers
- Servant-minded culture

WEAKNESSES
- Previous lack of formal training process for drivers
- Intradepartmental communication
- Lack of working capital
- Managing growth

OPPORTUNITIES
- Grow via ecommerce
- Partnerships with carriers
- Improve route and backhaul efficiency
- Expand business with current customers
- Upscale with new customers
- Expand into health care logistics
- Grow service line and footprint via acquisitions

THREATS
- Independent contractor legislation and other regulations
- Competing carriers
- Fuel prices
- Insurance rate increases
- Economic downturn

AN OLD TOOL BUT A GOOD ONE

Have you conducted a SWOT analysis with an eye on what makes your company a winner (your competitive advantages)? Have you figured out how you can better focus on those advantages?

If you've ever participated in one of my seminars, you know I am a huge advocate of using the SWOT exercise to assess your business, as well as your personal relationships. What you can/will discover in both is priceless.

Figure 7.1 is a SWOT analysis that I picked up from a logistics company's team planning session. This is another invaluable one-page management tool to laminate and keep handy for reference.

I'm still shocked at how many owners and management teams don't agree on their company's competitive advantage, much less the threats to its sustainability. I consider ignorance, uncertainty or fuzziness regarding why customers buy and a failure to protect and improve on that reason as tantamount to malpractice. So, bring your leadership team together and conduct a SWOT analysis. I promise you it will help you unearth your distinct barriers to entry and help you fortify them. It will also expose where you might have some holes in your castle walls.

UNLESS YOUR MARGIN IS BETTER, YOU DON'T HAVE A COMPETITIVE ADVANTAGE

If you tell me, as most owners do, "Of course my company has competitive advantages!" I'll listen politely, then I'll ask to see your company's income statement. If it fails to demonstrate consistent and sustainable outsized gross margins in your industry cohort, your competitive advantage is not a provable reality. Gross margins prove whether you are really doing more with less and doing it better because of your secret sauce. Your margins signal whether your company's additional "value add" allows you to charge significantly higher prices (and thus expand margin even further).

> An underestimated metric of competitive advantage is gross margin.

Of course, a gross margin is specific to an industry. You can't compare the gross margins of an HVAC distributor to a SaaS company's. Or a grocer's to that of a niche sporting goods ecommerce company. You have to compare apples to apples. And when you do, you know where you stand. You can track and improve your gross margins.

> If you don't have outsized gross margins, you might not have any competitive advantages. And without competitive advantages, you have no barriers to entry and can't protect your market share.

If your company's margins are lower than your industry cohorts', it tells me you may be less efficient, don't have the pricing power of competitors, are a low-price supplier, etc. If your margins are higher than your competitors', it tells me you have some advantage, some secret sauce. Perhaps your operational systems and processes are stellar. Maybe you've recruited a more talented, productive team. Great margins tell everyone that something exciting is happening. Higher margins, not surprisingly, generate the interest of potential buyers because higher margins generate healthier cash flow. Of course, cash flow doesn't just benefit future owners; it benefits you today.

No Excuses, Please.

Many owners will tell me (always before they get to know me) that their companies simply aren't "the type" to generate a competitive advantage. I'll often ask what "type" they mean. The following are some of the most common answers I hear.

Poor Excuse No. 1. Mine is a service company!

In today's marketplace, many technology consulting/service firms have failed to build the technological infrastructures that would transform them from low-value, staff-augmentation firms to powerful, asset-based consultancies that score well on a 17 Reasons Assessment.™ Those who succeed—not only in growing profits but also in building real enterprise value—are the professional services firms that have built asset-based services companies. They are widening the moats around their companies through continuous improvements to their talent, processes, methodologies and automation. They have added the tools and systems that allow them to provide the essential trifecta: people, processes and technology.

I've seen numerous pure project-based service companies transform themselves into tech-enabled service companies and reap the benefits from a significant increase in valuation multiples from 3x to 4x TTM EBITDA to 8x to 9x TTM EBITDA. Do the math. A project-based services company doing $1.5MM in EBITDA can increase its valuation from the $6MM range to the $13.5MM range. The greater multiple reflects the margin and barrier advantage that technology can offer a service business.

Poor Excuse No. 2. We're growing too fast to build margins!

Too many managers of fast-growth companies tell me that it is "just too difficult" to develop top-tier margins in a fast-growth company. I totally get the "too difficult" argument when it comes to your EBITDA margins, because you are investing in growth. But your gross margins should be a focus no matter your growth rate. How efficient (as measured by your cost of goods sold) are you in delivering on your value proposition to customers? Can you deliver crazy value to them while maintaining your pricing power? If you can, you are creating value! You are making a product or delivering a service better and/or more inexpensively than your competitors. Your company has a competitive advantage.

I'm sympathetic to fast-growing companies who lack high profit margins because they are so focused on growth that they are investing in operations (e.g., hiring more people, investing in technology, marketing aggressively, building a sales infrastructure, starting up production, expanding into new markets). Still, you must focus on your EBITDA margins, since they indicate how efficient you are within your operations (SG&A). But if you can't focus on both, gross margins are at the heart of your business model. If you get your gross margins right, you can manage to grow your EBITDA margins as your company scales and matures.

Even rapidly growing companies should have healthy gross margins relative to their industries and be able to demonstrate how these margins will expand over time.

Poor Excuse No. 3. My company's products aren't one of a kind!

Owners of product-based (rather than service-based) companies will tell me that only companies with one-of-a-kind products can generate more Return On Invested Capital (ROIC) than their competitors and have competitive advantages that last beyond the first imitator. (ROIC is a performance ratio that aims to measure the percentage return that investors in a company are earning from their invested capital.)

There are at least three fallacies in this argument.

- **Fallacy 1. Only one-of-a-kind products build barriers.**

Meet "Ezekiel," an owner whose company's product was virtually a commodity.

"EZ8" was a manufacturer of oxygen concentrators (a medical device used to deliver oxygen to patients). Ezekiel, its owner, had developed a growing business in a marketplace full of large manufacturers offering largely similar functionality and price points.

Fully aware that competing on functionality and price would not create the kind of company he wanted, Ezekiel turned to distribution channels. He built his company's moat by setting up and supporting local distributors in underserved countries across the globe. Once he understood the culture of an area, Ezekiel invested resources in recruiting, training and supporting distributors there.

This strategic path was time-consuming and fraught with unique challenges, but it was one that the large distributors weren't willing to take. Over time, Ezekiel leveraged the moat of "relational equity" in these off-the-radar international markets to create a high-margin business in an apparently commoditized medical products business. In doing so, he built a substantial barrier to entry.

Coca-Cola and McDonald's have mastered the art of using distribution-channel domination, product consistency and strong internationally recognized brands to create nearly invincible moats. Many of us would not name Coke as our favorite soft drink or identify the Big Mac® as the best hamburger we've ever tasted. Both, however, are the undisputed brand leaders in their categories because we can buy a Coke or Big Mac® almost anywhere in the world and they'll be exactly as we expect. If McDonald's added donuts to its menu tomorrow, it would be the leading seller of donuts in the world, not because its doughnuts were the highest quality or best tasting, but because McDonald's has a distribution network that competitors cannot easily replicate.

- **Fallacy 2. Only companies making one-of-a-kind products can generate more ROIC than their competitors.**

Even companies that sell commodity products can produce outsized ROIC if they are run by highly capable management teams that allocate capital well. Stellar management teams have a keen understanding of opportunity cost, and they invest company resources in the optimal strategic initiatives. Examples of these initiatives are plant modernization, technology investments, international expansion and cost control programs.

- **Fallacy 3. Any barriers that product-based companies do manage to build only hold until the first imitator comes along.**

I will concede that no secret sauce lasts forever. But, as one of my clients learned, limited shelf life is no excuse for failing to create the kind of competitive advantage that can build a moat around your company.

I remember the day that the owner of "QuantiPhi" called to tell me that his company's product had attracted the notice of a large state's department of education. After observing several districts leverage the data generated by his student learning applications, the state was launching a study to determine if it could build its own similar system with the help of a leading software engineering firm. If there were ever a test to see whether Goliath could swim David's moat, this would be it.

Years earlier, this owner (a former math teacher, turned principal, turned entrepreneur) had devel-

oped proprietary algorithms to help school districts collect and analyze detailed student performance data. The software application used this data to identify at-risk students in grades K through 12 and followed up with customized learning modules to help put students back on track.

QuantiPhi then offered district administrators a series of short, digital assessments to track student progress over entire school years. Over time, QuantiPhi gathered substantial longitudinal data sets about each student that proved to be reliable predictors of student performance on statewide criterion-referenced tests as well as on national norm-referenced tests. These data sets gave teachers and schools valuable information about patterns, so they were better able to assist individual students and accelerate their learning/progress.

QuantiPhi gained traction in key cities and districts throughout the Midwest. At regional and national conferences, curriculum coordinators gave glowing reviews to the system and its creators. As word spread, large national assessment companies and state departments of education began to take notice.

Did Goliath set an Olympic record crossing QuantiPhi's moat? Far from it. Eight months after our phone call, the interested state mandated that all its districts install QuantiPhi's assessment and data collection system. The state recognized QuantiPhi's value, but, more importantly, it realized that it could not easily replicate the functionality or valuable byproduct—instructional data. The state desperately needed the longitudinal data that QuantiPhi had collected over several years and that ONLY QuantiPhi possessed.

This longitudinal data—performance data from weekly quizzes and periodic end-of-unit assessments—provided QuantiPhi a deep barrier to entry. QuantiPhi had designed its system so that extracting these data jewels and importing them into other student information systems would be difficult if not impossible. On top of that, teachers were using and impressed with QuantiPhi's suite of easy-to-use report writers and highly graphical performance dashboards.

By collecting valuable data from its operational software, QuantiPhi created a moat that its competitors could not overcome. Every additional data point created and stored within its system was one more hungry alligator in QuantiPhi's moat, waiting for its next meal. No one could match QuantiPhi's constantly growing body of valuable longitudinal data.

QuantiPhi is a great example of a company building a moat by first developing something unique and then doing what it takes to keep it defensible. It's also a great example of the value investors place on deep moats. Soon after that state mandate, a public educational monolith purchased QuantiPhi at a handsome revenue multiple.

We can all imagine other situations in which Goliath would one day figure out the ingredients in David's secret sauce (i.e., substantial longitudinal data sets about thousands of students). But will Goliath be able to "execute" on it? It isn't just knowing the secret-sauce ingredient that gives David the advantage. The advantage that Goliath cannot replicate is David's ability to use the ingredients to produce instructional data (i.e., information about patterns that teachers can use to better assist their students and accelerate student learning).

Unfortunately, secret sauces don't last forever, so owners of investment-grade companies must:

1. Repeatedly ask the hard "Why do you buy from us?" question.
2. Be so possessed by the desire to win that they are willing to listen to and learn from prospects that chose their competitors.
3. Be humble enough to accept that they don't know everything and smart enough to seek input from the folks on the front line.

4. Be on the lookout for stronger, longer-lasting barriers.

BARRIERS IN TECH-ENABLED COMPANIES

Yes, like steel, barriers come in different strengths. And like steel, the stronger the barrier, the more valuable it is. Jeff Totten, (CEO of Evergreen Services Group, former private equity investor and friend), has made a hobby of studying the intricacies of barriers in tech-enabled companies. A few years back, I invited Jeff to kick off one of my Silicon Y'all Summits[29]—an annual event that brings together 60 high-growth technology entrepreneurs for two days of networking and expert-led discussions of growth, value and industry trends. Jeff blew away the group with his professional insight into barriers. Dozens of the tech entrepreneurs who attended reported that Jeff's recommendations would shape their barrier-building strategies as soon as they got back home.

I can't outdo Jeff's presentation on barrier strength in software companies, but I do have Jeff's permission to summarize it here, and I encourage you to apply each of the concepts to your specific industry.

As you can see in Figure 7.2, Jeff places the most common barriers to entry in software companies on a continuum.

FIG. 7.2 Common Barriers In Software Companies

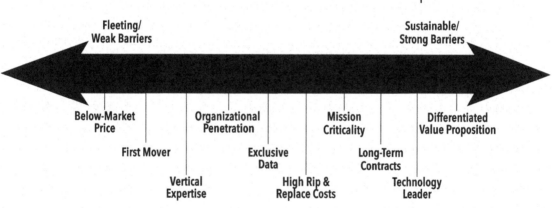

Since most of the listed barriers are fairly straightforward, we'll run through them quickly.

Below-Market Price

A lower price can be a barrier if the price is disproportionately below value delivered or the prevailing market price. Making the claim that "They're good, but we're cheaper" carries a real risk of moving down market rather than up. It is also a claim most often made by companies with small development budgets.

First Mover

Being the first mover is a decent barrier—while it lasts. Typically, it's short-lived because there is always someone with more funding out there to compete with the first mover. While it holds, however, it provides a short-term opportunity to build more defensible long-term barriers.

Vertical Expertise

Bones Billing (in Reason 4) was a great example of dominating a smaller market before expanding scope. If your company has that kind of deep expertise, you've erected a barrier against more general competitors.

Organizational Penetration

Do you know how dependent your customers are on your software? Do customers rely on it as a system of record and have they integrated it into daily workflows? Who in their organizations uses it and how often? If your software is ingrained in your customers' workflows, you've created a powerful barrier against switching.

Exclusive Data

The longitudinal data that QuantiPhi provided its customers was key to its ability to offer valuable and targeted instruction. Its unique and proprietary data added significant value to its educational customers' operations.

High Rip And Replacement Costs

Ideally, your software product becomes so embedded in your customers' environment that the costs of switching to a competitor are prohibitive.

Mission Criticality

The risk and cost of switching also depends on how critical your software is to your customers' core business. Do they depend on it to operate their business? Would their operations be impaired if they turned off your software?

Long-Term Contracts

Long-term contracts (1+ years) are near-perfect barriers—during their term. Unfortunately, it has become increasingly difficult to secure long-term contracts in today's SaaS market. Jeff suggested that owners combine: (A) high customer retention (90+ percent) and (B) revenue retention (100+ percent—this occurs when existing customers buy more each year) to create a sustainable barrier. A + B is a pretty sticky model. He also noted that online SaaS delivery, versus on-premise installation, puts teeth in contracts since providers can more easily pull the plug.

> While technology can create a temporarily unbreachable moat, there's very little about operating systems, database architectures, workflow user interfaces, server farms and microprocessors that—given time—competitors can't replicate.

Technology Leader

Owners who invest up front and heavily in their technology teams build three of the barriers we've listed above (high rip and replacement costs, mission criticality and long-term contracts). In addition, the technology leader in a marketplace can charge the most and sign customers to the longest contracts.

Differentiated Value Proposition

A differentiated value proposition combines technology leadership with a blue ocean to sell into. The idea is that technology leaders are able to offer a replacement that is superior to the existing product. Consider how Netflix replaced Blockbuster's brick-and-mortar model.

WHY CUSTOMERS BUY IS YOUR INVESTMENT CRITERIA.

Once our customers tell us why they buy from us and not from our competitors, we can dig into the really interesting questions—the ones that tell us which processes to invest in and which to divest or farm out.

- Which factors enable you to produce your product or service at higher margins?
- What is it that enables your company to provide the same or a better customer experience for the same cost structure or for much less?
- What produces the increased value that customers prefer: your company's technology, people, processes and/or go-to-market strategy?

CAN YOU EXPLAIN YOUR COMPANY'S SECRET SAUCE?

If your financials (margins) tell you that your company has a competitive advantage, but you can't tell me exactly what it is, you are not alone. You are not the first owner to be so focused on keeping the train running that dissecting the fuel it runs on just isn't a priority.

If you want to attract a great investor, it's time to change that. Not only do you have to know what fuels your margins and grows and protects your market share, you need to be able to communicate both to prospective investors. Owners who rely on assumptions rather than hard data to identify their companies' secret sauce signal to investors that they have not intentionally invested in that sauce. They are also incapable of explaining to potential investors or buyers why their companies enjoy the margins they do. Investors expect you to know the "why" behind your numbers.

Against the 1000 proposals that come across Bryce Youngren's desk—all of them primed by investment bankers who only make money if they find buyers—how will your company compare? If you want to be the company that excites him, I suggest that the day to figure out how to explain your margins—the measure of the strength of your company's competitive advantages—is today.

If your company has a competitive advantage, prospective buyers will find it but won't tell you. That's not their job. Their job is to use the advantage to build synergies to make more money from your company under their ownership than you did.

> We look at about 1000 possible acquisitions in a year and narrow the funnel quickly to the five we'll invest in. We look for management teams who can articulate their barriers and why those barriers are sustainable and strong.
>
> Bryce Youngren
> Managing Partner
> Polaris Growth Fund

It is your job as an owner to know what competitive advantage your company offers to customers. Once you do, you have to assess its value, be able and well prepared to articulate it, and persuade a buyer to pay for it.

IF YOUR COMPANY HAS A COMPETITIVE ADVANTAGE, PROTECT IT!

If you haven't already done so, put a black box around your key processes and the proprietary methods within these processes. Mask them, limit access to them and guard them with your life. Processes, especially those related to order and sequencing, take years to build and should be as deeply buried as that family secret about crazy Uncle Harry. Don't underestimate the value of your processes to a competitor.

You might not be able to attract investors or buyers if almost anyone can set up shop and compete with your company, and your company's gross margins are not greater than your competitors'.

RECOMMENDATIONS

1. Understand your company's competitive advantages and how to enhance them.
Have you asked customers why they buy from you rather than your competitors?

2. If you think you have a competitive advantage, have you compared yourself to competitors in your industry?

3. If your company does not have a competitive advantage, create one.
Simplify a complex process, or radically innovate an existing one. New processes can inspire unique products and better solutions to everyday problems. Eliminating customers' pain points is a proven strategy to secure a competitive edge.
- Have you conducted a SWOT analysis?
- Have you determined how to exploit your competitors' weaknesses?

4. Deliberately budget to bolster your competitive advantages, and make them part of your company's strategic plan.
- Are your best people incentivized to strengthen your company's advantages?
- Do you engineer remarkability into products, services or processes and invest in them?
- Does your company spend more money on engineering than it does on sales?

5. Gross margin demonstrates your competitive advantage, so adopt an intense bias toward a high-margin business model.
- Do you track your peers' margins?
- Are you driven to be a top-quartile performer?

6. If your margins are lower than your competitors', don't make excuses. Figure out why.
Every company can develop a competitive advantage, including fast growth, commodity-products and service-based companies.
- Have you built a unit economic model to demonstrate margin expansion?
- Are you examining the input costs of your products and services and diligently working to lower these costs? If you do more with less and do it better, customers will gladly pay your price.
- How much do you invest in product engineering to drive more value for your customers so you can raise prices?

7. Use competitive advantages to direct capital investment.
- Have you ranked your competitive advantages by their relative contributions to your overall business strategy?
- Are you investing your attention and capital expenditures in the products and services that have the highest margins?

- Do you have the capital to continually deepen and widen your moat?
- Are you making suboptimal business decisions because your company is undercapitalized?

The competitor with the most money/resources to invest in people, tools, technology, consulting and brand awareness usually wins. Proper capitalization is the ultimate offensive and defensive weapon.

8. **Be prepared and able to articulate your company's competitive advantages to prospective investors.**
    - Can you provide a concise explanation of your company's competitive advantages?
    - Does your company's financial performance prove that a competitive advantage truly exists?

9. **Protect your advantages/barriers.**
    - Have you limited access to your key processes?

TAKEAWAYS

1. **Competitive advantages have many benefits:**
    - They increase valuations and purchase prices.
    - They maintain, and often even expand, gross margins.
    - They give investors a scalable foundation from which to grow.

2. **Your competitive advantage is the reason customers buy from you over your competitors.**

3. **Every aspect of your company is a potential source of competitive advantages.**

4. **Healthy gross and net margins prove the existence of a competitive advantage.**

5. **To excite buyers, your company must have margins that exceed the industry norm.**

6. **Defining and showcasing your company's competitive advantage is your responsibility as an owner.** Don't expect a prospective investor to do the heavy lifting for you.

7. **The real competitive advantage in any business can be summed up in one word: people.**

Your Company Lacks Owner-Independent Sales And Marketing Processes.

DOCUMENT SALES AND MARKETING PROCESSES, AND RELY ON MOTIVATED PEOPLE TO DEPLOY THEM.

L et's start with two definitions: (1) marketing means cultivating the soil for sales, and (2) sales involves the ask and conversion.

In investment-grade companies, both sales and marketing are more process-centric than people-centric. That's what "Hank" learned from a large private equity buyer during the first (and only) management meeting.

Hank was as confident walking into our meeting with one of the private equity groups interested in his municipal services company, as he'd been facing ace major league pitchers 20 years earlier.

Given his career as a former MLB player, the polite preliminaries between seller and prospective buyer lasted longer than usual. When the PEG reps finally got down to business, they opened with an easy, easy throw. "We're impressed by the two large state contracts listed on your customer list. Tell us how you landed them."

Hank leaned into the pitch and took his first swing. "I personally worked for 18 months to reel in these big fish!"

"Strike one," I thought to myself.

"I've got some good friends from the old days in powerful places," he continued, "but I wasn't comfortable putting them on the spot. Instead, I hired a few crack lobbyists to make sure my friends knew that

my company was a contender."

Strike two.

Like any good coach, I tried to signal Hank to settle down. We'd talked about highlighting systems, but I could see that he hadn't connected sales with systems. Before I could pull Hank out of the batter's box, he continued proudly, "I made it clear that, if I got 'em, these two clients could depend on me to be available 24/7."

Hank looked at me as if he'd hit a pitch out of the park, but I knew he hadn't read my signals.

The PEG reps threw a couple more easy pitches over the plate, but the game was over. Without knowing it, Hank had spooked his prospective buyer.

On the surface, the two contracts looked like gold: great revenue, fabulous margins, everything you could ask for. But the private equity team saw that Hank's sales lineup had no depth. Hank was the sole reason for these two contracts. Customers were doing business with Hank, NOT with his company.

Hank's company's sales efforts depended on personal relationships rather than finely tuned processes designed to produce predictable sales and cash flow. Once Hank left the business, there was no reason to think that these "personal" customer relationships wouldn't leave with him. Contrast Hank's approach to that of "Marcus."

Marcus' 30-person company, GPAlert, developed a retention management software system that over 400 colleges and universities used to track the performance of both athletes and at-risk students.

Marcus and I were sitting in the conference room of a large public company, taking in the view of lower Manhattan. As a result of a targeted auction, three strong potential partners emerged. This was our first meeting with the COO and senior vice president of strategy for one of the suitors. As the two executives reviewed GPAlert's customer list, they singled out Arizona State University.

"You know," the COO began, "ASU is one of the largest universities in the country. How did a little software company down in the Deep South manage to land them?"

Marcus hesitated. He looked at me for a signal, unsure about how to handle the pitch. Luckily, I'd heard the story before, and I nodded at Marcus to continue.

"I really don't know," he began. "I've never met them." Both the COO and senior VP dialed up their attention level by a factor of 10.

Marcus continued, "Our automated marketing programs do a great job of consistently adding strong prospects to our sales funnels. Once that happens, our inside reps initiate a series of demonstrations and follow-up contacts. Ultimately, the qualified prospect merits a call from our outside rep. I could find out which reps handled that client if you'd like."

As quickly as Hank had struck out, Marcus had struck gold. These executives were convinced that GPAlert relied on sales and marketing processes that delivered predictable sales growth independent of charismatic salespeople.

Ideally, your company's sales process:

- Produces new business/revenue as predictably as a highly organized manufacturing plant produces sophisticated jet engines.
- Uses a lead generation system to identify, research and contact prospective clients.
- Has defined benchmarks and sale-cycle timelines so your team can track progress through a pipeline (e.g., the 30-day process to close).

- Is "improvable" in measurable ways (e.g., can reduce sales cycles from 30 days to 25).
- Determines the personality and skill set in the people you hire.
- Is the backbone of the curriculum for training new hires.
- Uses a sales methodology that is implemented through a well-adopted Customer Relationship Management (CRM) system.

People fit within the guardrails of a process, not the other way around. But systems without people are worthless, so let's focus on how you create a culture and compensation systems that motivate your people to operate your systems at top efficiency.

THE PEOPLE PART OF THE SALES PROCESS

While you can outsource some of the 17 Reasons, you can't outsource sales or marketing. These processes are intrinsic to value creation. You might outsource components such as graphics, appointment-making, lead generation, call centers, and event planning for your annual users' conference. But never hand over to an outsider the processes you use to convert and retain clients.

Create A Healthy Sales Culture.

We've all heard the stories about (or even experienced) cutthroat work environments in which sales reps do whatever it takes to hit their quotas. Competition is a good thing, but, when left unchecked, it can create a toxic culture that will kill an organization, or at least the organization's long-term success.

Those of us who've been around long enough have also run into organizations that put a fence around their sales departments. Other departments don't see themselves as part of sales or marketing, and they expect "that group of extroverts over in sales" to magically bring in clients every month. These companies are not holistically focused on acquiring, retaining and delighting customers.

Contrast that view of sales with the one adopted by highly functional organizations. In these companies, everyone sees themselves in sales AND service, so cross-pollination is standard operating procedure. In these companies, leadership teams constantly highlight how all team members are critical to winning the customers' business and loyalty.

Cross-pollination among teams does not always come naturally. It requires CEOs to conduct frequent, informal stand-up meetings and schedule regular meetings (monthly or quarterly) for sales and marketing teams to meet, share and coordinate their activities with product management teams. Product teams need customers and prospects to let them know in real time what they want, need and don't like so product teams know which features and functions to develop next. Ideally, you want your teams to hold regular, informal check-ins guided by the aggregated data from your CRM system and automated marketing tools.

I was in a board meeting one morning when one of the members dropped this little gem into the conversation: "The goal of sales and marketing is to solve customer problems profitably." I'd never thought about sales and marketing quite that way before. This executive focused on building a culture/organization in which every member knows the challenges or problems those in its target market face, and is adept at communicating exactly how they (and their organization) solve those problems.

You can't build a scalable organization if sales employees don't understand, appreciate and promote cross-pollination. Any team member (independent of role or responsibility) should be able to benefit from closing a deal if they played a key role in bringing it in the door. Clear boundaries (in terms of territory, client type, etc.) are fine, but it makes sense to reward team members for handing off leads to an appropriate team member who is in a better position to close the deal.

Volumes have been written about creating team-selling cultures, but this is a tricky challenge in the real world. I suggest that you make every player on your sales team appreciate the value of being trained in, and adept at, other team members' roles; communicate openly and frequently with your sales teams; and continuously solicit their thoughts on how to foster teamwork through creative incentive plans. (See Reason 6 for more ideas about creating a culture that supports teamwork.)

> To create an investment-grade company, you define the behavior you desire, and you put in place the "carrots" and "sticks" to reward/hold accountable your employees for their behavior.

Reward The Behavior You Claim To Value.

Compensation plans should clearly reflect your corporate goals and, if your company is in growth mode, it makes sense to tie a majority of a sales rep's compensation to new client sales.

How do you come up with a compensation system that is consistent with your culture and goals, and motivates sales reps to do what it takes to sell and retain clients? Hire a compensation expert!

Many (if not most) owners have never made a living based on commissions, so they don't know what it's like to meet a quota to cover the monthly mortgage. Fewer still have been in sales management, so it isn't surprising that they view the complex and highly technical process of designing compensation plans for their sales teams as one big, scary mystery. Scary because they know that mistakes take a huge toll on business performance and that there's an art to the continual A/B testing necessary for improvement.

Achieving sales results is reward-worthy behavior, but so is maintaining a valuable corporate asset: CRM data. While I can't name one sales professional who just loves devoting time and effort to updating information in a CRM system, I know plenty of buyers who love pristine, up-to-date customer and prospect data. I also know several owners on their way to building investment-grade companies who do not pay commissions unless their sales reps have fully updated their CRM records. No CRM update means no commission, because CRM data is the objective version of the truth.

Finally, don't forget to reward sales reps who, by guiding customers' buying decisions rather than simply walking them through the features of your solution, are true consultants. Consulting behavior results in a shorter sales cycle.

Hire A Specialist.

The rapid growth in digital platforms and analytical capabilities has created the need for a new player on today's sales and marketing team: the Marketing Technologist. This MarTech professional bridges the gap between automated systems and marketing initiatives in an effort to put the right content in the right place at right time for the right person. He or she helps you assess your company's performance in market automation and can develop a workable plan to install and implement the right set of tools.

SALES AND MARKETING SYSTEMS

By observing a number of highly successful companies, I've learned a few things about well-designed sales and marketing systems or processes:

1. They are consistent with the values and mission of the organization and its leaders.
2. They carefully define each step involved.
3. They document the time it takes to perform each step.
4. They depend on adhering to the procedures defined in each step operating them and on the technology that supports them to be successful.
5. They are used as a basis for compensation and accountability.
6. They are continually monitored and improved.
7. They produce quantifiable, trackable results.

> Taking a client out hunting in the hope that he'll keep buying is not a sales system. It's a quid pro quo.

The underlying principles of sales and marketing haven't changed, but the sales and marketing tools we use today are very different from those of the past. The best systems are organized around a seamless handoff of data generated from automated marketing technologies and collected by employees after each customer interaction (and recorded in your CRM system) to humans who use that information to create relationships.

If you do not collect and capture data systematically, you:

- Are missing important buying signals.
- Can't objectively analyze data and take appropriate and timely action to accelerate growth.
- Can't use data to predict future revenue streams.

Don't Reinvent The Wheel.

Today there are more effective sales methodologies and sales and marketing solutions on the market than there were even five years ago. Strategic Selling™ (Miller Heiman®), SPIN Selling, SNAP Selling, Solution selling, Consultative selling, The Challenger Sale, CustomerCentric Selling® and the ValueSelling Framework® are just a few.

Of course, your job is to pick the methodology that best suits your organization and its goals. The critical question to ask is whether the system will equip your company to produce revenue in a proven and systematic way without relying on ad hoc personal efforts of individuals. Once you pick a methodology: (1) implement a CRM system, (2) train your people to use it and hold them accountable; and (3) hook it all up to automated or content marketing that's appropriate for your business.

If you need suggestions or guidance, hire a consultant or poll the players in your industry (or those in adjacent markets) that are sales and marketing rock stars.

Understand How Your Customer Buys.

Do your customers follow the traditional purchasing process of awareness, interest, desire and then action (AIDA)? Well-respected researchers argue that this model is no longer complete or relevant in today's marketplace. Instead, internet-savvy customers follow the less sequential, more dynamic path of explore, evaluate, engage and then experience.[31] Today most customers identify their own needs, research solutions, and discover potential providers. Increasingly, B2B customers desire (and sometimes expect) pilots or trials before making a final decision.

Use High-Tech Tools.

Web analytics, conversion optimization, search engine marketing, remarketing, email, and automated marketing are powerful components of highly automated processes that constantly identify, score, rank and educate potential leads. Since the MarTech tool landscape continues to evolve at a rapid pace, I suggest that you identify a thought leader in your market segment and follow them. You may not need all of these platforms, but your sales and marketing toolkit is not complete without the majority of them.

Educate Your Customer.

With the internet making it easy for customers to research products and services before they buy, education becomes a powerful and logical marketing tool. Rather than pushing a customer to buy, education:

> Yes, my bias is showing. I'm a fan of leaders who look outside for advice. I've found that companies that do not seek consulting advice don't do as well as organizations that ask, pay for and act on expert help.

- Helps prospects navigate the purchasing decision and identify unmet needs.
- Self-selects prospects and makes them better qualified than others.
- Can make your company the source of insight and expertise (the thought leader) on a particular topic.

As we'll discuss in Reason 10, education also builds brand making it a high barrier for competitors to overcome.

> Building more valuable content than your competitors differentiates you in the marketplace.

In a world of specialized services, the person who educates freely wins. That's a lesson I learned from "Juan," the owner of a company that sold a variety of electric fireplaces.

Juan packed his company's website with loads of information about the costs and savings of various heat-saving strategies. The site's learning center included industry articles, research from the Department of Energy, buyer's guides and videos.

Juan believed that customers would appreciate the investment his company made in educating them about various products and services, and he was right. His site was an SEO superstar, and analytics indicated superior dwell time. Post-purchase surveys told Juan that the website was the first point of contact for a majority of his customers.

Using educational content, Juan's company established itself as one of the (if not the) leading experts in zone heating. The site successfully attracted customers, drove sales, created repeat customers, and ultimately generated huge value for Juan's company.

When you care enough to invest in providing education for your customers, it highlights that you are passionate about your industry, solutions and your value proposition. That's attractive to investors. In Juan's case, he could prove to prospective buyers that: (1) his company's site was more effective than his competitors' in driving sales, and (2) there was a direct link between the content on the website (education) and sales and repeat sales.

If you haven't already built a platform to educate prospective customers, you can begin by building a list of themes or topics that your team recognizes as important to your current and potential customers (e.g., typical pain points, industry trends, articles and surveys). Track prospective customers as they move along the purchasing path, and insert sales reps into the process only when prospects are "lathered up and ready to go."

Once your content library has reached critical mass, make this data accessible and searchable for all stakeholders to use and enjoy. Producing quality content also advances your reputation with search engines, so when prospects are ready to buy, you are at the top of their lists.

Strategic Partnerships

If you structure and nurture them, strategic sales partnerships can bring tremendous value to your organization. Partners typically tap into one another's expertise to provide expert-level information that is incredibly valuable to customers. When partners' product offerings benefit the same customers, they can host lunch-and-learns, social events and conferences to multiply their pool of warm leads at a lower per-customer acquisition cost. If the partners already share customers, shared events strengthen these relationships.

> In my experience, it is extremely common for strategic **partners** to evolve into strategic **buyers** of your company. Both of my tech companies partnered (i.e., forged licensing and distribution relationships) with the public companies that eventually purchased my companies.

If appropriate in your industry, you may be able to structure these relationships to benefit each partner financially, thus motivating teams to collaborate. You can provide access to one another's blog posts, interviews and webinars.

Think about where your company will be several years from now, and recruit partners in adjacent industries to your future company. In every partnership, find the exit before you enter, so it is easy to walk away should the relationship not work out.

No Documentation: No System, No Success

It is hard to describe the sick feeling I get in the pit of my stomach when I hear a CEO proudly describe his sales and marketing process to a prospective investor with the statement "My team is just that good" or "I know in my gut that my team is A+."

On the flip side, it is easy to describe the sound I hear when CEOs articulate how their sales and marketing processes address every step of their target markets' "purchase journey." If they can show me a one-page laminated summary of their company's data-driven, process-oriented sales and marketing culture and meticulously describe their sales cycles and closing funnels, I hear the joyful singing of heavenly choirs. What's strange is that the sound is remarkably similar to the scratch of a buyer's pen on a huge check payable to an owner.

As an investment banker who is a C-minus tenor at best but loves the sounds of choirs and of big checks being signed, I just can't overemphasize the power that sales data has on buyers during a transaction. For example, during the diligence process, buyers ask CEOs to describe their companies' sales pipelines. Those who produce a few names and rough revenue figures increase their buyer's perception of risk. Those who generate reports that include confidence weights, the location of a prospect in the sales cycle, revenue projections, and accurate or approximate calculations of the lifetime value (LTV) of customers keep their buyers at the closing table.

My friend Paul Rafferty (founder and CEO of Sales Engine International LLC) created a diagram to illustrate the automated marketing process that his company Sales Engine Media uses. When he showed it to me, I don't think I said a word for at least a minute. I was busy absorbing the logic behind it and being awed by a level of detail that reminded me of a schematic for a complex manufacturing process.

Paul's "Integrated Marketing Map" clearly showed how multiple inputs fed into different silos and interacted (or did not) at three major and five supplementary stages. Each stage was defined and included metrics expressed as percentages and gross numbers and specific actions to move prospects (or "suspects" as Paul labeled them) from one level to the next. Once Paul walked me through the professionally designed, full-color flowchart, I was even more excited about his model and the value he was building in his selling process and, therefore, his company.

Your sales process might be simpler than Paul's. That's okay. Simple is good, especially if simplicity helps you focus on each step necessary to document the process from stem (the universe of *prospects*)—to stern (*customers*).

Once you document the nuances of each step in your sales process, don't skip any as you perform the process! If you do, you can't accurately spot weaknesses in the journey from prospect to customer, much less fix them.

This level of precise documentation equips you to:

- Audit, troubleshoot and improve your sales strategy.
- Hold people accountable.
- Calculate the ROI of various initiatives.

And for buyers, it:

- Adds predictability to your sales strategy.
- Is scalable.

The point is to document each step in your sales process and track it as carefully as you would a raw material through a manufacturing process.

> The distinction between a formal and informal pipeline is simple: A formal pipeline documents what is real and verifiable, while an informal pipeline reflects a hope–a gleam in the eye of the beholder. A formal pipeline (constructed with great attention to detail) defines prospects, measures the length of the sales cycle, yields critical customer data, and, most importantly, predicts revenue accurately.

You Can't Improve What You Don't Measure.

You should track your sales team's historical performance with the devotion of Penelope to Ulysses or Romeo to Juliet. Okay, I'll admit that I might be exaggerating, but only a little. Without a metrics-driven sales culture, you cannot identify meaningful trends, improve your approach or take action quickly.

While visiting the office of a senior VP of sales for a light-assembly manufacturing company, I noticed a five-bar, multicolored meter on her computer screen. When I asked what it was, she explained, "That's my daily gauge of my team's top five KPIs. It shows me whether, on a daily basis, my team is focused on the best opportunities." I asked her to explain to me what five key performance indicators she was tracking.

KPI 1: The number of open opportunities each sales professional is working at any given time—by count and size.

KPI 2: The number of opportunities the sales team closed out in the CRM, including both closed-won and closed-lost opportunities.

KPI 3: The average sale price (deal size) of all closed-won deals.

KPI 4: The number of closed-won opportunities (win rate).

KPI 5: The average time (sales cycle) to win a deal.

If this is the level of tracking that you are using, congratulations! If not, you are sacrificing value in your business today and decreasing the value an investor or buyer will ascribe to your business in the future.

What's Working? What's Not?

It is quite common for prospective buyers to tell me, "Zane, we love that this company has made the right investments in sales and marketing." I've learned not to celebrate prematurely because often they continue, "Too bad it's done minimal tracking and, worse, has no data related to ROI."

Owner "Randy" was a good example. He spent over $300,000 per year on industry trade shows but didn't know each show's ROI. The buyer asked the logical questions:

- If Randy doesn't know how many leads and business partnerships a show generates and how these leads convert to customers, how does he choose which shows to attend?
- Should he expand or downsize his show presence?

Obviously, trade shows contribute to brand and overall awareness of a company, but unless you accurately document the ROI on each of your sales initiatives (including trade shows), you are as uninformed as Randy.

Believe me that when (not if) a sophisticated buyer asks to see data related to your sales process, you will feel and appear dull if you can't produce it easily. Tracking investment to return isn't a perfect science, but with analytics and attribution, you have the tools to track, calculate and improve the ROI of your company's marketing efforts.

Understanding what drives ROI for your company is important in all of the 17 Reasons. Professionalized businesses operated by strong management teams track data in order to make better/more informed decisions. Weak owners/operators manage by gut and emotion. Are you a data-driven steward of an investment-grade business, or are you flying by the seat of your pants?

Why Sales And Marketing Processes Matter To Buyers

Scalability

Processes are scalable. People are not. For that reason, buyers and investors discount people-centric sales and marketing cultures, especially when sales and marketing rely on one or two people.

> When it comes to sales cycles, buyers want predictability, scalability and replicability.

"But I'm really good at sales!" you argue. Well, in a company's start-up years, Visionary Founder = Top Salesperson is a workable equation. It is not a recipe for ongoing success.

If you haven't already done so, you, visionary founder, need to: (1) transfer your sales skill set to others, and (2) document your sales process.

When I think of owners who created marketing machines, my close friend "Tim" comes to mind. I mentioned one of his companies in Reason 4 as an example of focusing on a niche and reaping the benefits.

Tim developed an expertise in the financial services space through his first two ventures—ones he ultimately sold. His third start-up company offered compliance solutions to community banks.

From day one, Tim made it a priority to document how sales reps were to use his company's CRM system. First, he rewarded employees (through additional compensation) for recording conversations and collecting data about current and potential clients. Then, Tim trained his sales staff to mine the database for those nuggets to use in marketing pieces and sales pitches.

Over time, the company's database grew into a massive treasure trove of golden nuggets regarding a large number of players in the community bank market. Not surprisingly, the company's sales materials "spoke" to existing and prospective customers with a level of expertise and intimacy that competitors could not match.

In collecting customer data, Tim developed a deep understanding of his customers' businesses, their pain points, and how they structured their purchasing decisions. Armed with these insights, he priced his core software model below the threshold that typically required approval by a bank's board of directors. Without that roadblock in the sales cycle, Tim's company amassed significant market share very quickly and, after building up credibility with customers, began to offer higher-priced, ancillary products at a greater margin.

Buyers and investors absolutely love companies that have taken the time to document the key decision-makers within their customers' organizations and whose managers can describe in detail how those customers make their buying decisions.

Buyers will accept a deficiency in sales and marketing only if your company is growing.

An Exception

If your company is growing and its products and services are selling better than your competitors'—despite your anemic lead-generation or sales process—you may get lucky. It is possible to attract one of the many buyers and investors who see sales and marketing as low hanging fruit that they can exploit after the purchase.

Pretend for a moment that you are shopping for an investment property and come across a home in the right neighborhood, but whose carpets stink to high heaven. You know that you can replace the carpets for $4,000 and sell the house for at least $40,000 more than you paid.

Similarly, if you've failed to install a strong sales and marketing system, buyers know that they can install and implement one and quickly generate additional qualified leads and, therefore, sales.

When I'm involved in marketing a company with "stinky carpet" to prospective buyers, I'll certainly promote this potential pickup to the buyers. As a former IBM sales and marketing guy, however, I'm partial to companies that truly understand their markets and put the processes, people and systems in place early on to create highly effective sales and marketing machines. I can assure you, if you wait and let a buyer replace your stinky carpet, you'll leave significant value on the table.

You might not be able to attract investors or buyers if you do not have well-documented sales and marketing processes capable of systematically producing predictable revenue.

RECOMMENDATIONS

1. If you are your company's No. 1 salesperson, resolve to become No. 10.
Would you buy a company whose sales depended on the relationships of its departing owner or on one salesperson? I didn't think so.
- If your No. 1 salesperson left, how would that impact your company financially?
- How quickly could you hire, train and replace that lost expertise?
- Do you know who your competitors' top salespeople are? You should be recruiting them.

2. Establish lead generation systems to identify, contact and nurture prospective clients.
Continually design and test methods to fill the top of your marketing funnel with qualified leads.
- Does your process provide automated follow-ups?

- Does your process generate tracking reports and attribution statistics that provide key metrics around sales cycle and resources expended?

3. Build a collaborative, data-driven sales culture.

In a high-growth tech company:

- EVERYONE is in sales.
- EVERYONE is in service.
- EVERYONE on your sales and customer service teams (and ideally everyone in your company) should be able to articulate the ideal and current customer profile, the roles within client organizations that influence the buying decision, and how your product or service meets a need.
- EVERYONE should be excited and feel great about evangelizing. If your employees aren't excited about what your company delivers, don't let the door hit them on the way out when you show them the exit.
- How well is your marketing team actively collaborating with the sales team (and vice versa)?
- How well do your employees understand your target customer profile, how customers buy and who makes the buying decision?

4. If you aren't an expert in compensation systems, use an industry consultant.

Consultants can help you: (1) avoid common mistakes, and (2) constantly improve your compensation system.

- Are you honest with yourself about your limited sales compensation design experience?
- Do you really understand the importance that compensation design/implementation has on your company's success and ultimate valuation?

5. Set your goals, and then structure compensation accordingly.

As we've discussed, investors value highly engaged, delighted, loyal customers. That said, if yours is an early-stage company, you should probably reward sales reps for new orders, but it may be tricky to restructure compensation after a couple of years to place a heavier emphasis on retention. Consider compensating sales reps for:

- Spending time in account management (e.g., collecting data on customers, entering it into a CRM system, and building a database of invaluable data) and renewal.
- Improving marketing tactics or initiatives.

Rewards aren't ongoing benefits. They are creative motivators to get and keep people moving in the right direction.

- Is your sales reps' compensation structure aligned with the company's overall goals?
- Are your company's sales compensation plans competitive in the industry?
- Does your compensation system reward teamwork?
- Is intracompany competition costing you new customers?
- Do you have/need a customer retention budget?
- How is your team actively working on customer retention?

6. Adopt a sales methodology.

Pick a sales system that fits your industry, products, people and prospects. Choosing the right system (including CRM) is not simple, so seek outside help from an experienced marketing automation consultant if needed. Industry-specific CRM systems can save headaches and eliminate the need (time and expense) to customize a one-size-fits-all platform.

- Once you choose your system is it standardized so that:
  - Everyone in your organization consistently speaks the same sales language and documents sales activities appropriately and consistently in your CRM system and forecasts? (If everyone in your organization defines "quality lead" or "just about closed" differently, you lack a basis for decision-making.)
  - Your staff can engage in a higher level of thinking and be proactive?
  - You can hold your team accountable?
  - The risk associated with losing your best sales rep diminishes?
- Does your company have defined marketing and sales strategies?
- How can you make your company's strategies more dynamic and agile?
- How quickly can you standardize them?
- What tools/strategies do your successful competitors use?

7. Document, document, document.

At the drop of a hat, you should be able to hand an interested party a well-conceived (preferably laminated) summary of your sales process. If your documentation lacks any of the following elements, you're doing a disservice to your customers and failing to achieve investment-grade status. Investment-grade companies track the following information for every customer:

- The recommender, influencer and ultimate buyer.
- Their general met and unmet needs.
- The key facets of their purchasing process.

And their sales processes define:

- Milestones of the sales cycle.
- Key roles/responsibilities.
- General timing for each step.
- Average conversion rates at steps along the path.
- Core marketing strategies and how each channel or component drives new business.
- The retention cycles and loss/risk processes.

Ask yourself:

- What sales and marketing processes can you document to better streamline efforts?
- What metrics do you track?
- What metrics should you be tracking?
- How do you measure the ROI of marketing initiatives?

8. Create information-based content that integrates with automated marketing.

Continually create valuable information for your stakeholders. Build a reputation as a generous giver, rather than as just another taker trolling for a sale. Speak at industry conferences, write white papers on topics that matter to your customers, and make instructional videos.

- How do you use automated marketing to move leads through the funnel?
- How do you educate prospective customers?

9. Identify and nurture strategic relationships.

Yes, strategic partnerships can be a time suck and expensive if you (and your management team) don't vet them well and align them with your corporate objectives. Explore ways to structure these types of partnerships to make them a win-win for both parties.

- What adjacent players have access to your prospective customer base?
- How do you build a win-win strategic partnership with each of these players?

TAKEAWAYS

1. Sales and marketing are core processes.

You can't outsource sales and marketing. You can leverage outside consultants to help you design and set up your systems. It is your job to constantly tweak sales strategy and content to test response and conversion.

2. Sales and marketing are systems.

They are created and operated by talented employees but not solely dependent on people with good people skills.

3. If it isn't documented, it isn't a process.

Documented processes are the foundation for the scalability of your business and ultimately increase equity value. Documented sales and marketing processes identify key operational procedures, track relationships and quantify the strength of those relationships.

4. Educate and create content that differentiates.

Producing and disseminating informative and valuable content is a key way to differentiate your company in the marketplace. Some companies compete well above their weight class simply because of their intimate understanding of customers and approach to prospect education and customer support.

REAS🔆N

Your Company Relies On Too Few Customers.

DIVERSIFY, DILUTE

AND BE DELIVERED!

"Acme" was a star. It had an excellent reputation in its industry, a blue-chip customer base, strong growth, nice EBITDA margins, expanding market share, and an experienced management team.

I f you expect that this is the beginning of another success story, prepare to be surprised. Despite our best efforts, not one of the 18 reputable firms that initially expressed enthusiastic interest in Acme made an offer to invest growth capital. Not one. But every one of them was willing to tell us why it chose to pass on the opportunity: They were not willing to assume the risk that they saw in the company's top-heavy customer list.

Acme's owners hired us to raise capital to support the company's rapid growth trajectory: a compound annual growth rate (CAGR) of 41 percent over the past five years. Acme needed the capital to fund the start-up costs of entering new geographic markets.

The two founding partners had met and become fast friends on the little league baseball circuit. When they were in their mid-20s, one came into enough seed capital to launch a business and recruited the other to be COO. When I met them, the two were in their late 30s and had become an impressive duo with strong corporate experience. They had created a privately held business services company that, by consistently exceeding customer expectations, had attracted a roster of household, brand-name customers. Acme retained these large publicly traded companies for an average of eight years, losing only a couple in its 12-year history.

Whenever its top customers asked Acme to serve them in new markets, Acme obliged. What management team wouldn't be excited to follow its national brand customers' growth into new markets? Growth was addictive and easy. But by constantly entering new markets for existing customers, Acme's customer concentration balance entered dangerous territory. We learned just how dangerous when we analyzed Acme's revenue per customer during the prior three years. (Figure 9.1).

FIG. 9.1 Acme's Customer Concentration

	YEAR 1		YEAR 2		YEAR 3	
Customer 1	$10,066,118	48%	$12,246,338	44%	$14,979,754	41%
Customer 2	$4,725,406	23%	$5,973,993	21%	$5,743,685	16%
Customer 3	$0	0%	$406,085	1%	$4,099,399	11%
Customer 4	$1,535,334	7%	$3,448,540	12%	$3,991,237	11%
Customer 5	$1,917,617	9%	$2,412,231	9%	$2,502,263	7%
Customer 6	$485,510	2%	$705,043	3%	$934,408	3%
Customer 7	$447,489	2%	$766,654	3%	$850,051	2%
Customer 8	$20,374	0%	$160,768	1%	$560,607	2%
Customer 9	$0	0%	$59,885	0%	$471,330	1%
Customer 10	$296,812	1%	$336,168	1%	$405,212	1%
All Others	$1,507,001	7%	$1,370,672	5%	$2,376,949	6%
Total	$21,001,661	100%	$27,886,377	100%	$36,914,895	100%

In Year 3, Acme's top 10 customers accounted for 95 percent of its revenue. The top five generated 86 percent of its revenue, and its largest customer weighed in at a titanic 41 percent of revenue. Fixing a customer concentration issue of this magnitude takes years, but Acme needed capital yesterday to fund its expansion into new geographies.

Management's options were clear:

1. Find an investor that appreciated all of Acme's great attributes and would inject much-needed capital despite this level of concentration, or

2. Labor under its own weight and sink into slow growth and mundane offerings.

When we warned Acme's management team that this level of concentration would make raising capital difficult, the COO said all the right things. "We're aware that we're approaching the red zone, so we're addressing it." When we asked him to tell us how, he said, "We've set up a contest for our sales reps. The one who brings in the most new customers in the next six months wins a Mediterranean cruise!" That was not the disciplined approach we were looking for to forgo unhealthy revenue growth from top customers.

Over the next few months, updated monthly financials indicated that: (1) the sales reps were indeed bringing new accounts onboard, (2) Acme could not raise prices high enough to cover its new client *onboarding/start-up costs, and (3) the company was starting to lose money.*

Still, revenue growth from its largest customers continued to outpace the rest of the customer base. Still, management continued to favor top-line growth over profitability and ignored the tough choices required to diversify the customer base. Still, the COO was so concerned about disappointing, and possibly losing, top customers that his team made suboptimal decisions when it came to pricing and profitability.

As more and more prospective investors dropped out of the process, Acme's management continued to focus on revenue growth rather than profitability. They just couldn't say no to their largest clients.

We finally got Acme's owners' reluctant agreement to postpone the market process until the company could sustain an acceptable level of profitability and balance the revenue growth across more clients.

Pulling a company off the market is not something we do lightly, but keeping Acme on the market for the length of time it would take to fix its customer concentration problem would create another issue. Prospective buyers can begin to view companies that don't quickly attract the right investor/buyer as shopworn. If companies are in a market auction too long, the assumption is that they might have some issues or have been picked over and not worth the investment of a deep review.

But what happened to Acme?

Plan to go to market one time and one time only. If you are ever tempted to "test the waters" by putting your company on the market, make sure you are prepared and deal ready. Remember that there's a potential price to pay for being shopworn.

WINNERS UNDERSTAND THE POWER OF NO.

One of my favorite mentors often says, "It isn't the business (customer) I don't get that hurts me the most; it is the BAD business I win that I wish I hadn't." Great companies know the characteristics of good business and say no to the rest. The difference between successful people (and businesses) and VERY successful people (and businesses) is that VERY successful people (and businesses) say no more often.

When Acme's owners ultimately acknowledged that there was no financial lifeboat coming to rescue their sinking ship, we recommended that they bring in a fractional CFO to examine the key financial metrics on each customer. She subsequently demonstrated to Acme's entire leadership team that the gross margin Acme earned from serving one of its largest customers was well below the level it required to achieve its profitability goals.

This discovery finally woke up Acme's owners. They bit the bullet and made the tough choices:

- *It systematically discontinued service for customers whose business did not satisfy its target margins.*
- *It renegotiated some of the pricing with its two largest customers to move them to a profitable top tier.*

These large customers accepted the price increase. They recognized that they'd not only incur significant costs to find a new supplier but also to train that supplier to deliver the same quality of service that Acme did. Ultimately, customers determined that it would take too much effort to change from Acme to one of its competitors.

How Many Customers Have You Delighted Today?

I assume that you have figured out how to delight your customers, but are you delighting too few? Happy, loyal customers decrease the risk of defection and increase the potential for additional value—but only if a few customers don't dominate the list.

"A few" is subjective because the optimal level of customer diversification largely depends on the industry in which you operate. In a technology-enabled services company, an acceptable level of concentration is one in which:

- No one customer accounts for greater than 10 percent of revenue, and
- The top 10 customers account for less than half of revenue.

Since each industry has its nuances, consult with industry subject-matter experts to determine what the acceptable customer concentration metrics are for your company.

The Price Of Doing Business With Bigfoot

You know that if your company loses its biggest customer, revenue and net income will decline immediately. Quick recovery will likely be difficult, and you may have to cut costs, reduce your workforce or operate at a loss.

So how do you sleep at night? Let me guess. You rationalize that:

- Your company, in the early growth stage, is dependent on the revenue that your biggest customer ("Bigfoot") generates.
- While the profit margin on Bigfoot's business isn't great, profit is profit and revenue growth is exciting!
- Bigfoot is a great reference, and prospects are impressed by its logo.
- Bigfoot is demanding, but you've got a contract.
- Bigfoot is behind some great custom products that you have developed based on his request. And who doesn't like customer-funded development (CFD)?
- If you don't accept Bigfoot's terms, your competitors will. (That, my friend, is indentured servitude.)

Revenue In Early Growth Companies

It's natural in early-stage[31] service businesses for a few customers (or even a single customer) to generate the majority of revenue. These large customers are incredibly valuable at the outset, but they create significant risk down the road, particularly to private equity groups. If Bigfoot runs off with another supplier, a PEG will not meet its return expectations. After all, buyers use some multiple of revenue or EBITDA to value companies. Losing 30 percent of revenue or EBITDA makes it challenging to generate an acceptable rate of return on that investment and lowers the operating cash that PEGs need to service the debt that they typically use in their buyouts.

If your company is in that early stage, expand your business with the profits these customers generate. When capital is tight, large customers (assuming they are large companies) may be willing to directly fund additional projects and innovation—if pleased with the service you are delivering.

Margin Matters

If Bigfoot provides half of your company's revenue, and if the profit margin on Bigfoot's work is 2 percent, losing Bigfoot will affect your revenue but will not damage profitability. Alternatively, if Lillian Lilliput generates 10 percent of your company's revenue at a profit margin of 50 percent, losing Lillian will significantly damage profitability. Over time—and to minimize the risk to revenue, growth and profitability—it is necessary to recruit more Lillians.

When (not if) Bigfoot turns up the pricing pressure, profit margins get squashed. In Acme's case, its Big Foot was responsible for 41 percent of revenue, so Bigfoot set the price he paid. Acme's CEO accepted the lower price because the company could still eke out a tiny profit. Once you set your breaking point (or floor below which you will not go), knowing your margin by customer enables you to determine which customers are profitable. If your business objective is to make money, isn't it better to fire unprofitable customers no matter how large they are?

Logo References Win New Business.

It's really nice to list Bigfoot as a reference, and prospects are impressed when you first "flash" the company's logo. However, sophisticated clients/prospects understand that you do "special things" to keep your Bigfoot happy: things that might not be "business as usual" for your less influential accounts. You'll have to prove to them that your business systems consistently provide stellar service to all your customers, not just the big, hairy ones.

When Nudges Become Shoves

Large customers like Bigfoot manipulate service-level agreements to best meet their needs, because they can. If Bigfoot chooses to pay in 45 days instead of 30, he can. If he demands service in three business days instead of five, you provide it. If he wants your product stacked in pyramids and shrink-wrapped in pink plastic outside his cave, you will train your delivery people in the finer points of pink pyramid building. If Bigfoot makes an unexpected demand for more products or services, your management team forsakes all others to accommodate. If he asks you to use his cousin, Yeti, as a supplier, you start importing from the Himalayas.

Customer Funded Development (CFD)

Big customers can act as the instigators for some great custom services, product modules and enhancements. That motivation can be a good thing if the modules and enhancements that your company produces at their request are needed by the broader market and can be included in your base offerings. Can there be a downside to CFD? Absolutely. If Bigfoot's individual needs knock you off your strategic product road map,[32] you end up with a custom product for one customer instead of a configurable product for the entire market.

The Price Of Indentured Servitude

If you and your team scramble to serve your largest customer, I'll bet that you are ignoring the needs of other customers. Hyperfocus on one customer does that. It clouds your ability to: (1) keep the entire market in perspective, and (2) make optimal decisions that align with your product management strategy. You spend so much time focused on one customer that you lose perspective of the needs of your entire target market. Owning a niche market, not one big customer, is what moves the value needle.

DIVERSIFY, DILUTE AND BE DELIVERED!

High customer concentration is not a death sentence. Even Acme, given enough time, could have diluted its customer concentration. But addressing the issue requires intentionally building a new, top-to-bottom culture that supports you—and every member of your team—as you exit your comfort zones to create and grow new accounts.

Build A Beyond-The-Comfort-Zone New-Account-Focused Culture.

Your entire culture must celebrate new customers if you want to inoculate your business against the valuation killer of customer concentration. If you haven't extended a recruiting premium to everyone who brings in a new customer (e.g., current customers, vendors and all company employees), you aren't thinking big enough. Recognizing and rewarding everyone for bringing in new customers is what I mean by a sales culture.

Let's look at how an owner built a new-account sales culture in an engineering firm.

After a successful run as an NCAA Division I volleyball player, "Chris" joined a well-known management consulting firm. As he gained experience, he recognized the enormous opportunity in meeting the cybersecurity needs of financial institutions, and he started his own consultancy company, SpikeDeep Security, at the ripe old age of 29.

Chris understood the market and the value of his company's services to financial clients. Right out of the gate, Chris snagged annual contracts with two large West Coast firms and created two flagship security products for them. These big-name clients were extremely profitable, so in the early days, SpikeDeep had a strong profit margin, and all 14 of its engineers were generously compensated. Everything seemed to be going well on Chris' side of the net.

From the outset, Chris understood the importance of growth and diversification, and he dreamed of building—and one day selling—a company with "platform value." Chris' exit number was $25 million—a value threshold that relied on a highly satisfied and diversified customer base.

Chris recognized that he and his engineering team shared similar attributes: While they were great at solving technical problems, they were less skilled at building relationships. They liked solving problems, not talking with people. Still, Chris knew he needed to build a new account culture that celebrated and valued new additions to the SpikeDeep's family of clients.

If the sales culture Chris envisioned was to take shape, his current team had to understand that diversifying the customer base was a critical component of a valuable and sustainable business. First, Chris created a skills profile for an experienced sales recruiter—one who wouldn't share the engineers' aversion to knocking on doors and making calls. Second, he set up incentives for engineers who uncovered leads for the new, charismatic salesperson he planned to hire.

Once the engineers understood their role in a sales culture and the need for customer diversification, they got on board and enjoyed collecting the finder's fee Chris paid for passing on leads. Chris then hired "Trey," a self-described "new account hound."

Trey joined SpikeDeep and quickly armed himself with: (1) a compelling value proposition, (2) an ROI calculator for the company's service and tools, and (3) two strong logo references. He began preaching the SpikeDeep message to its target market. Chris gave and Trey used funds to cover taking a different engineer to lunch every week. It was magic and had the engineering and sales departments singing from the same hymnbook.

Within 12 months SpikeDeep had onboarded eight nice-sized banking clients who signed annual contracts. Chris gave the green light for another new account hire, and his two salespeople brought in 19 new accounts within 18 months, resulting in a very diverse customer base, with none making up more than 10 percent of SpikeDeep's revenues.

I can't say that building a sales culture within an engineering firm is always easy, but Chris proved that it is do-able. Chris created the framework for a team that valued new accounts. He understood that he had to make bringing on new business a key performance indicator (KPI) and that success required getting the right talent on the bus. He recognized that it takes a special skill set and personality type to drive new business, and he was willing to recruit, hire and reward talent that had the personality and motives he needed at SpikeDeep.

Four years and one month after starting the company, Chris received an email from the CFO of a $275 million PEG-backed cybersecurity platform company. It read, "Congratulations on your reputation/traction as a top regional consultancy in the financial institution cybersecurity segment. Our firm is looking to roll up top-tier providers in your market and would like to discuss your potential interest."

Chris called a meeting of his advisory board to discuss possible next steps. It recommended that SpikeDeep prepare for a targeted process in which it would hold discussions with five potential best-fit buyers. Six months later, Chris closed a deal with the PEG-backed company that had reached out to him months earlier. In an effort to keep SpikeDeep out of the hands of competing buyers, this buyer increased its initial offer of $22 million (including an earnout) to a $32 million all-cash deal. Chris could thank SpikeDeep's growing, sticky and diverse client list for his deal-table success.

INVESTORS AND CONCENTRATION

Financial investors (e.g., private equity groups) operate under mandates that require them to achieve certain returns on their holdings, and if a portfolio company's loss of a large customer causes a significant drop in revenue/profitability, returns suffer.

Let's look at how buyers calculate the risk inherent to high customer concentration.

"Diversification Capital (DC)" is a private equity group required to achieve a return on holdings over its five-year investment horizon of 125 percent, or 25 percent per year. DC is considering the acquisition of "Manufacturing, Inc. (MI)," whose largest customer, "Really Big, Inc.," accounts for 30 percent of MI's revenue.

- *MI's annual revenue = $10,000,000*
- *Revenue from Really Big, Inc. = $3,000,000 (30 percent concentration)*
- *EBITDA at time of purchase = $1,000,000 (10 percent margin)*
- *Purchase Price = $5,000,000 (5x EBITDA)*
- *Holding Period = 5 years*
- *MI's Projected Annual Revenue Growth Rate = 20 percent over the five-year holding period*

DC acquires MI, and initially everything goes according to plan. As Figure 9.2 illustrates, with a 20-percent annual growth rate and conservatively underwriting the deal with an exit multiple of five times EBITDA, DC's return on MI over five years would be 149 percent (roughly 30 percent per year).

Now let's pretend that several months after the acquisition, MI's management team informs DC that Really Big, Inc. is no longer a customer because it has found a competitor who will accept its payment terms. As a result, revenue for Year 1 will be 30 percent less than projected. Even if MI manages to grow revenue by 20 percent in each of the subsequent four years, Figure 9.3 shows that DC's return will be half of what it had projected: 75 percent over five years (or 15 percent annually).

The imbalance that Really Big, Inc. created in MI's customer base added significant risk to DC's acquisition. That type of imbalance creates risk in almost all acquisitions—especially when a company's biggest customers are very large companies. I say "almost all" because there are two exceptions.

FIG. 9.2 MI's Annual Return With Really Big, Inc. As A Customer

	AT PURCHASE	YEAR 1	YEAR 2	YEAR 3	YEAR 4	YEAR 5
Revenue	$10,000,000	$12,000,000	$14,400,000	$17,280,000	$20,736,000	$24,883,200
EBITDA	$1,000,000	$1,200,000	$1,440,000	$1,728,000	$2,073,600	$2,488,320

EXIT VALUATION	ROI	ANNUAL RETURN
$12,441,600	149%	30%

FIG. 9.3 MI's Annual Return Without Really Big, Inc. As A Customer

	AT PURCHASE	YEAR 1	YEAR 2	YEAR 3	YEAR 4	YEAR 5
Revenue	$10,000,000	$8,400,000	$10,080,000	$12,096,000	$14,515,200	$17,418,240
EBITDA	$1,000,000	$840,000	$1,008,000	$1,209,600	$1,451,520	$1,741,824

EXIT VALUATION	ROI	ANNUAL RETURN
$8,709,120	74%	15%

EXCEPTION 1: A strategic acquirer does not view industry segment concentration or geographic concentration as significant a risk as private equity groups do. Typically, strategic acquirers' motives for buying a company include obtaining intellectual property, gaining access to a customer list or certain geographies, or expanding its product/service line.

EXCEPTION 2: As a result of an acquisition, a strategic buyer dilutes its customer concentration, as it is able to spread its revenues across a larger customer base. The seller's large customers become small customers of the buyer, but they are new customers nonetheless.

"Victor," a talented entrepreneur nearing retirement age (and ready to diversify his wealth), provides a great example of Exception 1.

Victor's company (AsclePAID) had created and developed a workflow system that allowed physicians to more accurately code procedures and efficiently bill insurance providers. AsclePAID had amassed an impressive client list of over 75 cardiology practices within a 250-mile radius of a major city in the Southwest. Some of these practices, however, were large and represented a significant percentage of AsclePAID's business.

While preparing to take the business to market, our team found that the company had strong funda-mentals and that the largest acquirers in the industry were keenly interested in breaking into AsclePAID's market niche. Acquirers could start marketing to this niche (cardiac surgery practices) from scratch or use the AsclePAID's existing relationships to quickly gain traction. For this reason, we forecasted, and Victor expected, the outsized valuation that the market soon confirmed.

Strategic buyers—IT-managed service providers, outsourced billing companies, health care education companies and medical software companies—quickly responded. They recognized the opportunity to cross-sell their complementary products to AsclePAID's loyal group of customers. Knowing that it would take significant time and resources to build this customer base from scratch, these buyers preferred to simply acquire a customer list instead. Ultimately, each made a premium offer for AsclePAID, despite the customer concentration due to Victor's largest clients.

Situations like these, however, are exceptions to the rule because financial investors (such as private equity groups) rarely ignore the risk associated with asymmetries in industry, geographic and revenue concentration. This buyer weighed the risk of all customers being involved in one industry and in one geographic area against the benefit of access to its niche customer list and happily paid a healthy purchase price.

Greater Risk = Financing Hurdles

Investors aren't the only ones who will pass on investing in companies with high levels of customer con-centration. Lenders also generally pass on loan opportunities, provide less than the desired loan amount, or offer borrowers (strategic buyers) suboptimal terms in order to mitigate risk. Higher financing costs reduce expected return and point prospective buyers toward either a lower valuation than expected or more lucrative opportunities.

Investors Love New Customers For Reasons Besides Customer Dilution.

Did you know that as much as buyers love longtime, loyal customers, they often assign a greater value to revenue generated from newly onboarded customers than they do to revenue earned from existing ones? Call-ing on new customers/prospects is hard work, so to increase your number of new customers, you'll need to install some systems and incentives to motivate your salespeople—and that means everyone in your company.

I see company founders every week who resist bringing on salespeople. They think salespeople are hard to manage and don't justify the payroll expense. To those founders let me say this as clearly as I can: To build value you must build a sales system and culture.

Sure, building growing revenue streams that buyers value can be accomplished through resellers, white-la-bel licensing agreements and other types of distribution, but you still need a sales system, a sales process or salespeople to manage your channels and licenses. Resellers can drop your product and choose a competitor's. White-label partners can phase out your product as they build their own competitive product. Your lack of control over distribution—compared to a direct channel—leaves you rudderless and can and will hurt your overall valuation. You need to control access to your customers and markets and hold accountable the people responsible for doing so. Control is dangerous in human relationships but beautiful in the context of customer access.

Industry Sector Concentration

Once you review each customer and their effect on customer concentration, take a step back and consider the industries in which your customers operate. Are they cycle-hard industries, such as construction, oil and gas, and real estate? Are your customers from one or just a few industries? Even if no one customer dominates revenue, concentration is still a risk if customers in one boom-or-bust industry account for a large portion of revenue.

The few exceptions to this concentration rule apply only to industries with a minimal number of players, e.g., federal government agencies, credit card issuers or airlines. In these cases, there are only a limited number of swimmers in the prospective customer pool. If your customer pool has only one or two swimmers per lane, it is critical to sell a greater variety of products to decision-makers in multiple divisions. In that way, you can decrease the influence of any one decision-maker within the larger organization. Multiple relationships make you less vulnerable to a single point of failure.

> **You might not be able to attract investors or buyers if your business depends too heavily on a few key customers.**

RECOMMENDATIONS

1. Analyze your customer list.

Buyers look at concentration in four forms: revenue, profit margin attributable to top customers, geography and industry sector. Review your customer list, meet with your management team, and address any imbalances.

- Do you track customer concentration by revenue?
  If so, does that concentration meet or exceed your industry's standards?
- Do you track customer concentration by profit margin?
  If so, what actions do you take to ensure that a few customers are not producing the lion's share of your profits?
- Do you track customer concentration by geography?
- If you serve a narrow geography, do your target customer profiles translate to other regions of the country and world?
- Do you track customer concentration by industry sector?
- If so, does that concentration meet or exceed your industry's standards?
- Do you serve any cycle-hard industries?

2. Build a new-account culture to keep customer concentration at bay.

In order to add new customers, you must create an environment that supports creating new accounts.

- If you've managed to achieve a strong retention rate for existing customers, is your success rate for adding new customers as impressive?

- Do you put a premium on new accounts?
- Whom do you reward for bringing in new customers?
  - Salespeople?
  - Everyone in the company?
  - Vendors?
  - Other customers?

3. If your industry pool has only a few players, sell deeper.

Salespeople like the familiar, and it is easier to call on current customers than to pursue new ones. However, the best of both worlds is to sell additional products and services to more points of contact within your customers' organizations.

- Have you identified additional needs in existing customers?
- What efforts have you made to sell multiple products or services to multiple decision-makers in multiple divisions of your largest customers' organizations?

4. Consider the effect concentration has on your decision-making.

It is easy to make suboptimal decisions in an effort to retain a major customer. After all, that total revenue column is sweet.

- Are you devoting significant company resources to a large, but marginally profitable, customer?

TAKEAWAYS

1. Healthy companies add new clients at a faster pace than their competitors.

New customers are the lifeblood of a company. They prove that you are relevant in the market, meaning your products and services add real value to your target market, and are taking new territory from your competitors. Who doesn't love that?

2. Bigger is not always better.

Large customers can dictate pricing, payment terms, contracts and service-level agreements. If you and your employees are bending over backward for them, that hurts other customers and your company.

3. Customer concentration comes in four types:

- Revenue.
- Profit margin.
- Industry sector.
- Geography.

4. Unless you reach out to new customers, you really don't know whether your company makes a compelling offer to the ever-changing marketplace.

5. High customer concentration = risk to your company and to prospective investors.

If you seek any type of recapitalization or strategic sale while you have a significant customer concentration issue, investors will either pass or significantly discount their offers.

6. Even niche operators must go wide.

A wide customer base is especially valuable to buyers of niche companies because acquirers desire to cross-sell their own products and services to the customers in the seller's niche.

7. There is an exception.

Strategic acquirers don't consider customer concentration to be as much of a threat as financial buyers do. Their motives for buying a company can be obtaining intellectual property, recruiting a management team, gaining access to certain geographies, or expanding its product or service line.

REAS⚙N 10

Your Company's Brand Does Not Translate Into Client Acquisition.

DEFINE WHO YOU ARE, AND INVEST IN MAKING THAT IDENTITY A REALITY FOR YOUR CUSTOMERS.

"I'm sorry, but what's the name of your company again?" The first time he heard those words from a competitor at a trade show, Sam figured he was being gaslighted.

"Of course he knows my company," Sam thought.

The second time he heard them, Sam felt queasy. But the third time? "I'm angry," Sam told me. "I thought I'd been in the arena with these guys long enough to at least inspire a little fear, but they don't even know who we are!"

Fear, love, loyalty, trust, security and respect are all feelings, and feelings point to the existence of a brand. The depth of those feelings measure the strength of a brand.

> If the name of your company doesn't elicit a positive feeling on the part of customers, employees, prospects and potential future investors, you have no brand—or, at best, a weak one.

- If your employees are not excited about your brand, they won't evangelize or go the extra mile for you. They will not take impeccable care of your customers. Sales will suffer, and growth will be hard to come by.
- If your competitors don't recognize you at trade shows or prospective customers have never heard of you, how can you expect to compete in your market segments for customers, talent and ultimately suitors?
- If prospective employees don't have a clue who you are, do you really think the best candidates will compete to work for your company?
- If potential suitors don't even know you exist, can you blame them for walking right by?

Your long list of stakeholders includes customers, employees, competitors, prospects and potential future investors, but length is no excuse for so many of us to focus solely on our customers.

Let's look more closely at these potential suitors.

Why Brand Matters To Buyers And Investors

Buyers hate risk. I know: I've said it before and you get it! But a strong brand plays an important role in reducing risk, because a brand that resonates with customers translates into efficient client acquisition and retention. Buyers like knowing that customers will continue to do business with the company in the days, months and years after the buyers acquire it. A solid brand also drives growth, enhances pricing power, attracts better employees, and, therefore, increases cash flow.

As intensely as they hate risk, buyers love upside potential. They know that companies with established and trusted brands are much more efficient at rolling out new products. Just look at the line outside any Apple Store next time Apple announces a new product.

When a company is irrelevant to its stakeholders, it rarely attracts the attention of sophisticated buyers and investors. If it does, poor branding won't necessarily kill a deal, but it affects the caliber of the buyer at the closing table and alters the valuation multiple a buyer assigns to a company.

The Basics Of Brand

There are some great books out there completely devoted to brand. (Debbie Millman's *Brand Thinking and Other Noble Pursuits* comes to mind.) If you haven't read one, do. This chapter won't give you 10 percent of the information that these books will, but I hope it will help you appreciate the important role that brand plays in increasing your company's value, and inspire you to become a student of brand building.

> If your company's reputation is poor, trying to build enterprise value is a waste of time.

This chapter includes what I've learned, both from the experience of those who own companies and those who buy them, about the importance of brand. And I warn you that these teachers can be blunt.

When creating an investment-grade company, I think that the most important facts to remember about brands are:

1. Branding is in the eye of the beholder, or perception is reality.
2. Branding is an ongoing process.
3. Brands are fragile so we must defend them.
4. Brands no longer take generations to establish.
5. Brands tell people inside and outside of our companies where to focus.
6. Branding helps us stand out in a noisy marketplace.

Today our stakeholders are well informed and tech-savvy. They form strong opinions quickly and know exactly how to broadcast their opinions to others. Aren't we lucky?

Perception Is Reality.

I said brand was about feelings. I didn't say your feelings.

If brand were about how *we* feel about our companies or how *we* represent our companies in the marketplace (e.g., logos, brochures, messaging and advertising), there would be no need for brand strength to be one of the 17 Reasons. Our brands would be as great as the strong, positive feelings we have for our companies.

> The Walt Disney Company summarizes, in one sentence, what I'm taking a chapter to say: "Emotional connection creates economic outcome."

But brand isn't about our feelings; it is about the feelings of every one of our company's stakeholders. When it comes to brand, it is "all in *their* heads." Our stakeholders' perception is 100 percent our reality.

Great brands arise from the creativity, consistency and success with which our business systems, processes and people make positive connections with stakeholders at every possible touch point.

What Have You Done For Me Lately?

Stakeholders can be a lot like teenagers. As parents, we're only as popular as the last time we let them borrow the car, endured a slumber party or bought the tickets to the big event. Customers and employees are a demanding bunch that really does not care about our last successful project, installation or Vendor of the Year award. We have to deliver "fresh every morning," just like a bakery.

What Have You Done For Them Lately?

Too many of us assume that our customers truly understand the value of our daily efforts, reliable products or high-quality services. We believe that our company and the value we offer is top of mind. Therefore, we don't take time to ask our customers to tell us what our product or service means to them, and we are shocked when we lose them. This pattern can apply to our personal relationships as well: We get lazy and take loved ones for granted.

A valuable brand builder is to show gratitude to our stakeholders. When thanking others, leverage your style and brand as one of my friends, a proud native Louisianan, does.

> Scot owns a highly successful financial-tech company in Covington, Louisiana, and each year, about two weeks before Christmas, he sends personalized notes of gratitude and king cakes to his customers and suppliers. Not one to do things halfway, Scot sends cakes from the king cake king, Manny Randazzo.
>
> This unique gift has nothing to do with Scot's company's services. Instead, it highlights Scot's pride in his roots and his love of southern traditions. These king cakes are conversation-starting treats that recipients serve their families and holiday guests. Everyone loves the prospect of finding the hidden plastic baby, and Southerners understand that the one who finds the baby hosts the next party or provides the next king cake.

Before closing a transaction, most buyers and investors I know (with the sellers' approval) contact key customers and vendors to guage their satisfaction. Of course, they don't reveal that they are potential buyers or why they are gathering information. Can you really expect customers who are confused about what you do or who don't find significant value in what you do to recommend you to others, much less impress a prospective buyer with a powerful endorsement of value? Can you expect customers to stick with you when your competitor calls on them and makes a shiny new value proposition?

> In the current online culture, you can't hide anything. So don't even try.

There Is No Place To Hide.

In today's online jungle, more stakeholders have easier access to more comment/review forums than at any time in history. There is—or soon will be—a forum to review just about anything. People are not shy about voicing their opinions—especially negative ones. Twenty years ago, quality was the differentiator. Today quality is the requirement. You will not survive long in today's marketplace if your customers are indifferent to the value proposition your company delivers.

Recently, I helped a national consultancy choose one of two strategic buyers who were competing hard to win their deal. My client wrestled mightily with the choice because the companies and their offers were remarkably similar. Then my client checked reviews for both companies on Glassdoor. com. Suddenly, there was no contest: The reviews were night and day. This exercise immediately broke the tie, and my client made its choice.

We Live In A Petaflop World.

Consider the amount of time and money it took for GE, IBM and Coca-Cola to build their brands. Compare that to the meteoric rise of international brands such as WhatsApp, Facebook, Amazon, The Honest Company, Instacart, Spotify, Airbnb and Uber. In our no-place-to-hide world, each of your customers is a publisher (blogs, reviews and/or social media) and a video producer (YouTube and Instagram). If every reviewable experience with your company does not create a brand evangelist, your brand is vulnerable.

Your Four Words

My granddad, PaPa, understood our family's brand. Before I'd go on a date or school trip or meet new people, he'd tell me, "Remember who you are." In four words he reminded me that I was part of my family's brand. In four words he told me to be consistent in action, attitude and speech with our family's values.

I can't say that I was a perfect brand ambassador in all my "shareholder interactions," but I definitely knew what PaPa was talking about and what he expected. I had watched him and other family members model the Tarence Brand: serve, don't be a taker, give, don't withhold; be grateful, not thoughtless. His voice resonated in my head every time I was tempted to stray from our values/brand.

In business, brand tells our management teams and employees where to focus their attention, and a strong brand helps attract top-tier talent in a highly competitive job market.

Brand Your Employees.

If employees don't "get" our brand and love living it out, that's our fault. We're the crazy ones if we expect confused or indifferent employees to deliver a distinct feel or experience to every customer. Happy employees (like happy customers) are advocates of a company's brand.

Brand tells employees how to do their jobs when the boss is not around and training manuals are silent. Brand is the high-level directive that aligns employee actions with the owner's vision. If you are the only person in your company who understands why you do what you do, you—not your employees—have a serious problem.

Brand starts with you. If you live your brand and communicate it clearly and frequently to your employees, your voice will resonate in their heads as PaPa's does in mine. You can't expect your team to share your vision of your company's brand if you don't model it.

Customers Notice Wow Experiences.

Several years ago, my daughters pooled their funds and went all out on my Father's Day gift: a YETI® soft cooler. "Well, it isn't a tie," I thought as I looked at the gift and smiled. "But a cooler? They bought me a cooler?"

Maybe they saw through my lame smile because the youngest said, "Lizby's dad loves his. Just wait 'til you try it."

Well, I did try it. And, wow, did that cooler perform on hot southern lake days. It retained ice two to three times longer than any cooler I'd ever used. After one of those days, I called Lizby to thank her for giving my daughter the best idea ever for a Father's Day gift.

I'll admit it: I was a latecomer to the YETI® party, but that company exemplifies my last brand lesson: Get noticed and, if possible, get noticed first.

If you provide "wow" experiences to your customers, they'll want to talk about them. We can't help ourselves. Shoot, I ended up on the phone with a 14-year-old girl, raving about a cooler. It is human nature to share amazing experiences. (We talk more about this topic in Reason 12.)

The only time it is appropriate to fly under the radar is when we are creating a new product in a highly competitive marketplace. For most of us, most of the time, existing and potential stakeholders need to know that we are players in the market we serve, and that groups and individuals that they trust have vetted us.

The only thing worse than being talked about is not being talked about.

Oscar Wilde[33]

If our companies are boring, meaning we don't stand out in the marketplace of customer choices and potential suitors, we can chug along but we won't thrive. Worse, our companies won't hold much enterprise value and certainly won't attract the attention of potential investors.

As owners, we have to be experts in "magnification" of our companies and their offerings if we are to capture the attention of prospects and suitors. Our websites and white papers have to be compelling, effective, great looking and insightful. Our annual conferences must be epic and feature the biggest-name speakers we can manage. Ideally, potential suitors will "bump into you" everywhere and find you interesting long before you ever go to market.

Ingenuity, amazing products, outstanding service, wow interactions, culture, great communication, and discipline—not jaw-dropping expenditures—create unique, defensible and valuable brands.

THE PRICE OF A STRONG BRAND

A good name is rather to be chosen than great riches, and loving favour rather than silver and gold.

Proverbs 22:1 (King James)

I can almost hear you thinking, "Nice quote, but there isn't enough silver and gold in my budget to create the kind of brand he's talking about."

Huge marketing budgets are not the only source of great brands. I'd argue that the biggest budgets are rarely the source of the greatest brands. Owner ingenuity is.

One ingenious owner who comes to mind is "Herb," a classically trained chemical engineer. He was precise, rigorous in his thinking and, as are most chemical engineers, crazy bright.

Herb landed his first job in a lab of one of the biggest chemical companies in the world, but after four years he was bored. He pivoted into commercial banking, but after only three years he was bored again. This time he started his own company to monitor the online reputations of banks and other financial institutions.

Herb knew from experience that few regional banks and credit unions have the internal resources and know-how to actively manage online content outside their own websites. By offering a well-designed tool on a subscription basis at a very reasonable price point, Herb's company rapidly captured significant market share and developed an exceptional reputation in the banking marketplace. His company's reputation for quality and his product's outstanding performance fueled growth as customers quickly became evangelists. Herb was enjoying the fruits of product-market fit and the resulting strong brand it created.

Another one of my clients, "Jeff," also took a creative approach to creating a strong brand. He understood that in the technology world, it is important that subject-matter experts know who you are and that your company's products or services are associated with the best solutions in your industry niche. He also recognized that while he had the best product on the market, he didn't have the budget to be a platinum sponsor of industry conferences or host extravagant parties.

Jeff decided to invest significant time and resources to educate "MFR/AO" (my favorite research/analysis organization) about his company's products so it would ultimately include his business in its vendor landscape for that particular niche. Once Jeff earned MFR/AO's endorsement/mention, he leveraged it to promote and market his company to customers. Influential consultants in the space took note of Jeff's position in MFR/AO's "Excellent Sextant," dug in to learn more, and eventually recommended his solution to their clients.

Jeff used MFR/AO but there are several organizations (e.g., Yankee Group and International Data Corporation) that provide market research and intelligence in the technology space. Jeff's branding strategy paid off when a sophisticated buyer/investor that tracked industry-specific research paid an outsized valuation for Jeff's company. The buyer recognized Jeff's company as the leading player in its market niche.

Jeff didn't rely on Facebook, Twitter and LinkedIn to "connect" his company with its target customers. Instead, he cemented himself and his brand to niche industry experts and shared the value of those relationships with his customers.

Conferences provide great opportunities to expose your customers to recognized industry consultants and influencers and, of course, to your company. They also give you the chance to collect feedback, identify issues and requests, bolster user engagement, and nurture customer relationships.

Invest In Your Customers.

Some of the more forward-thinking companies invest in their customers and industry consultants by hosting annual users' conferences. These can be expensive but, once again, a little ingenuity goes a long way to creating a memorable event on a reasonable budget.

Once your conferences run like finely tuned machines, you can always add potential investors or private equity groups to your invitation list so they can see and experience the value you provide to your customers.

That's what our investment banking team does each year at our annual Silicon Y'all SaaS & Internet Summit (*http://siliconyall.com*). Every October we invite 60 really talented CEOs and 15 representatives from leading private equity groups to spend two days with us. We exchange best practices, trade stories, play golf, shoot skeet, kick back and get to know one another. We do it all with Southern flair, hospitality and cuisine, and the event would greatly please the business mentor who taught me to "weaponize Southern hospitality."

Hosting this event is not inexpensive. We like to do things right, but we don't highlight or explicitly promote our firm. Instead, we take this time to invest in relationships. It doesn't matter if it will be years before CEOs sell or if they sold years before. Our brand is hospitality and building relationships with our prospects, clients and referral sources. We believe in the power of fellowship, and at Silicon Y'all we live it. Silicon Y'all continues to provide a strong return on our firm's investment and never fails to strengthen our brand and, therefore, our firm's value.

There is no excuse for hiding your light under a bushel, because nothing fuels the "velocity of trust" more effectively than being recognized as the most generous thought-leader in your industry.

Use Education To Build Brand.

Customer education is not only a powerful way to drive sales; in a world of specialized services, it also builds brand. Back in Reason 8 (See page 114.) we met "Juan," the owner who used customer education to create huge value in his company. By sharing valuable expertise, he also positioned his company as a thought leader.

If you don't have the in-house talent to write white papers about your company's products and services, hire a top-notch contract writer. Train knowledgeable customer support reps; build in-depth online knowledge bases; host regular "tips and tricks" webinars; and create informative drip-marketing campaigns that address key customer questions. Never turn down opportunities to speak at your industry's trade shows. If you are a poor public speaker, hire a coach so you can make presentations at industry conferences and accelerate your brand.

Who you know, who knows you, and what they think of you matter a lot.

A Good Brand Is A Terrible Thing To Waste.

As difficult as great brands are to build, they are super easy to damage and even destroy. That's the lesson a client of mine learned the hard way early one Saturday morning. "Jason" was a serial AdTech entrepreneur with a real knack for designing and building code that provided data to advertisers about what was (or wasn't) driving their advertising ROI.

I remember picking up Jason's call on my cell phone as I was finishing my favorite trail run. Without so much as a "Hi, Zane. How are you?" he shouted, "Have you seen the news? Remember that group I licensed my solution to? It turns out that they're a bunch of crooks!"

Before I could tell Jason that I hadn't yet heard, he continued, "With my company now tied to theirs, my brand is toast."

As unfair as it was for the public to associate Jason's company with the actions of that month's face of corporate dirty dealings, the damage was done. Various trade blogs and message boards linked Jason's company to these bad actors and indelibly marked Jason's company in the industry. Over $20 million in value went up in smoke in about the same amount of time it took me to complete a four-mile run, because Jason made a common mistake: He failed to consider how every stakeholder has the potential to enhance or destroy a brand.

The news about Jason's licensee was big enough to hit the mainstream media, so the online reputation-monitoring tool he'd invested in simply confirmed what we all would read in every trade and financial publication.

But you and I operate in the same real-time, always-connected economy that Jason did. That makes monitoring our brands' digital reputation part of doing business as an investment-grade company. Monitoring tools make it possible to listen—in real time—to the digital buzz concerning our businesses, products, services and employees. Hopefully (unlike Jason's case) we can quickly detect and correct potential issues with our brands.

Who Are You?

Your brand is as unique as you are, because your brand should reflect who you are. Brand is not a fake-it-'til-you-make-it thing. Try to be something you're not, and the market will call you out faster than a hot knife slides through butter. As is true of all of the 17 Reasons, brand and culture overlap. They are linked, yet distinct. Your culture is a key component of your brand, and your brand reflects your culture.

Shattering Brand Perceptions

What image comes to mind when I say "investment banker"? Let me guess: a professional wearing a tailored suit, carrying a miniaturized Ivy League degree in his or her wallet, and just barely hiding an eagerness to take your money and run. Am I close?

You might say that we investment bankers have an image problem.

My partner Duane knew that when he founded our investment banking firm. He could either play to the perception—build the fanciest offices on the highest floor of the newest building in the "hottest" part of town, hire only Ivy League MBAs, and go for the quick hits—or he could build a company that reflected who he wanted us to be.

So we sat down to figure out who we were and who and what we wanted to be. We started with a list of our values:

- Relationships, fellowship and hospitality
- Service
- Order
- Accountability
- Truth
- Growth

Then we defined each value and decided how it would affect the qualities we would look for in employees and how we would compensate them; our choice of which projects to take on and which to pass up; how we would prioritize tasks; and areas in which we'd take risk. Our values determined our nonnegotiables. If these values were to stand up as our brand, we had to make sure they were front and center for us and for everyone we hired.

We aren't perfect. Far from it. But we do bust our butts to make sure that all of our actions and choices are consistent with our values. We also hold one another accountable when we see any level of compromise in these areas.

Fellowship and hospitality don't require any backside busting. In fact, they make doing what we do a whole lot more satisfying and fun. To us, fellowship means sharing in a congenial atmosphere and with a community of people with common interests. And we don't shy away from the spiritual roots of the word "fellowship" in our conversations, events or communication. It is who we are and how we were raised.

Hospitality is how we create that congenial atmosphere and share who we are with our clients, industry leaders, employees and representatives of private equity groups. Sharing takes all kinds of forms: spending time together, introducing them to our hobbies, and eating a great meal all come to mind.

In the heat of the Louisiana bayou summer, Duane, an avid fisherman and outdoorsman, rounds up a group of oilfield and industrial service executives and owners for two days of marsh fishing, gator hunting and enjoying Cajun culinary delights. It doesn't matter if owners have never baited a hook; Duane's enthusiasm for the sport, the sun and the mosquitoes is infectious.

And after a day catching (or not catching) whatever he's after, Duane loves to share stories at long tables heaped high with good Southern cooking. As an example, here are three menus that Duane and his partner in cholesterol crime, Mrs. Vicki, cooked up for one of his events.

Appetizer of smoked boudin and hogshead cheese
Smoked duck and andouille gumbo with Vicki's special potato salad
French bread pudding with pecans and whiskey sauce

Appetizer of fresh fried alligator tail with Cajun dipping sauce
Crawfish pie with panfried speckled trout almandine
Bananas Foster

*Appetizer of grilled bacon-wrapped wild teal (duck) poppers stuffed with cream cheese
    and jalapeño peppers*
Rabbit in sauce piquante with a touch of cream sherry served over pasta with fresh garlic bread
Homemade apple pie with vanilla ice cream

Now that is some good eating.

Fellowship and hospitality help us get to know people, earn their trust, and genuinely care about them and their personal goals. Fellowship creates relationships that are bigger and deeper than transactions. Our firm leadership is open about who we are (and tries not to fake what we are not) and vulnerable if our values make some people uncomfortable. The risk is worth it to us because over the years we've established friendships that last long beyond any trip to the closing table. Relationships and connections result in fulfillment and opportunities.

Our prospects, clients, strategic partners and employees tell us that they can feel the value we place on relationships. And feeling has everything to do with brand.

You might not be able to attract investors or buyers if your company's brand is weak and doesn't elicit positive emotions in your market niche.

RECOMMENDATIONS

1. Figure out who you are, and be the best you can be.

You have unique talents, abilities, resources, gifts and drive. Branding is a ruthless consistency to be who you are, and it communicates the value you provide in every interaction.

- Is your brand an authentic extension of who you are?
- Have you asked your employees, customers and every stakeholder you can think of how consistent you as a leader are in upholding this brand?
- How is your company's brand different from that of your closest competitors?
- Is there any data to substantiate how your company's brand compares to your closest competitors'?

2. Spend more time on product or service delivery than on advertising.

There is no trickery or magic to building a brand. It isn't about how much you spend; it is about being who you are and the value you provide in every interaction. It is about delivering "wow" experiences through remarkable products and services. Shortcuts in performance are the fast track to a short-lived reputation. You have to deliver on your brand promise—even if that means admitting your mistakes.

- What promises do you make to customers?
- How do you ensure that your company delivers on those promises?
- When was the last time your company asked key stakeholders what value your business provides and where your company misses the mark?
- How does your company handle mistakes?

3. Recruit to your brand.

Employer reviews are available on sites such as Glassdoor.com. Your prospective employees will check them, and so might investors.

- Have you checked the perception of your company in the job market?
- Are you a student of generational trends?
- Have you figured out how to best convey your corporate values and culture to members of the generations you employ?
- Are your employees brand evangelizers?

4. Use your brand to guide employees.

- Can you and your core management team articulate what the business does, your values and the overall value proposition?
- Do you empower your employees to take action and make decisions that are consistent with your company's brand?

5. Invest in and thank your customers.

It is tough to measure return on the investments you make in your customers but try.

- Do you know your customer retention metrics? What actions have you taken to improve them?
- How often do you thank your customers?
- Are the ways you thank your customers meaningful to them? Be creative in showing gratitude.

6. Magnify your attributes.

When we begin to lose our battle with gravity, we all work to minimize the negative and accentuate the positive. It's time to apply that skill to making your company look bigger and more influential in a market than it really is.

- Do you personally promote continuing education initiatives, community involvement and any other team-building programs you have in place?
- If your company provides a specialized service, are you providing the reliable, informative content that consumers need?
- Who are the influential thought leaders in your industry?
  - What can you do to connect with these leaders?
- Which industry research reports should you be tracking?
- Are you sharing your expertise with your customers?
- Does your ideal buyer or investor know that you exist?

7. Let your light shine online.

- What is your company's online reputation?
- What are you actively doing to improve your digital brand?

8. Invest in an online monitoring tool, and protect your brand.

As both soapbox and megaphone, the internet allows customers to promote (or attack) your brand. Online chatter about anything having to do with your company can just as easily turn good customers into detractors as convert prospects into customers.

- What online reputation-monitoring tool does your company use?
- Are you prepared to move quickly if your brand is tarnished?
- What are you actively doing to protect your brand?

TAKEAWAYS

1. It's all about you—and it's not.

Your brand is an extension of who you are—your values and your talents. It is your job to communicate your brand to your team, employees, customers, competitors and prospective buyers. But, at the end of the day, your brand is how these same groups of people feel about you. Their perception is your brand reality.

2. Walk your talk.

Once you know what your brand is, deliver it. Every time. And when you make a mistake, admit it. Own it. We all hope that our products and services work perfectly every time, but buyers and investors understand that mistakes happen.

3. Don't take shortcuts.

Building a brand isn't about logos, ads or useless flash. It is about a ruthless consistency to be who you are and the value you bring to every interaction. When you take a shortcut to building your brand, you are on the fast track to a short-lived reputation.

4. Never underestimate the power of the internet.

The internet has created information overload and so much noise that it is tough to cut through it all. Still, a negative review of your company can carry significant weight and have a tremendous impact on future earnings. Be fanatical about monitoring and protecting your company's image, both online and offline.

5. Be visible where it counts.

Show up well where it matters by:

- Participating in critical industry trade shows and gatherings.
- Maintaining a first-class web presence with leading educational content that adds value to your prospects and clients.
- Authoring insightful blogs and white papers so your prospects find you when searching online.
- Serving your community and employees.
- Aligning yourself and your company with winners.

6. Protect your brand.

Every stakeholder—employees, customers and strategic partners—has the potential to help or harm your brand. Protect your brand like a mama bear would her cub. Put systems in place to alert you if poor reviews appear or customers don't have "wow" experiences with your company. Make it safe for your team to share bad news quickly so you can take immediate, positive action.

7. Compare your brand to your competitors'.

As is the case with all of the 17 Reasons, what matters is how your company compares to its competitors and industry cohort.

Your Company Is Not Hungry To Innovate.

CREATE AN ENVIRONMENT WHERE INNOVATION IS SAFE, VALUED AND REWARDED.

Whether you are content with the good thing you've got going or want to grow large enough to attract a buyer's attention, innovation is necessary simply to survive in today's global, instantly connected and warp-speed market. Look at the intense competition for market share or at consumers who never hit the pause button. Today your organization must be a better innovator than your competitors or be left behind. In this economy, the day—or the minute—your company ceases to innovate, grow, evolve and adapt, it begins to die.

> Learning and innovation go hand in hand. The arrogance of success is to think that what you did yesterday will be sufficient for tomorrow.
>
> *William Pollard, 1911-1989*
> *Physicist and Episcopal priest*

Before we discuss innovation as a strategy to build an investment-grade company and attract investor attention, let's define it. Generically, innovation is a new method, idea or product. In the context of building an investment-grade company, innovation applies to the products, services, culture, systems and processes (as well as the technology that supports all of these) that your company uses to meet and exceed its customers' needs.

INVESTORS INVEST IN GAME CHANGERS.

Private equity buyers are often most attracted to companies that have predictable revenue streams, are dominant in a niche market and have a low risk profile. They get really excited when a target has these three characteristics and has mastered innovation, because the combination is a tremendous pickup. Adding innovation to the mix improves their chances of dominating the segment over time and creating more value.

Investors assign value to innovation because it translates directly into higher margins, barriers to entry, sustainability and scalability. Innovation is also an activity that can slowly petrify in large companies due to layers of bureaucracy, institutional formality, regulatory compliance and risk management practices.

Buyers lust after nimble, innovative firms because they appreciate the firms' value and have dim, but fond, memories of once having been innovative themselves. Large public companies in particular prefer to purchase innovation rather than greenfield it. Funding innovation internally through huge R&D budgets or digital transformation projects is possible, but the most insightful public companies are not narcissists; they acknowledge that much industry-changing innovation comes from outside their walls. They also know that they are slow! Like Blockbuster or Yellow Cab, they risk being driven out of business or severely threatened by innovative upstarts at any moment.

All the benefits of innovation make large companies willing to pay outsized valuations for innovative teams/cultures. Recognize that there's leverage in innovation that can drive enterprise value and ultimately your investor's value as well.

INNOVATIVE COMPANIES

Innovative companies are beautiful ecosystems in which all factors, especially leaders and key people, create an environment that encourages, supports and rewards innovation.

Leaders

In an innovative company, leaders are obsessed with "better." They know how well their company champions and implements innovation compared to its competitors. They actively invite innovation, new ideas and out-of-the-box thinking; celebrate every time they move the chains;[34] and reward employees for contributing to innovation.

True innovators appreciate that their companies face constant change—change that can come from unexpected events inside and outside of their companies. In response, they stay current with industry trends, pay attention to a wide range of inputs and maintain a sense of curiosity about the world. They are humble enough to address difficult discussions head-on, creative enough to find ways to improve, and courageous enough to act.

Innovative leaders are those who conduct meetings that energize people rather than drain them. They routinely ask, "How can we do X better?" and then listen to the responses and act accordingly. They respectfully ask their key people the hard questions about the processes they're responsible for.

Key People

The key people in innovative companies are also about the "better." They constantly ask, "How can we do business better, culture better, products better and customer service better?" They want to know whether they are beating competitors on every level.

As individuals key people are lifelong learners who thrive in cultures that value innovation. They are intellectually curious, humble enough to listen before they speak, and mature enough to act on feedback. They know that their bosses really do prefer to hear the "bitter truth," because they've watched innovators excel while sycophants lose ground. They know which processes and systems are "their babies," and they are attached to them and have the authority to improve them.

All stakeholders in an innovative company understand its goals, connect personally to its mission and share a passion for continuous improvement.

Disciplined Leadership

As owners we often prefer to work on certain areas or aspects of our companies more than others. If we love product development, we'll spend countless hours and resources on it but practically ignore sales. Some of us will pour our passion into our implementation methodology but rarely work on how we recruit talent. For example, I get excited about working on the sales systems in my companies, but I struggle to invest the same amount of energy to innovate around my financial systems and KPI reporting.

Doing what we love or what we're best at is natural, but we've got to be disciplined enough to work on and innovate in those areas we aren't naturally drawn to or don't enjoy. And if we lack the necessary expertise, we must recruit a talented team of individuals who each obsess over their respective functional areas.

Think of the discipline of innovation (or lack of it) in terms of the gym guy who loves working his upper body but is less inclined to do squats and hard-hitting leg workouts. In his quest for great "mirror muscles" (arms, shoulders and pecs), he ends up looking like a powerlifter on bird legs. This lack of balance is not a pretty sight.

The same thing can happen to a company when its leader concentrates on only one area of the business. As leaders, we've got to innovate across the entire organization. We have to be disciplined enough to give equal time to all of our systems and processes, and invest accordingly. If we don't, we end up like that top-heavy guy with bird legs.

Humble Leadership

Innovation comes from those who are intellectually humble and curious enough to ask questions. It comes from continual learners, learners like Sam Walton who "sought first and foremost to learn" throughout his career and even from a group of Brazilian CEOs who wanted to pick his brain about discount retailing.[35] It comes from the everyday innovators you've never heard of. Innovators like "Molly."

Molly had a knack for understanding her target market's needs, and that knack translated into one home-run product after another, perfectly suited to her target market. If I didn't know better, I'd think she had access to their email and was reading and delivering every

> Your best competitors are focused on "out-innovating" you. If you ignore the importance of being an innovative company, be prepared to lose market share to your competitors and damage your ability to attract an investor.

> In innovation, as in any other endeavor, there is talent, there is ingenuity, and there is knowledge. But when all is said and done, what innovation requires is hard, focused, purposeful work. If diligence, persistence, and commitment are lacking, talent, ingenuity, and knowledge are of no avail.
>
> Peter F. Drucker
> "The Discipline of Innovation"
> *The Harvard Business Review,*
> August 2002

item on their wish lists.

Molly was a gifted merchandizer, but (like all of us) she had a weakness—one she'd been aware of, but only during a breakout session at a trade show realized was holding her business back.

"Zane, I admit it," she started, "data isn't my thing. That's why I wasn't really interested in a session called 'Mining for Data Gold' at last month's conference. But a friend who is totally into the whole analytics thing dragged me along."

I knew that she had over 70,000 loyal customers in her database, but Molly was telling me that she had done nothing to leverage her sales and customer data to better understand these customers and use that data to drive more loyalty through customized marketing programs and offers.

As she spoke, I tried not to let my jaw drop. "Sure, we keep track of who has purchased what and when," she explained, "but this speaker talked about dividing customers into cohorts, finding the buying patterns, using A/B testing and using this data to increase sales. We've never done any of that. I had no idea that we're sitting on a treasure trove of actionable data."

"Molly, this guy is right. You are sitting on a gold mine!" I exclaimed. "So, what's your plan?"

"I've got one breakout session's worth of expertise," Molly admitted. "And honestly, I'm more excited by the result—getting products that more of my clients want into their hands—than I am by the process."

"Is there anyone in your organization who has expertise in this area?" I asked.

"If there is, they aren't stepping up and volunteering to go data mining for me," Molly observed.

"Then hire a consultant," I recommended. "There are people out there who eat, breathe and sleep data mining."

The next time I ran into Molly, she was a convert to the benefits of data mining. She'd taken the information her consultant had generated (e.g., amazing patterns around sales attribution by product line) and had begun to leverage it. Molly crafted campaigns targeted to identified cohorts and watched her same-client sales increase by over 125 percent in one year. That innovation in managing customer data drove substantial value in the business, even though it originated from an outsourced resource.

Courageous Leadership

If you want to cultivate a culture innovation, you need to be a leader who encourages and undertakes long-term experiments and trials. You must have the patience to stick with experiments through the inevitable disruption they create in the status quo and discomfort they cause for stakeholders. Most importantly, you must accept that errors are the cost of innovation and willingly pay the price.

> Your company does not have to do everything internally. Sometimes the best way to innovate is to choose an innovative partner or service provider.

> A hallmark of a healthy creative culture is that its people feel free to share ideas, opinions, and criticisms. Our decision making is better when we draw on the collective knowledge and unvarnished opinions of the group. Lack of candor leads to dysfunctional environments.[36]
>
> Ed Catmull
> Co-founder of Pixar Studios
> and Former President of
> Walt Disney Animation Studios

Do you encourage people to innovate, or do you penalize them for taking risks and making mistakes? As the leader, do you take risks and freely admit when your ideas bomb?

The innovation you want around your products and services will come from people, but only if they are swimming in a culture that values innovation over the status quo.

Curious Leadership

Innovators are always on the lookout for the best practices in other industries. They ask questions and then take the best practices and apply them to their own market segments.

Everywhere I travel (to India on business trips or to my neighborhood butcher) I consciously look for how service providers innovate and produce outsized outcomes. I observe what they do well and not so well and the systems and processes they use. I analyze what sets their people and brands apart from competitors, and I ask myself whether I can implement any of their best practices in my business.

One company that consistently impresses me is Chick-fil-A®. It has set the bar for my expectations in the quick-serve restaurant (QSR) space. The service and efficiency of its employees are markedly different—no, crazy different—from those at other fast-food restaurants.

My usual No. 6 grilled chicken club sandwich meal with double tomatoes is exceptional, but I'm not satisfied unless the cashier is cheerful, efficient and servant hearted. Without exception, that teenager (or sometimes young adult) is all three. So how does Chick-fil-A® hire and train its people—recruited from the same labor pool as its competitors—to perform at a much higher level?

While I chew, I watch. I ask questions, and I take away the best practices that I can apply to my business. For example, on a recent visit I asked a manager, "How do you achieve this level of service?"

I should have expected her first answer. "Everyone else is just so bad at customer service that they make it easy to look good!" She had a point, but when she realized I was really interested, she said, "We hire people who love to serve and bring joy to other people. I guess what we do differently is the way we screen associates, the questions we ask. We hire our culture." She paused and added, "We also obsess over being an amazing place to work. We are relentlessly focused on being the QSR where employees are proud to work. With all that, we attract the very best from the pool of potential employees."

I saw the immediate application to our investment bank: We can innovate by enhancing our value proposition to target talent. We can take specific actions to make Founders Advisors a more attractive boutique bank to work for and an advisory firm that draws the best of Tier 1 university finance graduates to the South. (We discussed culture in Reason 6.)

As another example, the church I attend is one of the largest and fastest growing in the U.S. and it has an off-the-charts Net Promoter Score® (NPS®). Its leadership team has spent serious time studying data about why people aren't keen on organized religion these days. Based on that data, the team has created and marketed a weekend service experience that successfully attracts first-time churchgoers *and* keeps them coming back. Better yet, first-timers come back and bring their friends and family members along.

To be a successful innovator, it is necessary to have intuition/feeling about what is happening in the environment and industry. You need to be in a close relationship with your customers. They have the perspective and potential to help you in selecting the real innovation for your business.

Look around. Innovation is everywhere, and you can apply it to your specific business. Are you alert to the innovation you see and passionate about adapting it to your organization?

Innovation Value From Product Managers

Excellent product managers are innovation engines, because they constantly balance customer requirements against resource constraints and competitive pressures. It's what they do.

It is true that the type of company, its maturity level and the type of product or service it offers heavily influence a product manager's job description. It's also true that specific duties vary, so there are vastly different views on what a product manager's role is. It is no less true that the right person in that job can have a huge impact on a company's 17 Reasons Assessment Score. Product managers, or the person filling that role, can drive company valuations as much as, or more than, any other team member.

Stellar product managers:

- Own the long-term vision strategy and road map of a company's products or services.
- Act as master product strategy communicators to all company stakeholders.
- Arm themselves with evidence (data, metrics and customer feedback) to support their decisions.
- Constantly explain the "why" behind priorities.
- Balance dissenting opinions from large vocal clients against the constraints, time and talent of the engineering, finance, sales and marketing departments.

To accomplish this, they must:

- Be meticulous students of the markets and customers they serve.
- Study ideal prospects and competitors.
- Constantly manage the product road map as they filter mounds of data and listen to competing stakeholders.

> In relationships, questions are beautiful and powerful tools. When we ask questions the people we ask feel important, affirmed and loved. They see that we are genuinely curious about and interested in them. Clients love service providers who ask questions, and prospects love potential suppliers who ask questions. When we stop asking questions, that's a good indication that we no longer care. So keep asking questions!

WHERE DOES INNOVATION COME FROM?

Innovation is not typically accidental, though epiphanies or breakthrough ideas can happen.

On the Friday after Thanksgiving, 1995, my brother-in-law and I were in my basement man cave-watching Nebraska shut out Oklahoma. I was describing an elearning project that I was working on for one of my clients. Between plays, we talked about the importance of assessments (both formal and informal) in classroom learning and how testing would evolve online one day.

I'll never forget it. I was reaching for another chocolate-covered pretzel when my engineer brother-in-law said something like, "You could probably build an internet application that would mirror a Scantron bubble sheet. Instead of a No. 2 pencil, kids could use a mouse and radio button to enter answers to multiple-choice questions."

I thought about this idea for a few more plays and added that this data-collection method could apply to surveys, practice tests and even proctored tests. Later that evening, I typed out some initial thoughts about the requirements in a PowerPoint outline that I named "net.test."

For days after, the list repeated in my head like a certain Queen song that we hear at every ball game. I returned to my outline again and again and net.test morphed into CyberTest and became the core product of my future company Virtual Learning Technologies. Ultimately, that patented software changed my business life forever. Innovation can be sudden.

Innovation As A Process

Innovation can arise from moments of inspiration, but typically leaders of investment-grade companies must first create an innovation-friendly environment and then initiate a systematic, ongoing process. Far more and better innovation comes from systematic thinking and planning than from ad hoc brainstorming and creative outbursts.

A deliberate innovation process has two defining characteristics: It is constantly (not occasionally) collecting data, and it is owner led.

1. Innovation is a company's response to the information it gleans from: (1) constantly asking questions of clients, prospects, suppliers and team members; and (2) tracking, analyzing and predicting market trends.
2. After gathering data from all sources, owners set the stage for innovation when they take a step back and ask, "How can we improve what we are doing, and what investments will it take to make improvements quickly with minimal risk?" Innovation is born when you make those investments.

"Innovation Process Leader" is not a role you can pass off to one of your executive team members. You must be the chief innovator and head cheerleader for the best—not just better—method, system or approach. Let your team see your genuine excitement about improvement, and always be willing to throw out the old for the better, even—and especially—if the *old* way was *your* way. Set egos aside for things that work!

In a healthy, investment-grade company, business innovation is a never-ending process. If something is innovative today, it's not tomorrow. You must improve daily.

INNOVATE OR DIE.

I'm a student of wealth advisory groups and registered investment advisors (RIAs). RIAs provide financial advice for a fee, are regulated by the Financial Industry Regulatory Authority (FINRA) and, as fiduciaries, are legally obligated to act in the best interests of their clients.

The financial advisory industry, like many others, is going through massive change, and slow-to-innovate firms disappear weekly as clients and advisors move to more innovative platforms. Huge amounts of wealth are being transferred to members of the next generation who are rapidly replacing "Dad's investment guy" with more innovative, tech-savvy advisors.

> Excellent product managers don't please everyone all of the time. Instead, they umpire the actions of all competing parties while driving the optimal product strategy for the company. They are generally data-driven decision-makers rather than "feelers." They live to innovate but keenly understand trade-offs.

> Without change, there is no innovation, creativity, or incentive for improvement. Those who initiate change will have a better opportunity to manage the change that is inevitable.
>
> William Pollard

Members of the "next gen" expect wealth advisors to speak their language and implement the latest in technology and real-time reporting. They want a comprehensive, full-service menu that includes investment management, education and governance, accounting and taxes, estate planning and philanthropic giving, tech communication, family retreats, bill paying, vacation homes/property management, and more. Take a look at what happened when "Stay Rich Multifamily LLC" evolved while "Old School Asset Management" did not.

Relying on personal relationships, trust and solid performance, Old School Asset Management (OSAM) managed over $4 billion in assets from its clientele of Deep South families with deeper generational wealth. Cynthia started her career with OSAM, but at age 34 she reluctantly left when her efforts to push the firm toward a multifamily office concept failed to excite, much less interest, the managing partners. She recognized that families wanted one provider for a range of services and argued that offering these services would tie families to the firm in multiple ways. OSAM didn't embrace the multifamily office concept and wished Cynthia well.

Cynthia soon founded Stay Rich Multifamily LLC based on a holistic model of meeting the investment, estate planning, lifestyle, charitable giving, real estate management, and tax needs of affluent, younger families. By offering multiple services, she was able to compete with other wealth advisors whose fees were lower. Her company's services and technology were more compelling to busy, affluent clients than a basis point (or two) reduction in fees.

Cynthia built her firm around making the financial lives of affluent families easier while growing and protecting wealth. She customized services around each family's specific goals and invested in a best-of-breed tech infrastructure to provide the lowest costs, real-time client portals, advanced reporting and education.

But she didn't stop there. She created a compelling commission and ownership model to motivate other advisors to move their books of business to the Stay Rich Multifamily platform.

Within five years Cynthia grew Stay Rich to over $2 billion in assets under management (AUM). Once OSAM's partners realized what Cynthia had created, they couldn't innovate quickly enough. They were left scrambling as their top advisors moved to Stay Rich (and took their clients with them). Former OSAM clients made up more than 75 percent of Stay Rich's customer list.

Ultimately, OSAM's partners retained a few of the clients with whom they had entrenched personal relationships, but the damage to their firm and brand was done. Rather than listen, learn, innovate and invest, Old School chose to die.

Every innovation has the potential to become a deep moat that protects your company, because innovation usually drives margin expansion by enabling you to do more with less and do it better. (See Reason 11.) Are you innovating better and faster than your competitors? If not, remember what happened to Old School's partners.

Small, Swift, First *And* Smart

If your company is smaller than its competitors, you will be pleased to learn that innovation is one of the few areas where small can be better

> Innovation has nothing to do with how many R&D dollars you have. When Apple came up with the Mac, IBM was spending at least 100 times more on R&D. It's not about money. It's about the people you have, how you're led and how much you get it.[37]
>
> Steve Jobs, 1955-2011
> *Fortune,* 1998

than big. You can turn on a dime, test, change and react much faster because your organization is more entrepreneurial and less bureaucratic. You should be able to:

- React to market demands faster. First, as CEO, fewer levels on the organizational chart separate you from your customers. Second, you don't need dozens of meetings with global product managers and with finance, strategy, marketing and legal executives to gain approval for an initiative. You can ignite change as quickly as your market demands.

- Experiment boldly. It is far less risky for your small, nimble business to experiment with innovations than it is for your larger competitors. Large public companies must be much more risk averse because they have more to lose than you do. They are mired in risk committees and red tape. Organizational heft has its advantages, but implementing change and testing innovative ideas quickly are not among them.

Smaller companies can better exploit market opportunities and jump to the front of the pack quickly. "Quick-start-ability" can produce nice leads in attractive markets for companies that take the risk of being first. Like being the biggest, being first attracts attention.

Front-runners and trailblazers attract the interest of larger companies that would rather purchase the lead position than take the time and assume the expense and risk necessary to try to grab the lead themselves. Their impatience and incessant hunger for growth causes them to pay up for the convenience of taking the lead position right now. That, my friend, is enterprise value.

Always Be Smart.

If your company is smaller than its competitors, you are in a better position to understand intimately your market niche, its trends and all its nuances. You can better see around the corners. Innovators pinpoint the forces they believe are poised to transform their industries, envision the changes these

> Is innovation a critical building block for other barriers such as brand, switching costs, intellectual property and low-cost provider position? You bet it is!

forces will bring, and then create their products and services accordingly. But your nimble, up-close position does not mean you can deploy innovation strategies without careful thought.

Given your very limited time, resources and energy, focus is essential. You need to be right about where and how you spend your resources. It is costly and time-consuming for organizations of any size to chase the wrong strategy. CEOs of companies large and small must manage their innovation investments prudently. You must take the right shots, and if you miss (as we all do sometimes), reflect, reposition and shoot again. Bleeding resources at a slow ooze is simply too costly.

Business innovation doesn't always mean creating something new, although new can be great. Some of the most valuable innovation comes from improving something that already exists.

No Need To Reinvent The Wheel. Just Improve It.

Two clients make a better case than I can for the argument that: (1) improvement (not just invention) can produce greater enterprise value, and (2) you don't need to create innovation from scratch. The market values incremental improvement.

"Process Pioneer" is the company that two brothers ("Luke" and "Levi") started after working for a few years in industrial sales. Levi took a sales management position with one of the country's largest manufacturers of personal protective equipment (PPE).[38] He shared with Luke some of the inefficiencies his national-logo protein-plant customers were complaining about in the workflows around managing PPE.

(Protein plants process chicken, pork and beef.)

"I'm guessing that the way they're managing their PPE—never mind their tools and major equipment—wastes millions of dollars per plant per year," Levi observed.

"Meat processors aren't the only ones bleeding cash," Luke replied. "I could say the same of any of my manufacturing and services customers."

"So what's the problem?" Levi asked, not really expecting an answer.

"I don't think it's as much resistance to change as it is that these operators have no options," said Luke. "The systems they're using to manage their processes around PPE and tools and uniforms—everything—are ancient, but they're the best ones out there. Would it be that hard to give these folks an option?"

Levi, picking up Luke's train of thought, asked, "You mean a presentation interface that looks more like a video game than a character-based green screen from the '70s? Something highly intuitive for users that also generates a myriad of impactful reporting options?"

"Right!" Luke responded. "An Apple-fication of the front end of the enterprise system! We don't need to reengineer the database and back-end business logic. We could concentrate only on the plant workers' interface."

That conversation turned two salesmen into owners of a rapidly growing and valuable SaaS company. Within three years, Process Pioneer had installed "3T" (Talk-Tech-Time), its one-touch visual interface that manages PPE, in top meat processing plants across North America.

But Levi and Luke didn't stop there. They quickly introduced additional 3T one-touch visual interfaces to manage other antiquated processes for multiple industries

The brothers didn't come up with some complex mathematical insight. Instead, they responded to their customers' pain by improving an existing process. Their company's more intuitive and visual software interface provided operators of some of the largest companies in the U.S. with greater employee accountability and over-the-top ROI. And these customers provided Luke and Levi with more new leads than they could propose and implement.

I recently asked a friend that runs a respected private equity fund whether he looked for radical innovation in his portfolio companies.

> Innovation means continually increasing functionality, focusing on product enhancement, making products stickier and increasing the value proposition to the customer.

You'll notice that I did not ask about developing a novel form of urban personal mobility or a new algorithm that searches thousands of customer interactions in your CRM system to predict best-value actions. Both of those are cool, but innovation doesn't have to be profound or wildly complex. Innovations can be as simple as redesigning your weekly customer progress reports, simplifying your subscription contract, warming up the phone messages customers hear when they call your customer service department, or changing the subject line on a mass email to boost open rates. Not one item on this list is terribly exciting, but we can all improve something about our companies. Simple innovation can have phenomenal payback.

ORGANIZING INNOVATION

Systems innovation means constantly tweaking or overhauling systems and processes so that they deliver at a higher level. It is helpful to divide processes into two categories because there are so many: (1) outward-looking processes (e.g., customer service), and (2) inward-looking processes (e.g., financial management).

Once you list all the key business processes in each of these two categories, start by evaluating the ones that are typically ripe for innovation, such as order entry, billing, collections, content marketing, sales forecasting and KPI reporting. Then look at the documentation for each as objectively as you can, and determine whether the process can be simplified. Finally, refer to the Recommendations at the end of Reason 5 to assess the strength, documentation and scalability of each of your company's system and processes.

Focus On Your Customers' Pain.

There are three key areas to consider when determining where to focus your innovation efforts: (1) products and services, (2) systems and processes, and (3) culture and, therefore, talent.

As you assess how you could improve/innovate any one of these, think about your customers' point of view.

> Innovation is fundamentally about delivering real-world value to customers. It doesn't really matter to me how original or new or unusual an idea is. What really matters to Microsoft is how it translates into software that can help people solve old problems in new and better ways, or be more productive or more creative, or use information more effectively, or just have more fun.[39]
>
> Steve Ballmer, Former CEO
> Microsoft, 2000-2014

> Customers feel secure, delighted and appreciated when they do business with innovative partners who listen to them and continually tweak their products or services based on that feedback. When competitors try to tempt these customers with more features or functions, delighted customers say, "No, thanks. We're happy with our current provider." They expect that their innovative partner will continue to improve and give them exactly what they need. As a result, they have no reason to switch to a new provider.

First, what causes customers pain? Innovators (like the brothers we met on page 155) identify pain points and minimize or eliminate them. They know that pain points represent innovation opportunities, and they respond by changing the problematic aspect(s) of whatever is causing that pain, whether that's a product, service, system, process or culture.

What do your customers want? Do they want you to make something easier to use or less expensive to maintain? Would happy customers be happier if you occasionally made improvements? If that's the case, you have definitely failed to delight your customers.

Ask your team—especially your product manager and sales team—how your product or service compares to your competitors'. With your engineering team in the room, discuss what technology you'd have to invest in to make the improvements that would make your products or services better than your competitors'.

Use Technology To Supercharge Innovation.

I'm a technology guy. I've spent my entire career in the technology space. First I was at IBM selling and servicing hardware and software.

Then I moved to IBM Consulting Services, reengineering processes and designing, building and implementing software to enhance those processes. In my early 30s I transitioned to tech-entrepreneur, creating vertical software companies to better serve niche market segments. I pivoted again to tech investor and M&A advisor, personally investing in over 18 technology companies during the past 20 years and acting as the M&A advisor lead on over 80 tech transactions. So, yes, I am a strong believer that technology drives enterprise value. I've repeatedly seen it do just that. Technology accelerates, protects and creates value-driving innovation while:

- Creating barriers to entry.
- Supporting scale and, therefore, driving better unit economics.

Protect Innovation.

Remember how I described the feeling that grabs hold of investors when they see products, systems or technology that they'd rather purchase than build? I think I used the word "lust." Well, nothing extinguishes that ardor faster than learning that intellectual property isn't protected.

Here's how the World Intellectual Property Organization describes intellectual property: "Intellectual property (IP) refers to creations of the mind, such as inventions; literary and artistic works; designs; and symbols, names and images used in commerce. IP is protected by law. For example, patents, copyrights and trademarks, which enable people to earn recognition or financial benefit from what they invent or create. By striking the right balance between the interests of innovators and the wider public interest, the IP system aims to foster an environment in which creativity and innovation can flourish."[40]

Unfortunately, I regularly meet owners who have not documented, copyrighted and/or patented highly valuable IP. They have simply failed to put thought or effort into protecting their valuable assets.

If you ever want to raise capital or achieve liquidity, it is mandatory to put some protections in place. When a buyer learns that your IP is loosely protected or unprotected (and they will during due diligence), they will, at best, take a swing at your valuation. In the worst-case scenario, a failure to protect intellectual property will kill the deal altogether.

Ideally, you have developed some valuable IP and invested in enhancing and protecting it. We will talk about IP again in Reason 14.

You might not be able to attract investors or buyers if innovation is not foundational to your business and culture, and it is not embedded in your people, processes and implementation of technology.

RECOMMENDATIONS

1. Create an innovation process.

If you can't think of the last time your company tried a new and unproven idea or process, your company lacks a systematic process for encouraging innovation. It is high time—and your job—to design and implement a way for your team, customers and suppliers to document their innovation ideas.

- Do you offer a convenient way for employees to make innovation suggestions? Idea whiteboards in hallways, online forms, the old suggestion box and setting aside time during weekly/monthly meetings are all ways to introduce new ideas.
- Have you set aside time and monetary resources to analyze ideas?
- Do you share ideas quickly with your team members to vet the merits of an idea?

Product Innovation

- How do you continually improve your product or service to make it:
  - Easier to use?
  - Bring more delight to the user?
  - Less expensive to maintain?
  - More differentiated from competitors?

Process Innovation

- In what areas could your systems be reengineered or tweaked to reduce complexity or bolster quality?

2. Be a disciple of innovation.

Examples and sources of innovation are all around us—in organizations, people and books—and ideas we can apply to our own companies can pop up at any time.

- Do you keep track of innovative ideas? Put a pad and pen on your bedside table to record middle-of-the-night ideas. (I also use the voice-recording app on my phone or leave myself audio text messages to save good ideas.)
- Do you believe there is always room for improvement? How often do you ask your team "How can we do better?"
- What tools or resources do you need in order to create a better, faster, less expensive or bigger "wow" experience for our customers?
- Do you watch, or spend time with and learn from, the high achievers that have mastered winning in other fields (e.g., sports, education, military, religion)?
- Are you a voracious reader of authors in and outside of your industry?
- When was the last time you found an innovation in another industry and applied it to your company?
- Take advantage of "hired guns" that specialize in the areas of your business where you feel unqualified or unmotivated to innovate.

3. Create a culture of innovation.

- Do employee interviews include questions designed to uncover the following qualities in applicants: (1) ability to identify improvement opportunities, (2) decision-making agility, (3) strategic imagination, and (4) resilience in the face of rejection?
- Have you created a safe place for your team and clients to test an improvement or new idea?
- Do you allow employees to make mistakes and submit crazy ideas, or do you break their spirits when they suggest ideas that can't be implemented?
- Do you, as the leader, offer up ideas and allow others to shoot them down if they lack merit? In a safe culture for innovation, even the boss's suggestions don't make it to implementation.
- Do employees understand that innovation is vital to creating an ongoing competitive advantage?

- Do you motivate employees to ask, "What if?"

    Do you document and listen to their responses?
- Do employees leave meetings energized?

You need employees who don't settle for the status quo. You also need those who have the aptitude to mesh creative thinking with reality, and who demonstrate the fortitude to complete testing and implementation of new ideas.

4. Create awards/bonuses that inspire and reward innovation from employees, contractors and key vendors.

Not only is recognition from the top a great motivator, but it also signals to employees that they have your permission to experiment.

- Have you considered monetary gifts as well as T-shirts, gift cards and nights out on the town?

5. Use technology to make your products, services and processes better.

- Are you constantly looking for ways to leverage technology to bolster your workflows and valuable proprietary processes?
- Do you regularly review technology solutions from vendors that serve your industry? Do you attend software providers' webinars or review their solution demonstrations to look for new areas of innovation/ROI for your business?

6. Lock down your intellectual property.

- Have you created a list of all your company's valuable intellectual property?
- If today a prospective buyer asked you how your IP is protected, could you provide an answer that would keep the buyer interested?

TAKEAWAYS

1. You must be a disciple of innovation.

You should be fanatical about capturing, testing and implementing innovation at every level of your organization, always driving to make each aspect of your company better, faster, and more value-adding to your customers.

2. Innovation applies to every aspect of your business: product, services, systems, processes, people and culture.

3. To be an innovative company you must create an innovation-friendly environment.

- Every member of your company should be intellectually curious and love to innovate.
- Your upper-level managers must own every key process and constantly be looking for ways to improve their processes.
- You must communicate to lower-level team members that they are a valuable source for innovation because they are the closest to the customers, market and systems they deal with every day.

REAS🔆n

Your Company's Customers Are Indifferent To Your Value Proposition.

CREATE NET PROMOTERS.*

My wife and I believe in marriage retreats. We've recommended them for years to the younger couples we mentor, because getting away from the daily demands of life to focus on our relationship was always a healthy exercise for us.

Notice I said "healthy." Not "easy," "fun," "predictable" or even "safe," and I think the next story will explain why.

About 10 years into our marriage, my wife and I went on a weekend marriage retreat. No big issue pushed us to sign up—just good timing, a nice location in the mountains, and my parents volunteered to babysit our two-year-old twin daughters.

On the first morning, the leader described an exercise in which we'd use a "delight continuum" of 1 to 10 to rate our marriage. "Now this is a great retreat!" I thought. I had been worried that we might have been recommending retreats that focused on the negative rather than the positive.

I think I may have said, "Bring it on!" out loud because I was so pumped about where we were in our relationship. At the time, I felt my wife and I had a high-functioning marriage. We shared values and common goals, and there was plenty of respect, affection and romance.

I figured my wife would score our marriage a solid 9 (since that's what I scored it), and I could not wait to be validated when I saw her score. That 9 was going to reinforce my opinion of myself as the amazing husband I knew myself to be.

The leader instructed us to reveal to each other our ratings—in a nonthreatening manner, of course. I assumed that his comment was directed to any low-scoring couples in the room; obviously, they needed to feel they were in a "safe environment."

When my wife showed me the 3 that she had written on her pink index card, I was stunned. "Maybe that's the way she writes an 8?" I thought optimistically. Nope. The number was definitely a 3.

I may have blurted out, "WHAT??" But I know I said, "Sweetie, I think you may have misunderstood the rating system." My daughters call this "mansplaining," but I call it digging my hole even deeper.

"Denial," "digging," "delusional" and "defensive" all begin with the letter D…basically the grade my wife had given our marriage and, therefore, ME as a husband.

When her score finally permeated my shock and denial, I was upset. I started firing questions, "What are you talking about? How can this be? How long have you felt this way? Why didn't you express these feelings earlier if our marriage was so disappointing to you?"

It turns out I was completely out of touch with my wife's feelings.

Luckily, the leader had seen this scenario before. After he took me aside for some very insightful coaching—and a very long walk around the lake—I was ready to really listen to my wife.

I learned several lessons that day—the hard way—about my marriage, my wife and myself. I also had a choice: use the information to take action or not.

Ultimately, the benefits from the actions I took far outweighed the painful blow to my false reality and ego. On good days, my wife rates our marriage a consistent 8, but that rating can slip quickly if we are not constantly investing in it. I know our score because: (1) we try to do this exercise a couple of times each year just to keep it real, and (2) she says "old love" is SO much better than young love. She was right 20 years ago, and she's right today.

I know you see where I'm going. The lessons I took away from that rate-your-marriage exercise apply really, really well to customer service.

Lesson No. 1: It is common (probably because it takes no effort) to operate under false assumptions.

Lesson No. 2: Data dispels assumptions, but you have to be willing to ask for it.

Lesson No. 3: Once fighters know the score, we take action.

Lesson No. 4: Action isn't a one-time thing. It's an ongoing project.

Lesson No. 5: The benefits are huge.

Why Blow Up Your Assumptions?

I walked into that retreat as a happy husband. I just knew that my wife would give me an outstanding rating on the "delight continuum." She'd never registered a serious complaint, and we were chugging along just fine, raising happy babies and meeting our goals. Boy, was I wrong.

I expect you have made assumptions about what your customers think about your company, because you hear very few—if any—complaints. Revenues are moving in a positive direction, and your customer attrition rate is low. Everything is good, right?

Well, I hope you have the data to back up your assumptions. If you don't, I'll share with you the best ways I've found to gather data, but let's first review why gathering data is (or should be!) a high priority.

When happy customers refer your company to others, those are the cheapest sales you'll every make It costs five times as much to attract a new customer as it does to keep an existing one, and in my experience, solid referrals from delighted customers convert in about 25 percent less time and with 25 percent less effort and expense than leads from other sources. They require much less friction/cost to acquire than cold prospects, which translates into a dramatically lower Customer Acquisition Cost (CAC).

- Happy customers create recurring revenue when they continue to do business with your company. That's a basis upon which a buyer can continue to scale your company.

- Knowing where you win or lose sales enables you to invest resources appropriately in existing or new projects. Based on customer input, you can make strategic and operational decisions not only related to sales and advertising, but also to product engineering and design.
- It is more empowering to serve customers that value your company, service or product.
- If you don't have data to show a buyer or investor how customers view your company, you may never be able to sell your equity.

Sometimes The Truth Hurts.

I assumed that because I was happy in our relationship, my wife was as well. Then I asked her to give me a satisfaction rating. Ouch.

I'm going to guess that you have a similar relationship with your customers: For the most part, everything is going well. You're happy and, since they're doing business with you, you assume they're happy.

Well, I'll bet that some of your customers could surprise you. They might even completely blindside you. There's risk in testing our assumptions, risk in asking for opinions.

- Do you really want to know what your customers think of your company and the products or services it delivers?
- Can your ego handle the truth?
- Are you committed to acting on the data you collect?

My kindergarten teacher, Mrs. Burt, taught all her budding CEOs an important lesson, using a soft voice and cupping her ears with her hands. "Always have your listening ears on," she'd say. As a leader, you have to have high-level listening and questioning skills, or yours need to be improving quickly.

I'd add that you should always have your watchful eyes on as well. To stay abreast of the trends that affect your customers, read the publications that they read. You should know what challenges they face and how your company could help address or overcome them.

So, if you're ready to hear what your customers have to say, buckle up.

Ask For It.

Mature owners don't wait for customers to offer their opinions. Instead, they actively seek customer input so they can assess what their companies are doing well and take action to improve in those areas where they are performing poorly. They set up listening mechanisms or systems to collect input on a regular basis.

Let's look at one of the best ways I know of to zero in on your customers' level of satisfaction.

> If you can't commit to acting decisively and quickly on the information you gather, DON'T ASK!

Net Promoter Score®

In my opinion, a company's Net Promoter Score® (NPS®) is the single best predictor of a company's future growth. Judging by how much weight this number is given during due diligence, I think most buyers agree with me. This tool asks customers one simple question: How likely are you (on a scale of 0 to 10) to recommend a company to a friend or colleague? It then organizes the results.

A customer's numerical response fits into one of three categories:

- 0 to 6 indicate detractors.
- 7s and 8s are passive customers.
- 9s and 10s are promoters.

To calculate the NPS®, subtract the percentage of detractors from the percentage of promoters. For instance, if you survey 100 customers and 65 rate your company a 9 or 10, 25 customers assign a rating of 7 or 8, and 10 customers rate your company between 0 and 6, your NPS® score would be 55. According to Bain & Company:

> To establish the correlation between relative NPS and growth, Bain teams identified the relevant competitors in a business and measured the Net Promoter Scores of each competitor using the same methodology and sampling approach. These relative Net Promoter Scores were then correlated with organic growth measures. In most industries, Net Promoter Scores explained roughly 20% to 60% of the variation in organic growth rates among competitors. On average, *an industry's Net Promoter leader outgrew its competitors by a factor greater than two times.*[41]

As Figure 12.1 illustrates, Loyalty Leaders (companies that are adept at converting unhappy and indifferent customers into brand evangelizers) have steeper growth rates over time than Loyalty Laggards (companies that do not create brand evangelizers).

Promoters:
- Are delighted with your product or service.
- Create recurring revenue by sticking around.
- Refer your company to others.

As I've said before, you should compare your company to those in your industry cohort in all areas. Now

FIG. 12.1 Growth Rates Of Loyalty Leaders & Loyalty Laggards

that industry groups are beginning to offer NPS® data by industry segments, you can benchmark your company against these relevant data sets. Also, as you periodically survey your customers, you can begin to track trends. Higher scores are better than lower, and the more detractors you can covert to promoters, the faster your company is expected to grow.

The relationship between promoters and growth makes sense because promoters are exponentially more likely to reorder and stick with you. Detractors, on the other hand, are more likely to check out your competitors' offerings. Promoters create recurring revenue, and (as Reason 1 emphasized) recurring revenue is music to the ears of owners, investors and buyers.

I recently advised a company with a low Net Promoter Score® and whose pricing model was based on an annual subscription. Everyone in the organization was so focused on engaging and signing up new customers that existing customers received little attention. In fact, I couldn't find evidence that anyone was doing anything to help customers get maximum value from their subscriptions.

With the company's annual retention rates in the mid-70 percent range, employees were devoting an extraordinary amount of time, money and energy to replacing nearly 30 percent of revenue simply to maintain.

We brought in a new CEO to revitalize the company and charged him with turning his team's attention from the "next sale" to helping current customers realize value from their subscriptions. An improved renewal rate meant that each new customer the company attracted would add to, rather than replace, revenue.

Within three months, retention rates began to significantly improve as customers started to realize healthy ROI on their subscriptions.

I recommend that you dedicate 25 percent of your marketing budget to make sure that customers receive outsized value from your offerings. Be as obsessed with your renewal rates as, I assure you, your ultimate buyer will be.

With the NPS® as your starting point, use simple, annual, in-person phone or email surveys to ask your customers four "NPS® supporting questions:"

Question 1. Does our service or product live up to your expectations?

In other words, are you delivering the value and product or service customers believe they should be receiving?

Question 2. How does our service compare to your "ideal" service?

Compared to a best-case scenario, how are you performing? Are there opportunities to improve and go above and beyond?

Question 3. Overall, how satisfied are you with our company, and why?

This question is open-ended by design. It allows customers to dive deeper and provide insight into brand, market positioning against competitors, values and more. Responses can be a challenge to analyze, but they yield the most helpful information.

Question 4. Would you renew your contract/buy the product again?

Answers provide insight into whether your expectations of recurring or reoccurring revenue are realistic.

If you decide to ask a random statistical sample (and top customers) additional questions regarding demographic details (e.g., age, gender, income), geography and other metrics that can help drive marketing efforts, be sure the questions are unbiased and solicit meaningful responses that you can and do act on. Surveys can also help you gather testimonials and compelling marketing messages to use in attracting new customers.

But whatever you do:

- Keep surveys simple and efficient. Customers "ain't got time" for long-winded questionnaires and simply won't provide feedback if a survey is too lengthy.
- Be efficient. I regularly see companies over-survey their customers.

- ALWAYS commit to acting on feedback. In taking action, you demonstrate that you value the time and effort customers spend responding to your questions.
- Send a thank-you gift card when customers invest their time to give you feedback.

What Are You Going To Do About It?

After my wife shared how she scored our marriage, I took a long, long walk around a very big lake. You may need a longer or shorter walk, but I'm going to assume that your ego and the organizational culture you've built can handle the truth, and you will act.

If you just want your ears tickled, your ego is too fragile, and/or you can't commit adequate resources to act, then your company is not sustainable. When mature owners hear the truth and internalize it, they take massive action.

Fix The Systems.

Install in all of your systems and employees the importance of customer satisfaction. Retool every touchpoint (e.g., form, process or interaction whether written, online or personal) to demonstrate that you value your customers' time, loyalty and opinion.

> Great leaders run toward the things that need to be fixed in their companies and in their personal lives. Weak leaders deny the truth.

Multiple positive touchpoints move a customer's empathy needle from detractor or passive to promoter—not because you are a friend or the only provider available, but because your company consistently delivers on the promises it makes.

Delivering on promises requires systems that:

- Include detailed checklists designed to make all customers, not just the key ones, feel important and appreciated. (See Reason 5.)
- Guide and enable all of your employees to deliver positive results and listen empathetically.

Involve Your Employees.

Every one of your employees must understand their roles in making sure customers are satisfied—no, delighted—and grasp that the results the customers receive far exceed the price they're paying. Have you hired people with a passion for helping and serving others? Do your employees know that they are ambassadors for your company? Do you motivate them to treat customers with respect and intentionality?

Empathy comes from the Greek word "empatheia," which means passion. Maybe that's why there isn't a training program in the world that can instill the level of empathy that some of us possess innately. That doesn't mean people can't learn empathetic behaviors, but some people are naturals: nurses, pastors, social workers, counselors, teachers and paramedics. They're called "people helpers." You want employees who naturally create relationships with customers and take great joy when customers are delighted.

If you have not let your employees know that their actions, large and small, matter and that you are committed to your customers, don't be surprised if your NPS® is low. Until employees view each interaction with a customer as an opportunity to solve a problem, you have work to do.

The Ritz-Carlton "$2,000 Rule" is a great example of empowering employees to delight customers. Ritz employees can spend—without a manager's approval—up to $2,000 to fix or improve a guest experience. Keep in mind that this $2,000 is a per guest per day limit, not a per year limit. But perhaps the bigger point is that the Ritz-Carlton knows that lifetime value of customers is $250,000. Suddenly the $2,000 makes perfect sense.

Put On Your Listening Ears—24/7.

Consumers—especially tech consumers—are adept at leveraging the power of the internet to make their voices heard. Social media and online review sites have changed what your customers are saying, how quickly they say it, and how they say it.

Whether you respond to online comments or simply listen, these programs make it impossible to claim that you can't know what customers are saying/feeling about your company (your brand!) in real time.

When my wife told me the truth about our marriage, it was painful. But shock, disappointment and positive shame (assuming there is such a thing) is what it took to open my ears to our issues and her concerns. It took "healthy" truth to put me on the path to a 10 and show me how to delight my bride.

The path that took our marriage to an EIGHT 20+ years later wasn't as steep as you might imagine. To dramatically increase my score, my wife needed only two things from me:

> Owners who don't carefully listen to customers in real-time and respond quickly to their needs can't build sustainable companies, much less ones with value to institutional buyers.

1. Become a better listener. To her, "better" meant shedding my defensive armor. I had to stop interrupting in order to really hear her perspective. Only then could I respect it and stop trying to win her over to my way of thinking.

2. Be honest. My wife wanted 100-percent honesty, not "convenience honesty." You know what that is. It's the tell-her-what-I-think-she-wants-to-hear type of honesty. I wasn't courageous enough to trust her with my truth about my personal world and feelings, and she knew it.

With that feedback, I chose to take action—action that was actually doable.

1. To become a better listener takes time and practice. We set aside time every week (we call it a "holy of holies") to focus on our marriage and REALLY listen without any judgments or personal agendas.

2. We adopted the "100-percent honesty rule." For us that means working like heck to make our marriage a safe place where honesty breeds intimacy instead of intimidation or danger. We check ourselves to make sure we use truth for information versus ammunition.

If I hadn't known I was a THREE in our marriage, I'm absolutely confident that, over time, I would have slipped to a ZERO. Our marriage would have deteriorated along with my score. If you fail to act on the "healthy" truths your customers share with you, expect your relationships and your company to fail.

Talk Back.

When customers use their valuable time to make suggestions, set aside some of your time to take action. If you ask, customers will tell you how to improve your marketing programs, products or processes. What you learn may set priorities for your engineering department or help salespeople more productively engage prospective customers.

Once you make the changes, tell your customers. When folks give suggestions, they like to see action/effort.

Finally, thank the customers who tell you what you don't want to hear, because they are sincerely trying to help you get better and thrive. At a minimum, that deserves a written note. As mentioned earlier, you might give an online gift card, a special discount or company swag.

I learned later that it wasn't easy for my wife to rate our marriage a THREE, but, wow, am I grateful that she did. Over 20 years later I realize that the experience was—and still is—priceless. And I make sure my wife knows that's exactly how I feel.

Take Names.

So far, we've talked only about addressing customer complaints/suggestions, but even the TENS among us have some work to do.

Once you've identified your biggest fans—those promoters who are evangelists for your products, services or company—put them on a list to call when a key prospect wants to talk to a customer.

Being a strong reference for someone takes effort, so make sure you express your gratitude sincerely and often. Your references should receive amazing care from you in whatever love language they speak. Schedule time to thank them for acting as a reference. I guarantee that your efforts will pay off when you prepare for that lucrative exit. To buyers, glowing references are gold.

But What About THAT Customer?

We all know who THAT customer is. No matter how hard we try to satisfy them, THAT customer inevitably complains and is a huge pain for everyone in the organization.

It's easy to forget that a provider-customer relationship is just that, a two-sided arrangement in which both parties work together. Never-satisfied customers do not work or play well with others. They are toxic. So what does that say about the company that repeatedly bends over backward or bangs its head against a wall to please them?

Quality customer feedback can, and should, spur innovation and creativity and strengthen core offerings. If, however, customers are difficult simply to be difficult, the best companies quickly fire them before their negativity takes root and undermines their positive customer service attitudes.

If you find that there is an entire customer cohort that you simply cannot please, it might be time to abandon that segment and better define your ideal customer/prospect. Face it: Some people will never be satisfied. The sooner you fire THAT customer, the better off you, your team and your company will be.

Life is too short to work with anyone who tries to control a relationship by never being satisfied. Chronic complainers dishearten us and undermine our honest efforts to improve, so protect yourself from these ungrateful parasites. Send them to your competitors.

It is significantly more fun and empowering to serve customers who value you and your service or product and whom you can wow over and over again.

The Many Benefits Of Great Customer Relationships

Given the opportunity, my wife told me exactly what she thought of my performance as a husband. Once I was able to listen, she shared two specific ways I could improve. Most customers will do the same. They will not only tell you what they think of your company and service, but they'll tell you how to perfect or expand your company's product offering.

"Grayson" grew up around photography. His grandfather had established one of Atlanta's most respected studios—the go-to for debutantes, brides and wealthy families of Buckhead, Georgia. Grayson's father had carried on the tradition, and Grayson spent summer vacations working in the studio.

But Grayson didn't see his future behind a camera lens. Instead, he started an ecommerce company that produced digital add-ons for photography studios. Its products made touch-ups and digital photo editing so easy that customers could produce beautiful portraits and photos quickly and reliably. As photographers and photography enthusiasts shifted from film prints to digitized photos, Grayson's company led the industry in educating them about how to apply new technologies. Customers became evangelizers, telling colleagues about the company, and demand increased for both existing and new products.

I was curious about how Grayson made such a long string of successful product development decisions. Specifically, I wanted him to tell me about his robust product and market research efforts. "Zane, I don't have the cash to spend on product development or market research," Grayson responded.

"So you just have an innate feel for what the market wants?" I asked.

He laughed. "Hardly. Starting out, I asked my dad what products would make his job easier. Then I asked some of his colleagues. Once things got going, the natural people to ask were my customers."

Grayson may not have thought he was conducting product development or market research, but over the years Grayson put considerable thought into how to ask, what to ask, and how to motivate customers to respond (something he did through discounts on future purchases). He also created a way for customers to provide direct feedback on purchases and trained his employees to respond appropriately.

"I don't have to guess about the problems our customers want us to solve. They tell us," Grayson explained. "My team—sales, product development and HR—mines every customer interaction. Customers tell my sales team the features that matter most to them. They tell my development team which features to enhance. They tell my HR team which characteristics to look for when hiring our customer-facing employees."

"The guy's a genius," I thought "His company creates new products that his customers already want."

Happy Customers Make Happy Buyers.

Prospective buyers and investors love happy customers for the recurring revenue that they create. They base their calculations of future earnings in part upon how likely current customers are to stay with the company and buy more. High customer LTV is a wonderful thing. Assessments like the Net Promoter Score® carry HUGE weight with them because the recurring revenue that it predicts also functions as a barrier to entry and basis for scalability.

Throughout all of the transactions that we have orchestrated, we have yet to meet a buyer who did not want to talk to a seller's major customers during due diligence. "Major" typically means the top 10 for companies with less than 100 enterprise customers. If a company has a large customer base made up of SMBs (Small Medium Businesses), buyers will typically require sellers to conduct a broad audience survey.

Buyers are hugely influenced by what they learn during due diligence. Strong positive customer feedback gives them both the willingness and confidence to close on the terms offered in their LOIs. They understand that high levels of customer satisfaction signal that a company is filling a need and valued as a partner, and, since it is more likely to get more "at bats," is going to grow quickly.

Strategic buyers in the market for cross-selling opportunities look for companies with strong customer satisfaction as well. They know from experience that existing customers are likely to take a sales call and listen to a pitch about another product or offering. Like a strong reputation, positive testimonials tend to shorten the sales cycle.

Long before a buyer/investor does, you should know what your customers think, and you should use that data to improve. Collecting customer satisfaction data when your prospective buyer/investor does is crazy risky—and can be crazy costly when you are in the middle of a possible sale.

You might not be able to attract investors or buyers if your customers are not evangelists for your company and brand.

RECOMMENDATIONS

1. Be a leader.
Seek the truth with a sincere spirit. Be strong enough to take the sometimes hurtful—but always healthy—truth, and be committed enough to act on it.
- Do you know how satisfied your customers are?
- In addition to asking customers about their level of satisfaction, have you asked your employees, investors and yourself?
- Do you study WHY you lost a customer or why a certain cohort of customers is leaving?
- Do you know the top sources of dissatisfaction among your competitors' customers?
- How susceptible are you to losing your customers to the seductive promises of a competitor?
- Do you know what it costs to acquire a new customer vs. acquiring one through referral?
- How often do you discuss customer satisfaction trends in your management meetings?

2. Implement a multi-platform Voice of the Customer (VOC) program.
The detailed, systematic process of capturing customers' expectations, preferences and aversions makes your company better and more desirable to a buyer.
- Does the system you use to collect data include the longitudinal data necessary to show customer satisfaction trends?
- Who in your company is responsible for tracking overall customer satisfaction?
- If you choose to use and track your Net Promoter Score,® have you created a strategy to move customers into the promoter category?

3. Act!
Act quickly to perfect and expand your product offering and improve weak areas based on the VOC data that you collect.
- When was the last time you perfected or expanded your product offering or addressed a weakness based on customer input?

4. Don't overdo it.
Be sensitive about "wearing out" your customers with too many surveys and questions. Unless you are announcing new products and/or services and are asking for specific feedback on those new offerings, I recommend you ask for feedback no more than once per year.

Don't make the response process difficult or long-winded. If you use online surveys, use simple radio button options that respondents can click through quickly.

- Can your customers complete surveys in less than three minutes?
- Can customers add comments in an open-ended box at the end of the survey?

5. Fire THAT customer.

Imagine a conversation between THAT customer and a prospective buyer. Will it spoil the deal and cost you millions of dollars? If you can't make THAT customer happy, don't go crazy trying. Amicably part ways.

- Have you documented the process you use to handle an escalating or frequently occurring customer satisfaction issue?
- How long has it been since you fired a customer? You can actually do it in a life-giving way: "John, it pains us as an organization not to delight you, because our passion is giving 'wow' experiences to our customers. Let me recommend X, another supplier that potentially can give you the outcomes you deserve, but thank you for making us better. BYE."

6. Create a reference list.

Whom will you call when a prospective customer or buyer wants to talk to existing customers?

- Have you created a list of strong, positive customer references?
- Do you thank your referrals on a scheduled basis?
- How can you leverage these sources in your branding, sales and marketing programs?

7. Don't train empathy. Hire it.

Employees who naturally connect with customers are your best cross-sellers because customers trust them to do what's best for them.

- Develop interview questions and testing techniques that assess empathy capacity. Don't hire low-empathy candidates for jobs that involve interaction with customers or prospects—ever.
- As a leader, do you exhibit empathy? Ask your trusted colleagues if they see this trait in you.

TAKEAWAYS

1. **Delighting customers is the key to cash flow, profits, growth, sustainability and enterprise value.**

2. **Without a system to collect and act on data, you are assuming you know what your customers are thinking.**

3. **Customers who are promoters trump all other forms of publicity or advertising.**

4. **Make it fun to be one of your customers, empowering to be one of your employees and a winning acquisition for your ultimate buyer.**

5. **Expect buyer diligence related to customers.**

There is no hiding in the diligence process. If your most important customers are not happy, prospective buyers and investors will find out. They will use extremely sophisticated methods to collect data about how your customers REALLY feel about your company, product and service, and how committed they are for the long run.

REAS⚙n

Your Company's Financials Are Not Buttoned-Up And/Or You Cannot Relate Them To Your Business Model.

CLEAN THEM UP, UNDERSTAND THEM AND BASE DECISIONS ON THEM.

I was a young entrepreneur when Roy W. Gilbert Jr., a board member and one of the original investors in my first SaaS company, Virtual Learning Technologies (VLT), told me that "A set of organized, accurate and believable financial statements will have more influence on a buyer/investor than anything you say, do or promise."

He continued, "When owners cannot explain how they use their financials to manage their companies, I know that they don't. That's not the type of leadership I invest in."

Fast forward 20+ years, and this battle-scarred deal warrior can only say "Amen!" to both of Roy's comments.

Addressing poor financial reporting is key whether you plan to sell your business or just want to continue to own and run a better business. "Ulysses" is a great example of what I'm talking about.

> Poor financial record keeping and owners who fail to use financial data to manage their companies diminish a company's appeal to investors and affect how a company runs.

Whether You Do It Right Or Wrong, Be Consistent!

When our team first met with Ulysses, the CEO and owner of a niche digital media company, we were excited. The centerpiece of his 15-year-old media company was an exotic-travel-on-a-budget website that proved addictive to his target audience: highly educated millenni-

als. *Organic site traffic consistently topped 1.2 million unique visitors per month and was growing. Site visitors hung around and readily signed up for alerts and newsletters.*

After our introductions, Ulysses launched his rapid-fire rundown (a style we'd get to know well over the next few months). "I love travel. I love saving money. It's simple: I put the two together and created a website. During the past five years, traffic on the site has exploded. Our Alexa rank is insane. I want to—I need to—be out traveling. I need my team to keep up with everything else, but they can't. I need a partner."

As he took a breath, I grabbed my chance to jump in. "A partner for what?"

"I need," responded Ulysses, "someone who can inject some cash—cash to hire enough additional staff to continue to create exceptional content and to manage the site's massive traffic."

"From what I've seen," I said, "the site has lots of advertisers. I'm not sure, but I think that the income statements you brought in indicate mounting revenue. I just don't see a recent statement."

"No worries," Ulysses said. "I've figured out the ad-based model that brings traffic to the site and generates CPM (Cost Per Thousand Impressions) revenue—lots of it—from content views. We've also developed CPA (Cost Per Action) models that are extremely lucrative. My cousin Marley can get you whatever financials you need. It's my team that's the bottleneck. It's just too small to talk to all of the interested advertisers out there."

If only building a bigger, better team had been Ulysses' only problem. But at this point, our view was limited. Here is what we did know:

- *Ulysses had set the business model in motion and was primarily responsible for generating content.*
- *Bookkeeping was in the hands of his cousin, a CPA.*
- *Ulysses wanted us to find a partner who could inject the expertise and capital necessary to fully monetize his growing digital media business.*
- *Ulysses was on the way out of the country to attend several of his favorite band's concerts.*

"I gotta run, but here's Marley's number," he said as he texted me contact information. "I trust Marley with the books and the business. He can get you whatever you need. I'll call you when I get home to see what a share of my company is worth."

On the way to the elevator, I tried to explain that before we could give Ulysses even a thumbnail estimate of value, we needed recent financials. As the elevator doors closed, Ulysses reminded me, "Just call Marley!"

When we looked more closely at the income statements that Ulysses left with us, the number of Ulysses' problems multiplied.

1. *Ulysses, like many owners, was living out of his company's checkbook.*
2. *Disorganization and inaccuracies made it impossible for us to see how revenues and expenses were tracked or how the two related to each other. The company's cost of goods sold incorporated a variety of misplaced expenses. For example, in the marketing expenses category we found $1200 for four concert tickets. Every category was similarly inconsistent.*
3. *Ulysses had assured us that the investments he made in purchasing traffic were profitable. As far as we could tell, his financials told a different story. The company had been purchasing traffic that failed to generate "real" (human) views of the content. The financials didn't support the ROI Ulysses thought he was getting from his marketing campaigns.*

I have a crack team of experienced analysts who love to dig deep into financials to find buried gems. But if there were any gems in these financials, we couldn't find them.

When Ulysses returned to the States, I called a meeting. "I'm not going to sugarcoat this, Ulysses." It was my turn for a rapid-fire rundown. "Number 1: Marley is a great guy, but your company is growing too fast and is too complex for any part-time CPA to keep track of. Number 2: As they are, your financial records are unusable. Number 3: It will take four to six months to fix them, and it won't be a simple task. Number 4: Bring in a fractional CFO to create a financial reporting system. You can afford one, and the return on your investment will be great offers from prospective investors."

Ulysses was quiet, so I continued, "Based on what we've learned about the profitability of some of your marketing efforts, you have to overhaul your customer acquisition strategy. We'll put that on hold while we clean up your financials."

I'm not sure which part of my speech sunk in, but Ulysses snapped to attention. "Not happening, Zane. I need an investor now, not in four or six months! We market this thing now. If I don't get as much as I could with perfect financials, so be it."

"Ulysses," I countered, "I strongly advise against going to market now. Investors use financials to make their offers. They view your financials as your 'track record,' and you are ONLY as good as your record says you are. If we can even find an investor who's willing to invest, and they have enough patience to wade through these financials to make an offer, I guarantee that they will reduce their risk by slashing their valuation of your business."

Ulysses didn't buy my argument or want my guarantee. "What do I sign to start the process of finding an investor?"

We decided that a financial buyer was not an option due to the poor condition of Ulysses' accounting practices. However, we acquiesced and made two calls to large strategic buyers that we knew were interested in acquiring travel digital media companies with exponential rates of growth. Both groups expressed interest, but once they reviewed Ulysses' financials, neither was willing to move forward.

The complete lack of clarity in the financials proved to be an insurmountable obstacle.

Ulysses is not the only owner of a fast-growing company to be so focused on pressing issues that he let maintaining accurate and up-to-date financial statements slip to the bottom of his task list. In the early days of operating my software company, I thought that the only value of financial reporting was to create tax returns and convinced myself that I didn't need a CFO until I was closer to selling. I had to grow up some—and let Roy's advice sink in—before I understood that accounting and financial functions were absolutely critical to the management decisions I was making on a daily basis.

> Don't even think about a potential transaction if your financial house is in disarray.

YOUR FINANCIALS ARE BUTTONED-UP. ARE YOU?

Owners whose financial management practices are buttoned-up—*and who know how to use their financials*—enjoy countless benefits before a buyer ever appears on the scene. The top five benefits are:

1. Additional and more reliable data for real-time decision-making and strategic planning.
2. Better and more productive relationships with lenders and investors.

3. Clearer insights into opportunities to exploit competitive advantages.

4. Ability to institute highly creative incentive plans for key team members.

5. Peace—the sweet peace that comes from replacing worry about non-forecasted cash flow items with knowledge of where you stand financially.

In managing and growing a company, cash flow is king. That means you must understand the unit economic model of your business and where you stand in regard to cash flow at all times.

Uncertainty or confusion in this area is unnecessarily stressful for you while running your company, and it can be devastating when a prospective investor realizes that you don't use accurate financial information to make decisions. You must have a firm grasp on how your company makes *and* spends money today, and you must someday be able to communicate that to a buyer.

True: The combination of well-executed financial processes and owners who understand what the numbers mean is one that buyers cannot resist.

Also true: Nothing repels a suitor faster than an owner's confusion about how a company makes and spends money to generate a profit.

"Curtis" is a great example of an owner who took the first step to creating an investment-grade company by putting his CFO to work creating accurate financial statements. What he failed to do, however, was understand those statements and use the information productively. There's just no way to hide that failure from an investor.

I remember the day I received a call from the CEO of a public company—a guy I knew from a deal I'd done with his company a few years before. In the proprietary deal that we were now working on, his company was pursuing one of my software clients as a strategic acquisition. At this point, I'd had several conversations with the CEO's senior vice president of strategy and corporate development about the perfect fit between the two companies.

After a quick "How are ya doing, Zane?" the CEO got right to the point. "I'd like a call with your client Curtis. I want us to get to know each other and confirm that our goals are aligned." I agreed and set up a conference call for the three of us the following week.

The three-way call started out great: significant synergy and all good energy. But then the CEO rattled Curtis with a standard request. "Walk me through your economic model. I'd like to hear more about how you use your financial data to manage and operate your business."

Losing your grip on financial matters hinders your ability to make informed decisions related to managing and growing your company. It will also destroy buyer/investor trust and confidence in your company's investment potential.

In one breath, my client went from confident and competent to cloudy and confused. Curtis didn't have a handle on his gross margins by product line. He wasn't sure how he tracked his investments in marketing, much less how he forecasted his sales and expenses. As to how he'd designed the commission plans for his inside sales reps? He couldn't really remember. It was as if he hadn't looked at his financials in months.

The inevitable email followed. "I'm concerned that Curtis doesn't have a handle on the financials. I had thought that he was a natural to run this division post acquisition, but to be candid, he's not. This deal just doesn't make sense for us."

No banker likes those emails.

I hope Ulysses' story drives home the present and future value of organized, supportable, up-to-date financial reports, aka investment-grade financial reports. I hope that Curtis' experience illustrates that great financials aren't enough: You must understand them, use them and be able to communicate the story they tell investors. In other words, you need to be an investment-grade owner.

Are Your Financial Reports Investment Grade?

The Monthly Financial Statements Of Investment-Grade Companies Are Up-To-Date And Readily Available To Their Owners.

Most owners track financials on a monthly basis, but many reports lag weeks or months behind. In addition to annual financial statements, buyers require detailed monthly financial statements in order to perform the analysis necessary to determine whether or not to purchase or invest in a company.

Investment-Grade Companies Track Revenue To Expenses.

If, like Ulysses, you are not matching revenue to related expenses during the same accounting period, you cannot be sure your expenses are generating sufficient revenue to achieve your profitability goals. The matching principle is a basic accounting principle that creates consistency in income statements and balance sheets. Financial statements may provide a distorted picture of a company's financial position if expenses are recognized earlier than related revenue and vice versa. Recognizing an expense earlier than is appropriate lowers net income, and recognizing an expense later than appropriate raises it.

The Financials Of Investment-Grade Companies Are Easy To Follow.

If the only person who understands how your financials relate to both your business model and financial position is the person who created them, you have some work to do. If even that person isn't sure, you have some firing and hiring to do.

Investment-Grade Companies Forecast.

A forecast is not a budget, and financial forecasting is not sales forecasting. Budgets and sales forecasts both have their places in a well-run company, but they are not the same as financial forecasts.

Financial Forecasting:

- Tells you what's in your pipeline. It predicts your hit rate (percentage of deals that you close) based on past performance.
- Enables you to evaluate and improve your planning and budgeting methods.
- Demonstrates an ability to accurately predict financial performance.
- Increases the trust buyers place in your management team's competence and ability to continue to grow your company.
- Proves to buyers your claim that your company is able to generate future cash flow.

> Ulysses was lucky. When I was consulting, the owner of a construction company called for help with due diligence on a transaction. In the first hour I learned that the bookkeeper had not reconciled all accounts, and some assets on the books didn't even exist. This owner's suitor walked away, not because it suspected fraud, but because the financials it used as the basis for all decisions (including what multiple to pay) were not correct.
>
> Mike McCraw, CPA
> Managing Director
> Founders Advisors

Financials Of Investment-Grade Companies Are Prepared According To Generally Accepted Accounting Principles (GAAP).

Publicly traded companies are legally required to prepare their financial statements according to GAAP, and consequently must convert an acquisition target's financial statements to GAAP before moving forward with a purchase. Buyers use GAAP to compare apples to apples, i.e., one company's financial statements to another's. For that reason, most financial buyers or nonpublic strategic buyers will require a company to convert to GAAP-compliant statements.

ARE YOU AN INVESTMENT-GRADE OWNER?

Investment-Grade Owners Hire CFOs—Not Bookkeepers—To Do The Financial Heavy Lifting.

I've met many entrepreneurs who over-title their financial managers. Their "CFO" is really a controller, or their controller is really a bookkeeper. Maybe it's a benign case of job title inflation, but more often it comes from not understanding the distinction among the roles.

- Bookkeepers are record keepers.
- Controllers are responsible for the timeliness and accuracy of the financials.
- CFOs are future-looking strategists. They work with CEOs to create and execute a company's strategies related to growth, pricing and investment. They play a key role in pursuing the correct sources of capital and in balance sheet management.

You may argue that the size and/or resources of your company don't yet merit a full-time CFO. Fine. For $5,000 to $7,500 per month (depending on job scope), hire a fractional CFO.

Fractional CFOs are highly qualified financial professionals who have worked as full-time CFOs. They act as CFOs only as you need them, i.e., on a less than full-time (or fractional basis). Sometimes they are referred to as "outsourced CFOs."

A fractional CFO can set up an accounting system, financial controls, monthly reporting, KPI tracking and margin expansion initiatives. Once your company requires a full-time CFO, you will have a solid platform from which you and your CFO can create and execute a growth strategy.

Owners Of Investment-Grade Companies Do Not Live Out Of Their Businesses.

Ulysses wasn't the first owner to attribute personal expenses to a business, and he won't be the last. That's too bad because the practice:

- Signals to buyers that an owner has run the company as a lifestyle business instead of an investment-grade entity.
- Justifiably decreases a buyer's confidence in a company and its management because financials don't accurately indicate how the company generates operating profit.
- Is so common that advisors use a process called "recasting" to remove personal expenses from a company's financials.
- Reduces a company's valuation.

Using your company to fund personal expenses isn't the only hallmark of a lifestyle business. Figure 13.1 lists a few other actions typical of lifestyle businesses and compares them to those of growth equity companies.

FIG. 13.1 Lifestyle Businesses vs. Growth Equity Companies

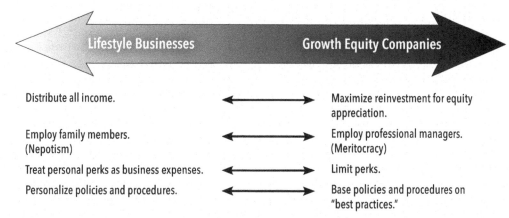

Lifestyle Businesses	Growth Equity Companies
Distribute all income.	Maximize reinvestment for equity appreciation.
Employ family members. (Nepotism)	Employ professional managers. (Meritocracy)
Treat personal perks as business expenses.	Limit perks.
Personalize policies and procedures.	Base policies and procedures on "best practices."

Don't get me wrong: Running a lifestyle business isn't a problem if that's what you decide to do *by choice*—not *by default*. A lifestyle business makes sense if it is mainly a hobby and tax write-off. But the purpose of this book is to help you create a company with salable equity—one that will attract and be valuable to buyers.

Investment-Grade Owners Develop And Constantly Monitor Key Performance Indicators.

Financial key performance indicators (KPIs) are the very powerful beacons that CEOs of investment-grade companies use to guide their decisions. You should pick three to five of your top metrics and dedicate yourself to tracking them like a hawk every month.

Which metrics? Choose the ones that have the greatest effect on your company's top and bottom lines. I recommend that you track percentages or ratios rather than numbers, because they're better gauges than raw numbers. If you aren't sure which metrics are the most critical for your company, find out which ones your competitors or publicly traded companies use.

Examples of KPIs for a services company include:
- Revenue per employee.
- Utilization and realization rates.
- Gross margin by billable resource.
- Employee turnover rate.

Six critical KPIs for an SaaS company might be:
- Monthly/annual recurring revenue (MRR/ARR).
- Customer retention.
- Net revenue retention.
- Lifetime value of a customer.
- Customer acquisition cost.
- The ratio of Customer Lifetime Value (LTV) to Customer Acquisition Cost (CAC).

For an ecommerce company, KPIs include:
- Gross margin by product category.
- Average order size.

During my last checkup, I found myself dancing with my doctor the way owners dance with buyers when owners want buyers to overlook the numbers. In an attempt to explain why my LDL number (the "bad" cholesterol) had to be inaccurate, I argued that I had probably eaten something fatty before the blood draw. My doctor's simply repeated the number and asked if I'd like the prescription for the statins he recommended or wanted to take my chances with the type of stroke that disabled my dad at age 68. I reminded him that my dad's stroke was unrelated to high cholesterol. The doctor just rolled his eyes and wrote a prescription for the statin medication.

- Sales conversion rate.
- Repeat orders by customer segment.
- Email opt-in conversion rate.

Choose your make-or-break KPIs and then track them diligently (on a monthly, quarterly and annual basis) with your team and work to improve them. If you tie employee compensation to your KPIs, you can expect to work in a company full of KPI fanatics. As Peter Drucker said, "What gets measured gets improved."

ACCURATE FINANCIAL STATEMENTS: THE SMOKING GUN OF COMPANY VALUE

Whether your goal is to run a better business or attract a buyer to your company, the three most important financial statements are:

- Income statement.
- Balance sheet.
- Cash flow statement.

Transaction advisors use financial statements because they are the best proof of past performance and predictor of future performance. We use them to:

- Assess whether a company is salable.
- Estimate a company's likely market valuation.
- Persuade prospective buyers that a company is worth the buyer's offer.

When our team builds a business case and a model for a sale price to a buyer, we don't depend on conjecture or hopeful expectations. Instead, we present the best predictors of future performance: financials. You are only as good as your record says you are, and financials are your record.

Just as doctors use lab numbers (rather than patients' statements) to determine whether to prescribe, buyers use financial statements (rather than sellers' statements) to determine whether to purchase a company. With financial statements, buyers can estimate future cash flow and forecast their potential return (based on that cash flow) over the investment holding period. Strategic buyers use these statements to gain insight into the potential synergies they could gain by acquiring a company.

A WORD ABOUT AUDITS AND QUALITY OF EARNINGS REPORTS

Business owners frequently ask me if it's important for them to have audited financials, and whether the value truly outweighs the cost and effort of producing the documents. Audited financials do more, however, than just improve investor or buyer confidence. They contribute to a more streamlined due diligence process related to disclosure, compliance and taxation.

To owners preparing for a confidential market process I also recommend a sell-side quality of earnings (QOE) report. Quality of earnings due diligence is an independent analysis of a company's financial information. This can be the best money a seller ever spends because a detailed QOE analysis can maximize the value of the business while uncovering and mitigating any financial surprises that might otherwise emerge during the sale process. Addressing issues before the sale process begins accelerates the process once a company is on the market. Speed is a good thing because time kills deals.

RECASTING FINANCIALS

Transaction advisors commonly recast a company's financial statements to most accurately present a company's performance to the market. Recasting illustrates to buyers what the business would look like if it were in their hands. This process involves:

1. Removing personal expenses, and
2. Adjusting EBITDA by reorganizing items so that they match industry-standard reporting procedures. We remove one-time or extraordinary expenses or revenues that would cease in the event of a sale. We also correct mis-categorized expenses to accurately reflect margins. Finally, we match revenue to expense accounting for items like deferred revenue.

We remove personal items (such as vacation expenses, country club dues and automobile purchases) from financial statements because they artificially inflate the cost of running the business and consequently lower operating income in the eyes of buyers. Potential buyers want to see what it really costs to run a company, and owner-related expenses distort that evaluation.

Buyers are accustomed to seeing financial statements in a certain format, so we reorganize and recategorize items to match that format. Consistency facilitates more accurate analysis and comparison to other companies in the industry.

Finally, we add back or subtract from EBITDA any items that would not occur under a buyer's ownership. Typical adjustments include:

- Excess compensation. If the owners (or other employees, such as the owner's family members) receive compensation well above market rates, we add back the amount that exceeds market rates. Conversely, sometimes owners do not take salaries, but instead receive compensation only in the form of cash distributions from the company's profits. In this case, we add (as an expense) the market value of that owner's salary as CEO/COO/president.
- Charitable contributions.
- Investments that should be capitalized. Some owners expense items such as software and office equipment in an effort to reduce net income and lower taxes. Since doing so deflates EBITDA, we recast these investments as fixed assets.
- One-time or extraordinary expenses. Legal fees and lawsuit settlements, severance pay, major repairs and maintenance, start-up expenses associated with opening a new business line, and onetime professional

> In my experience, companies that have more than three years of audited financials absolutely trade for higher multiples than their counterparts whose financials are unaudited. Buyers have more confidence in their bids when a third party has examined a company's practices, financial accuracy, claims, records and reporting activities.

fees are examples of significant, nonrecurring expenses that we add back. They are either atypical or not required to operate the business in the future.

- Revenue and/or expenses related to another business. Sometimes owners record revenue/expenses that are not related to the business itself, but to another operation. For example, one client owned and leased property in addition to running his services business. He recorded the rental income and upkeep of the property on his business's income statement. Since this property would not be included in the sale of the company and was not related to the business model, we eliminated the rental income and added back the upkeep expenses when recasting the company's financial statements.

While recasted statements give buyers the most accurate picture of a company's performance, they also benefit sellers. Eliminating personal items and onetime expenses raise EBITDA, and, since multiples of EBITDA are typically used as a basis for valuation, it strongly benefits the seller to present the highest level of EBITDA possible.

If your financials are accurate, up-to-date and audited, buyers are more confident both in the quality of management and in their own ability to accurately gauge the value of investing in your company. Unless buyers can perform a thorough analysis on numbers they trust, they will either not make offers or make subpar offers to mitigate risks associated with the financial "unknowns."

You might not be able to attract investors or buyers if you don't do an excellent job of managing finances and aren't capable of explaining how they relate to your business model.

RECOMMENDATIONS

1. Get comfortable with your financial reports.
- Are you capable of explaining how your financials relate to your business model?
- Do you use them as a primary resource in meetings with your management team?
- Do you have monthly meetings to walk through your financials with your senior financial professional?

2. Hire a professional.
If you haven't done so already, hire a CFO. If your company is still small, at a minimum, hire a fractional CFO or controller. Charge them with setting up an accounting system with monthly reporting and KPIs. These professionals can help ensure that your financial statements are accurate, up-to-date and useful.
- Is the person currently responsible for creating your financial reports capable of creating—and explaining to a prospective buyer—clean financials that would pass a buyer's muster?

3. Have financial statements audited.
Audited financials are not required in order for a company to be considered investment grade, but the "anointing" from an objective third party lends valuable credibility to you, your team and your company in the eyes of buyers/investors. Audited financials also simplify and/or expedite the financial due diligence process.

Buyers differ in the number of years of audited financials they will request, but it is best to be prepared with audited financials for the three to four years prior to the date you wish to sell.

4. Start financial forecasting.

If you don't already employ a detailed forecasting method, work to implement one. Update your forecasts on a monthly basis to reflect the realities of your business.

- Are you using your financial reports for financial forecasting?

5. Choose the appropriate accounting method, and follow industry standard practices.

Compare yourself to publicly traded competitors, and do your homework to ensure that you follow industry standard practices for recording financials.

- Are your financials prepared according to GAAP standards?

6. Be consistent!

If you don't know whether you are recording something according to GAAP and/or industry standards, be consistent in your uncertainty—even if you are consistently wrong. Of course, a financial professional (see Recommendation No. 2) won't be unsure. Consistency simplifies recasting and reduces the amount of questions a buyer might ask.

7. Match revenues to expenses.

If your financials are audited, follow industry standards, and are accrual based, revenues will match expenses.

8. Close financial statements every month.

While you may be able to run the business with only quarterly or annual reports, buyers need to see much more detail. For example, buyers will want to analyze monthly revenue growth, revenue growth by customer by month, and trailing twelve months (TTM) revenue growth. This means you need to be ready to provide up-to-date, detailed monthly income statements.

Up-to-date means:

1. Financials (at whatever level of detail you use) should be closed within 10 days, reports within 15. When financials are late, unreconciled or inaccurate, they don't enable owners to make necessary changes.

2. The balance sheet is reconciled on a regular basis.

9. Stop living out of your business.

With every expense ask, "Is this expense company-related, or is it personal? Is the expense necessary to produce financial results for my company?" I doubt, for example, that you can attribute the cost of the gas you used to attend your daughter's tennis tournament (on the off chance that you'd run into a customer or prospect) to the financial performance of your company. Every personal expense that you attribute to your business reduces the value of your company and its EBITDA. In the end, the practice of living out of your business hurts you, not the buyer.

- Do your company's financials include personal expenses?
- Have you looked at your financials from an investor's perspective?
- Is your owner compensation consistent with other owners in your industry and geography? Do you know what the average compensation package is for the role you play in a company your size in your industry and in your region?

10. Obsess over your company's Key Performance Indicators.

Once you identify the three to five most important KPIs for your company and/or industry, track your company's performance regularly. Make sure your team understands what your KPIs are and how critical they are to measuring the success of your company.

- Have you identified the KPIs for your company and/or industry?
- Do you compare your company's performance to industry norms?
- Does your management team understand how critical KPIs are to measuring the success of your company?
- Is your team's compensation tied to your KPIs?

TAKEAWAYS

1. You are only as good as your financials say you are.

You may be the best salesperson on planet Earth, but you can't sell your way out of poor financial reporting.

2. Don't skimp on professional financial employees and advisors.

Many entrepreneurs I meet either underestimate the financial firepower they need or over-title the financial professionals they hire. Bad plan.

3. You must understand your financials.

Your financials tell the story of your business. Can you read it and tell it? You need to understand your economic model and clearly explain how you make, spend and invest money in your business.

4. Accurate financials are the basis for better decisions.

Your financials give you accurate data—rather than assumptions—on which to base management decisions.

5. Financials matter to buyers.

Going the extra mile with your financial reports not only helps you today, but it smooths some of the bumps on the road to a closing in the future. Financials are the bedrock for the trust (or lack of it) between every buyer and seller in every transaction I've ever orchestrated, and they set the tone for every buyer-seller interaction. If your financial records are fuzzy or less than completely accurate, they color a buyer's perception of everything else about you and your business. Buyers don't just pay more for companies with stellar financial records; they simply won't consider investing in companies that don't have them.

6. Know your three to five most important Key Performance Indicators.

Once you determine the best KPIs (the make-or-break metrics) for your company, you and your key managers should track them relentlessly. Your management team will be highly motivated to do so once you tie their compensation to them.

7. Audits and quality of earnings reports are wise investments.

They give buyers/investors more conviction as they make competitive offers, and they accelerate the due diligence process.

REAS⚙n

Your Company's Legal Housekeeping Will Not Win Any Awards.

INVEST IN A COMPREHENSIVE LEGAL REVIEW, AND REAP THE REWARDS AT YOUR EXIT.

I Feel Your Pain.

Most of us hate hiring lawyers. We'd rather walk across hot coals than spend our valuable time on issues that annoy us, we believe do not apply to us, or we would rather not think about. We prefer to spend our time and energy on new product designs, emerging markets and talented recruits. Most of us are risk-takers by nature and don't default to safety and compliance. Almost all of us swallow hard at attorney fees of $400 to $800 per hour, and I'll bet we've both avoided attorneys' calls.

Well, I used to avoid them, but years ago I saw the light.

What's behind my conversion from attorney-avoiding entrepreneur to advocate for the role attorneys can and should play in creating investment-grade companies? I chalk it up to experience—mine and others'—with "hairy" situations like this one from early in my career.

"It's been a great ride," Carl told me, "but I'm ready to cash out. Let's go to market." I was a little surprised, since Carl, then in his early 40s, was riding a juggernaut with no end in sight.

Carl's company had all the earmarks of a successful sale: It was growing rapidly and had a great EBITDA growth story. Carl had developed a unique process to track highly valuable assets for transportation companies and had created some strong barriers around it. The company's reputation was good, and his customers were enthusiastic brand evangelizers.

As my team gathered and analyzed Carl's operating documents, contracts and financial data, it was clear that Carl would never win any Good Legal Housekeeping Awards. Still, the basics were in place and I reassured my team, "There is hair on every deal, but the overall picture is good." ("Hair" is a catchall we use for the negative elements present in every deal.)

The confidential auction we executed produced 11 highly competitive IOIs from both financial and strategic buyers. As we pruned the buyer pool down to the last two parties, the price climbed. Carl was thrilled when one of the remaining buyers offered a significant options package, and he happily went exclusive with this buyer and signed its more detailed LOI.

About 20 days into the buyer's due diligence, the rep for Carl's buyer called me. "Sorry, Zane, but we are putting our pencils down on this deal. After digging into Carl's contract with XYZ (Carl's key technology supplier), we just aren't comfortable."

"Wait a minute," I sputtered. "The contract between Carl's company and that supplier grants Carl's company an exclusive right to the supplier's patented technology."

"It appears that way on the surface," the buyer's rep admitted, "but my legal due diligence team tells me that without breaching the contract, XYZ can sell or distribute its patented technology to any of Carl's competitors." He concluded, "This contract just doesn't offer us the protection and barrier we had anticipated."

This call was painful for me, but it was nearly devastating for Carl. Ultimately, we resurrected the deal, but only after Carl agreed to convert a portion of his cash payment to an earnout and give up a lucrative stock options package.

Carl wasn't the first (and sadly won't be the last) entrepreneur to be tripped up or knocked out on the way to the closing table by a totally avoidable legal issue. He was able to recover, but many entrepreneurs are not so lucky.

> The investment banker's job is to get you the highest and best price. The attorney's job is to make sure that you keep it.

You could employ the world's most talented investment banker, but if a company isn't legally buttoned-up, no amount of talent will get you to the closing table.

To help you put your legal house in order, I'm going to:

1. Show you the issues we see that have tripped up other owners in their efforts to extract optimal value from their companies.

2. Help you assess whether any of these issues could affect your company today or in the future.

3. Offer concrete recommendations to help you avoid hairy situations like Carl's.

If I succeed, when you finish reading, you'll start to spruce up your legal house and avoid the most common issues.

Top Legal Issues For Tech Companies

I've said it before, and I'll say it again: Buyers and investors hate risk. It's not hard to imagine that sloppiness in your legal issues creates A LOT of risk—for you and for a buyer.

Yes, I expect you have legal counsel, but how do you view them: as drains on cash flow or as an investment in your business's ultimate success and enterprise value?

According to several friends who have created substantial M&A-based legal practices, the most problematic legal issues they see in sales of tech companies are:

- Intellectual Property (IP) Transfer Agreements.
- Undocumented Agreements or Poorly Written Contracts.
- Tax Issues.

Who Owns Your IP?

After earning his degree in accounting, "Grant Dixon" fulfilled his promise to his deeply Southern mama: He snagged a "respectable" job with a major CPA firm, sat for and passed the CPA exam, and put in the long hours necessary to one day become partner.

Now-proud Mother Dixon had spent years fretting about Grant. "That boy spent hours messing around making games on that computer!" she told anyone who would listen. "But look at him now!"

By day, Grant was a bespectacled accountant. By night, however, he was a gamer and software developer.

On his 30th birthday, Grant broke his mama's heart. He left the accounting firm and told her, "I started a company two years ago, and I'm going to see where it goes." He reassured her, "I can always go back to accounting."

Two years after that, Grant's company was growing at an amazing pace. His company had developed a number of exceptional game applications, or brain teasers, geared to customers looking to "exercise" their brains. Several articles in reputable medical journals reported that the games were highly effective in stimulating users' brain activity and short-term memory. As a result, many physicians—including his mother's—were recommending these games to their patients.

Just before turning out the lights on an early November afternoon, Grant opened a message from the senior vice president of corporate development for one of the world's largest health education publishers. "I'm very interested in understanding your goals for your company," it read. "Let's set up a time to talk."

Grant's reaction was instant, outsized and totally understandable. "Could this public company be interested in acquiring my company in an all-cash purchase?" Not wanting to appear too eager, Grant let the message sit for the longest 24 hours of his life.

As soon as Grant responded, the race was on. By December 25, the buyer submitted, and Grant accepted, an LOI ($24 million—all cash), and Grant gave his mama a Christmas to remember.

In mid-February, three weeks into the buyer's due diligence, Grant received another message from the buyer—this time from the head of its legal team. "I'm very interested in understanding more about The Ultimate Geezer Teezer," it read. "Call me immediately."

Before making this call, Grant pulled out the documentation file for his company's most popular game. It all looked fine to him except for one missing assignment. Grant's stomach flipped, and then it flopped when he talked to the buyer's legal rep. "We can't find employment agreements for all of your employees, but we are especially concerned about 'Gideon' (the senior developer for Geezer Teezer). Without that assignment, we have no way to confirm that he has assigned to your company the rights to the IP he has created while an employee."

You guessed it: Grant couldn't come up with the contracts, and the buyer walked.

Ultimately, Grant was able to convince his employees—including Gideon—to sign over their IP rights to his company. Gideon's signature cost Grant a cool $2 million, but that's the price he paid to woo the buyer back to the closing table.

If you believe that you own everything your employees create and your company does not have customized IP agreements with every owner, employee, contractor and consultant who works for it, you are dead wrong. You have also failed to take a critical step in creating an investment-grade company.

There's small comfort in knowing that you are not alone because the three most common transfer agreement problems that many attorneys and I see are:

1. Owners have not had independent contractors and consultants sign transfer agreements.
2. Signed agreements do not delineate a clear line of ownership from creator of the IP (e.g., software, technical framework, unique method) to the company.
3. Signed agreements are not customized to the company's particular product, service or need.

As a result, contractors and consultants own their work product.

Everyone (e.g., employees, consultants, independent contractors) involved in the creation or development of your company's product or service should have assigned all rights to your company *prior* to working on that project or service.

As the italics in the prior sentence indicate, timing matters. The worst time to ask an employee to sign over IP rights is while cruising toward a closing. The best is at the outset of employment. Bring up the topic at any other time and you can expect cultural havoc. Employees will justifiably note, "This isn't how we do things around here!" And what leverage do you have? Once you are negotiating with a buyer, your employees have all the leverage and nothing to gain by signing over their IP rights.

Are You Sharing IP Ownership?

A Word Of Warning: Does your company retain employees, consultants or independent contractors who also work for universities? If so and their work on your product or service relates to their area of expertise, the universities they work for may have rights to "your" product.

A Contract Has To Be In Writing, Right?

IP transfer agreements are just the tip of the legal-housekeeping iceberg. Under the water level are poorly written contracts and those "agreements" we don't consider to be contracts at all. I'm talking about the "agreements" that many owners like "Jerome" make without realizing it.

Jerome was a black-belt software developer who built a leading financial services data analytics firm over five years. He ultimately sold to a large public IT services firm, but in the process not only did he lose a lifelong friend, but he also missed out on the feeling that a check for $38 million can give.

Two weeks before closing, Jerome learned that his longtime friend and sales manager, "Randy," had misinterpreted a comment Jerome had made three years earlier. While at dinner after landing a large new account, Jerome had said, "Randy, I appreciate your sacrifice, and I'll make it all worth your while if we ever have an exit." Randy left that dinner happy to have his efforts recognized with a promise for what he assumed would be a 5 to 7 percent ownership stake in the business.

Jerome didn't give his comment a second thought until he told Randy about the buyer's offer for the business. When Randy reminded Jerome about his "promise," Jerome suggested a thank-you bonus in the neighborhood of $100,000 to $150,000.

"After my sales efforts have driven this company's enterprise value and revenue growth?" Randy asked. But he was thinking, "Surely my good friend Jerome won't be a greedy '$%^&*' when he's walking off with serious cash."

Randy didn't keep these thoughts to himself for long. He expressed them to both Jerome and to the attorney he hired to represent him in a lawsuit naming Jerome and the company as defendants.

Lawsuits have a way of ending friendships and, in this case, would have ended Jerome's transaction as well had he not settled with Randy for over a million dollars.

Undocumented agreements of any kind—but especially those related to ownership/equity and intellectual property—have enormous potential for confusion and conflict. Because comments like "I'll take care of you" are not documented, they can mean "I'll pay you a million dollars" or they might mean "Have a great steak dinner with three of your friends—on me!"

I'm not a big fan of sweeping generalizations, but I make an exception here: In the case of undocumented agreements, money always changes hands, and it always flows from the employer to the employee.

If you can't refrain from these conversations (remember that loose lips sink ships), please, document them. Save yourself money, emotional damage and, most importantly, your relationships.

Poorly Written Contracts…There's No Excuse, But There Is A Price.

Over the years, I've seen a ton of poorly written contracts, and I'm not a lawyer. I can only guess why there are so many deficient contracts—maybe because there's no one right way to write a contract but so, so many wrong ways.

Here's a list of some of the biggest types of contract failures we see in our M&A practice.

Poorly written contracts:

- Share or give away IP rights (to customers or sales agents). I've seen more than a few contracts give full IP rights to a customer (including the right to resell it), with no mechanism to terminate the contract. In one, an industrial tech company had completely given away its IP to its customers. That sounds crazy, but these giveaways frequently happen when large customers (often public companies represented by very sophisticated attorneys) write the contracts and assure owners that the contracts are "standard" and simply reflect the arrangements that they have "with all of their vendors or collaborators."
- Fail to describe rights to use the IP in the narrowest way possible.
- Are assignable to the new owner of your company only with your customers' consent. (If you have 1000 customers, imagine seeking consent from every single one of them. Now imagine the new terms they may demand in return for their consent.)
- Grant exclusivity to a distributor or customer without an ability to rescind that right. Owners usually grant exclusive rights when they are trying to grow quickly. Imagine that you've granted exclusivity to a customer in health care. A year later you receive an LOI from a buyer in the health care space who just happens to be a direct competitor of the customer holding that exclusive right. Without an ability to rescind that right, you have excluded that buyer and possibly a number of other prospective buyers.
- Have conflicting clauses. For example, a contract's term is five years, but it is terminable with 30-days' notice.

Poorly or unwritten contracts are just two examples of lazy record keeping. Lazy record keeping also occurs when any of the following are missing, unsigned or nonexistent: board minutes, equity grants or options, records of grants, leases, bond agreements and/or promissory notes. Keeping track of all of your company's key documents may not be a job you want to undertake, but someone has to do it. How about your corporate secretary?

> When it comes to undocumented promises made to employees about future rewards, every owner defines "reasonable reward" differently. Too many tell me, "I will not pay one dime to that lousy so-and-so." I can only tell them that owners who won't part with dimes at the front end too often lose millions of dollars at the back end.

Top Tax Issues For Tech Companies

Legal, financial and operational aspects of a company aren't separate buckets. I've had to separate them for this book, but a chapter about legal issues is a great place to talk about an aspect of financial operations that can have enormous legal consequences on a company: taxes. I'm not going to tackle all possible tax issues since I'm NO tax expert. Instead, I share with you what I see as the three tax issues with the greatest potential to increase or decrease the value of your company in a market transaction.

> Owners tend to view their businesses as three separate buckets—legal, financial and operational—instead of seeing that all three must be operating well together if they are to achieve the owner's objectives and increase enterprise value in a market transaction.

- Sales & Use Tax
- GAAP Compliance
- Employment-Related Taxes

Sales & Use Tax

Are you collecting and paying all the sales tax required in all the jurisdictions where your company does business? Do you know which states require online sellers to charge and remit taxes, and which collect based on the location of your sales agents or customers? Your attorney does—or should.

"Not to worry, Zane. If we've messed up and a prospective buyer wants me to fix it, I will. We'll just 'fess up' and make things right with the IRS and everybody else when the time comes." Yep, that's what a successful FinTech guy told me during a recent Vistage® presentation. I didn't have enough time to list all the ways his "plan" could go wrong, so I went with my tried-and-true Time Kills Deals argument.

I've never run into a state revenue department that grants absolution to those confessing tax transgressions—at least not before putting the sinner through a time-sucking audit. I asked this gentleman one question: "After your prospective buyer sees that you've played fast and loose 'with the IRS and everybody else,' do you expect the buyer to hang around while you settle up?" He had no answer, but I did: I wouldn't bet the farm on it.

Compliance With Generally Accepted Accounting Principles (GAAP)

As we discussed in Reason 13, GAAP is a collection of commonly followed accounting rules and standards that enable transparent and consistent financial reporting across organizations. These standards matter because:

- GAAP compliance is a fundamental practice for large strategic buyers and private equity groups.
- If your company does not follow GAAP standards, sophisticated buyers and investors will likely recast your company's financial statements during due diligence. This exercise is necessary for them to model how valuable your company is to them and, therefore, what price they can pay.

Ah, recasting: the birthplace and breeding ground for deep and far-reaching disagreements between buyers and sellers about how deferred revenue impacts purchase price.

Let's say that your business recognizes revenue on a cash basis (i.e., upon receipt of payment). For that reason, you (like "Samantha" in the following case study) do not record liabilities for service that customers have paid for but that you will deliver at a future date. Your prospective buyer (or investor) using GAAP standards will calculate this deferred revenue and present to you revised financial statements based on its recalculation. If the deferred revenue liability is (as it can be) a significant dollar amount, it negatively impacts your company's working capital position.

Samantha entered the world of digital marketing by accident when her roommate at Auburn, the editor of the university's student newspaper, asked her to take over the "On the Cheap" column. Each week Samantha covered available student discounts from local merchants.

Just before finals, however, Samantha was too pressed for time to contact all the usual merchants. Instead, she submitted a story about how she used secondhand clothing to define her style. Within weeks, that column turned into a blog—CheapSheek. By graduation, Samantha's blog had nearly 10,000 subscribers, 100,000 repeat viewers per month and was totally monetized.

Samantha continued to leverage her digital marketing experience after graduation and, over the next 12 years, built a company that helped at-home business owners run automated sales campaigns. Her software was a hit—the biggest in her niche industry. By the time I met her at a tailgate party before our shared alma mater's first home game, her company's average 12-month contract—billed up front—was $3,800, and the company was producing over $9 million in annual recurring revenue (ARR).

As soon as Samantha learned what I did for a living, her story of the past six weeks came pouring out. "Out of the blue, a private equity group approached me with an offer of $40.5 million. Zane, that's 4.5x my ARR!"

"Samantha, in my industry we call that 'go home money,'" I replied.

She smiled and pressed on, "After signing the LOI, the PEG brought in its Big Four accounting firm to do its third-party due diligence. That's when the numbers started changing."

I cringed inwardly because I had a pretty good idea of what was coming.

Samantha continued, "The accountants said that I had failed to list our deferred revenue as a liability on our balance sheet. They were right! I booked all subscribers' 12-month revenue up front. What I didn't realize is that my CFO should have listed the corresponding liability necessary to service that revenue over the full contract period. It turns out that we had over $2.8 million of deferred revenue."

I asked, "So your buyer deducted the cost of delivering this revenue from its purchase price?"

Samantha nodded. "It deducted $840,000, or 30 percent of $2.8 million. That really hurt."

Employment-Related Taxes

Yes, we really have to talk about them. If I had not spent the last several years crisscrossing the U.S., speaking about the 17 Reasons to owners in all industry segments, I would not have considered the topic of employee taxes to be worthy of mention—certainly not in a book for seasoned, successful entrepreneurs.

So, I make two observations:

1. State and federal agencies are scrutinizing the classification of workers as either 1099 or W2 because the choice impacts whether or not it's proper to withhold taxes and health care coverage. If these agencies disagree with how you've classified employees, your company is subject to fines and back taxes.

2. Using employees' taxes to fund operations during a company's start-up years is a stretch that I don't recommend. I would not have imagined that owners would use that method beyond the start-up years.

Turns out, I have a very limited imagination.

If you are one of these owners, STOP!

If you are not, but sometimes you are tempted to play the float with your employees' taxes, know that the IRS can hold owners and directors personally liable.

Oldie-But-Goodie Legal Issues

During each year's Silicon Y'all (*http://siliconyall.com*), speakers bring the latest trends or best practices to the attention of our CEO attendees, but we also provide a quick review of the "Oldies But Goodies." When it comes to legal issues that affect companies, those are:

- Pending Lawsuits, aka Loose Cannons.
- Capitalization Table Issues aka Buyer Allergies.

Loose Cannons

Lawsuits—either pending or threatened—make most of us uncomfortable, at best. Buyers are no exception. But to buyers, all types of litigation are not equal. For example, a lawsuit filed by one of your customers will cause a buyer some concern, but a lawsuit threatened or filed by one of your former employees, an ex-founder or one of your ex-partners? These types of suits push all of a buyer's hot buttons.

Entrepreneurs are often very emotional people, so when their relationships with employees, co-founders or partners go sideways, they "solve" the problem by firing them.

Fired employees, discarded co-founders and spurned partners are rarely happy exes. Buyers, usually through experience, understand the enormous damage that these "loose cannons" can do to a company, and they will do everything they can to remove themselves from the line of fire, even if that means walking away from an otherwise profitable deal.

Buyer Allergies

Buyers prefer simple and clean capitalization tables for one reason: Buyers are highly allergic to risk! For the same reason, they are big fans of accurate, properly executed cap tables that list only those active in a company's operations. (Owners who do not work in a business rarely add value over time unless they are highly connected in the industry and are value-added advisors to the business.) Buyers love cap tables in which all parties listed have the same agenda.

But we can't always give buyers what they want, because many of our companies include shareholders with competing agendas (e.g., shareholders of different ages often differ in their reliance on the business for income).

Buyers are also allergic to ambiguity, so the minutes of your shareholder and director meetings cannot be silent (or unclear) about any prior sales of ownership. Are there "uninvited guests" at your table? These guests include those to whom you have committed a portion of ownership—but just haven't gotten around to executing the appropriate legal documents. Remember, "I'll take care of you" may mean 1 percent ownership to you but mean 10 percent to the listening employee.

I met "Delilah" (age 55) at a 17 Reasons Workshop in Dallas. During a break in my presentation, she took me aside to tell me that several possible investors had approached her during the past six months. She'd mentioned these inquiries to "Samson," her 38-year-old co-owner.

"I'd like to pursue the possibility of a liquidity event with one of these investors, even at the most conservative offer that's been floated: 5x EBITDA. But Samson isn't interested in even talking with these folks. He's sure that our business is at an inflection point and poised to achieve 40 percent revenue growth over the next 12 months. He could be right, but I'm just not sure I've got the time, energy or desire to ride this rocket into a completely new orbit."

Competing agendas happen, but they don't need to clash. There are ways to resolve issues so that everyone is happy. For example, I suggested to Delilah that she might choose an investor who shares Samson's goals. Together, they could buy her out (giving her the liquidity she desires) and take the company to the next level.

HOT LEGAL ISSUES

Legal issues in the oldies-but-goodies category aren't the only ones owners have to deal with. We are constantly managing new issues that are "hot buttons" for the buyers or investors whom we hope to attract. The three we'll tackle here are:
- Cybersecurity.
- Data Privacy.
- Health Care.

Cybersecurity

Every day company data is hacked. Companies that have been hacked in recent years include:

> Anthem, AT&T, Chick-fil-A, Domino's Pizza, eBay, Evernote, Google, Feedly, Home Depot, JPMorgan Chase, Jimmy John's, Kmart, LabCorp, Neiman Marcus, P.F. Chang's, Premera Blue Cross, Sony, Staples, Target, UPS, the U.S. Postal Service, U.S. Investigations Services, Viator.com and Yahoo! Mail.

Breaches in smaller technology companies are not as well publicized, so risk-haters that they are, buyers now ask sellers about all security breaches and about what owners have done to protect their companies.

Basic questions include:
- Has your company's data been hacked?
- What policies are in place to protect your data?
- Do you have cybersecurity insurance?
- How have you managed the security of your supply chain?
- If you are outsourcing any functions to vendors, how have you required them to notify you if they are hacked?
- Are you compliant with all payment card industry (PCI) security regulations?

Buyers will attempt to minimize their risk by having you sign applicable representations and warranties. If you have locked down your company's data security, great. If you haven't, hire a reputable cybersecurity firm to perform a security audit, and act immediately on its recommendations.

Data Privacy

While there is no single federal law regulating the collection and use of personal data in the U.S., there is a patchwork of regulations. Like all patches, some overlap, some clash, some are legally enforced by federal agencies (e.g., the Federal Trade Commission and the U.S. Department of Health and Human Services) and others are simply guidelines. The lack of standardization across agencies makes it a challenge to comply with the regulations that apply to all of your company's activities. Your immediate concerns are:
- Do you have a right to mine data you have collected?
- Do you have a right to sell it?
- Data usage may require customer approval.

If your CIO is not an expert in this area (or you are not), find a consultant who is.

Health Care

In the last few years, there have been several huge changes in health care: the adoption of ICD-10 (the 10th version of the International Classification of Diseases), the widespread implementation of electronic health records (EHRs), and the passage of the Patient Protection and Affordable Care Act. Add these to thousands of Medicare and HIPAA (Health Insurance Portability and Accountability Act) regulations and you have a labyrinth of significant and evolving compliance obligations.

If your company is even tangentially involved in health care, expect a buyer to shift any risk involved in assuming these obligations to you through representations and warranties.

If you operate in the health care space, please hire a legal firm with extensive health care experience. The pace of change in this industry segment demands expert legal counsel.

Due Diligence

Every time we check an online restaurant review, conduct background checks on prospective employees, or monitor the online activities of our children, we're doing due diligence. In every aspect of our lives, we take actions to cut through the hype to see what's behind the curtain. The greater the investment we have, or plan to make, in the person or activity, the more thorough we are in our diligence.

Buyers of multimillion-dollar companies are no different. Before they invest millions of dollars, buyers will poke, probe and squeeze every part of a target's business. When you are the one being poked, probed and squeezed, however, the process can feel endless, overdone and intrusive.

Do you remember that buyers are allergic to risk and ambiguity? Well, add drama to that list. Investors simply will not invest in companies that come with legal drama. Meaning, they steer clear of inconsistent contracts, loose personnel policies, poor distribution agreements and pending or threatened lawsuits. If your company has any of these, buyers will find them during due diligence. When they do, the best-case scenario is they assume that you (and/or your management team) are incompetent. The far more likely scenario is pencils down. Show over.

Suitors want quality, not drama. When they open the door of your company only to find it in legal disarray, they assume (and usually correctly) that there are more messy issues in other areas of the business.

I will grant you that *no company is perfect*, especially a fast-growing one. Still, you never want a buyer to discover an issue before you do. Even if the two of you find an issue simultaneously, you are behind the eight ball.

Your approach to legal issues should be to prevent, acknowledge and fix them.

> The time to start cleaning your house is not when the guest is knocking at the door.

To reduce the amount of time due diligence takes and to minimize the number and intensity of the probes, we highly recommend that you actively prepare for the process well in advance. Not only does preparation reduce the time and emotional energy you and your management team will devote to the due diligence process, careful preparation protects your purchase price.

Even if you never sell your business or raise capital from outside investors, when you put your legal house in order, you reap the benefits of operating a legally squared-away company. You can enjoy the confidence and peace of mind that come from building your company on a stable foundation.

You might not be able to attract investors or buyers if your business is not legally buttoned-up.

RECOMMENDATIONS

1. Don't skimp on the important stuff.

Invest in a relationship with stellar legal counsel—preferably an M&A attorney (with expertise in your industry) from a multidisciplinary law firm. No one person can do it all (taxes, patents, regulations, etc.), and when you hire a firm, you pay for what you need only when you need it.

2. Protect your IP because the sale of your company depends on it.

Every owner, employee, consultant and independent contractor involved in the creation or development of your company's product or service should assign all IP rights to your company. As a standard part of your new employee onboarding process, get signatures on non-solicitation agreements and noncompetes.

- Do you have signed IP transfer agreements with every:
  - · Current employee?
  - · Former employee?
  - · Consultant and independent contractor?
  - · Current and former owner?
- Are the rights to use your product or service as narrowly defined as possible?
- Are your contracts assignable to a buyer without customer consent?
- Do your contracts include the right to revoke an exclusive right to use or distribute your product or service?
- Do you have technology IP that is patentable?
- Do you have a timeline of submitted patents and their status?

3. Kill the zombies—now.

If you have mentioned—no matter how casually—sharing the bounty from a one-day sale, memorialize that conversation. To memorialize is to define in writing what you meant by "share." Use a stock warrant, stock option, stay bonus or "bonus upon sale agreement." Whatever you do, clarity and communication at the front end trump fuzzy, conflicting and always-expensive memories when a buyer appears on the scene.

Casual conversations are like zombies: You think they're dead, but they're not. Have you made any verbal agreements formally or informally? If so, confirm your understanding with the recipient and document it.

4. Clean house from top to bottom.

Clean, complete, current contracts have real value to buyers, so assign the task of cleaning up and maintaining all contracts to your corporate secretary, COO or CFO. Instruct them to start at the top: customer contracts. Then have them move on to those with suppliers/vendors, landlords, lenders, employees, contractors and consultants. Include in your supplier contracts a clause stating that the obligations of the contract "survive" a change of ownership of your company. This contractual "tweak" better positions you to garner a significant premium for your company.

5. Stop, just stop.

If you are "playing the float" on employee taxes to operate your company, knock it off. Now.

6. Disarm the cannons.

If you are involved in a lawsuit or you can see one on the horizon—especially one involving a former employee, an ex-founder or one of your ex-partners—make sure your attorney knows your time frame for seeking an investor or buyer. If necessary, find and make a reasonable settlement before you go to market.

7. Set a beautiful (cap) table.

If all company stock owners have not signed a Disclosure to Investors, Form D and all required federal and state-appropriate notices of filing, you have work to do.

8. If you or your CIO is not an expert in cybersecurity, hire a consultant.

Until you find the right person, do the following: Choose security over customer convenience. Purge data that is not relevant, purchase cybersecurity insurance, reinforce your firewalls, and contractually require vendors to notify you of security breaches.

TAKEAWAYS

1. Buyers hate risk.

Yes, I do realize how often I beat this drum, and I'll keep beating it in an attempt to help you create an investment-worthy company.

If your legal house isn't buyer ready (e.g., you have unprotected IP, inconsistent contracts and/or pending litigation), you will exit the Transaction Express at Due Diligence Station. Scratch that. You won't even ride the train to Letter of Intent Junction.

2. Build a solid foundation for your purchase price from day one.

The foundation for your company's purchase price is made up of best practices and clean contracts. Best practices include adherence to GAAP standards, privacy protection for data, security of your systems, organization of your cap table, and more. All of your contracts (with employees, contractors, consultants, vendors/suppliers, lenders and customers) must be appropriate to your company and free from hidden land mines. All rights to your IP must be nailed down.

3. Control what you can. That's your job.

Once you enter the sale process, bad things that you are unable to control can happen: a public company's stock price can fall, a large customer of yours may find a greener pasture, and/or the sales you expected to close don't. As a result, your company would fail to meet its projections. But if you have to deal with issues that you should before entering the sale process (e.g., cleanup contracts; settle a lawsuit; resolve a sales tax dispute; or secure signatures on all agreements from employees, former employees or former partners), you've been a poor steward of your time, talents and resources.

It isn't your responsibility to perform every job involved in legal housekeeping, but its on you to make sure that your house/company is buttoned-up and sale ready.

REAS💡N

You Cannot Explain Why Your Company Exists And/Or Cannot Tell Its Story.

CREATE, CONDENSE,
PRACTICE AND REFINE
A STORY THAT ENGAGES
YOUR STAKEHOLDERS
AND INVESTORS.

How do you respond when your mother-in-law asks, "Exactly what do you do for a living?" Your answer may not be as comprehensive as it is when prospective customers, employees, investors and buyers ask, but it should be no less compelling. Being able to deliver a great elevator pitch and having a data-driven executive summary (your pitch's counterpart) pay huge dividends well beyond your mother-in-law's peace of mind.

Most owners believe that they are absolutely capable of telling their company's story. As the following story illustrates, most owners are wrong.

Two years ago, I was invited to observe a daylong seminar for a handpicked group of business owners in South Florida. In a nondescript, over-air-conditioned conference room, the leader had assembled 16 CEOs of nice-sized agricultural import businesses ($5 million to $60 million in revenue) to talk about implementing business growth strategies. He opened the day with a request, "I'd like each of you to come to the front of the room and give us your three-minute elevator pitch about your business."

"A good warm-up exercise," I thought as he listed on a flip chart the questions that he expected each pitch to cover.

His very basic questions were:

1. What does your company do?

2. What problem do you solve for your target market?

3. Describe your target market and ideal customer.

4. Why do you win?

5. Why do you lose?

6. What is your current growth strategy?

7. What is your vision statement?

I expected owners to jump at the chance to deliver an uninterrupted monologue about one of their favorite topics—their companies—to a room full of CEOs. Instead, I sat amazed as owner after owner stumbled and struggled through this seemingly simple exercise.

What I witnessed was beyond embarrassing. It was heartbreaking and shocking—a true goat rodeo of purple prose, fuzzy thinking and rambling responses. It was as if the first six owners to respond were thinking about these questions for the first time.

Finally, the seventh CEO got up and crushed it. "Brooke" wasn't just a little better than the others; she was over-the-top better. Her three-minute pitch was a work of art. Everyone noticed the difference, and no one wanted to follow her organized and passionate address.

Brooke had masterfully articulated her reasons for being in business. She had painted a clear picture of how and why her company was going to grow and prosper alongside her clients. If prospective employees had been in that room, I don't doubt that they all would have picked Brooke as their employer. If prospective customers had heard her pitch, they'd have moved their business to her company. And if investors had been in the room, they would have been making plans to follow up with her as soon as the event ended.

> A great presentation or speech is the child of strong conviction and repeated practice. It is delivered with sincerity, vulnerability and deep feeling, but it is the practice, practice and more practice before you utter the first word that makes it yours.
>
> Dr. Paul Tarence
> My dad, and former rhetoric and public address professor

While employees and customers may tolerate vague, uninspiring pitches, buyers and investors do not. They don't have time to waste with leaders who can't articulate clear, highly rationalized strategies and execute them with precision. If investors can't see why your business deserves to exist, they won't waste their time—and certainly not their capital—on it. The ability to tell a great story is a requirement. In the minds of listeners, the story you tell frames who you are as a company, the "why" of the organization and your strategy. A compelling pitch paints a vivid picture of an enduring and thriving company and separates you from the pack.

If a great speech is the child of both conviction and practice, most of the presentations I heard in that Florida meeting room were from single-parent homes. I don't doubt that every one of those owners believed in their businesses with all their hearts. But Brooke's pitch stole the show; her delivery was natural, organized and compelling because she had practiced!

Let's look at what good pitches and executive summaries contain.

Your Elevator Pitch

In less than three minutes, your pitch should include four points:

1. Who you are and your reason for being in business.

2. How your company makes money.

3. How your company invests money.

4. Where your company is going and how will it grow.

Your Executive (Or Investment) Summary

Your executive summary is your elevator pitch in crystallized, written form. It makes no difference whether you first create your elevator pitch then executive summary, or vice versa. Nailing the content is what's key. Both must give outsiders a thumbnail, but holistic, understanding of your company, and do so in a way that holds their attention.

While their details are unique to your company, impactful executive summaries include:

1. **Revenue Model.** Answering the question "How do you make money?" is the most important element of your executive summary. In two to three sentences explain how your company generates revenue and how revenue links to your selling, general and administrative expenses (SG&A) and to your cost of goods sold (COGS).

2. **Value Proposition.** What need does your company address, or what problem does it solve for customers? Does your company bring any unique features, services, experience or qualities to addressing that need or solving that problem? What demonstrable ROI does your product or service deliver for your ideal customer?

3. **Financial Summary.** Not all versions of your summary will include financial details, but potential investors or buyers want a broad overview. This can be a simple P&L statement showing only totals for revenue, COGS, gross margin, operating expenses and net income. Pictures and graphs are often the best way to communicate numbers.

4. **Addressable Market.** Which industries do you serve? Who is your target customer? How large is the market? What is your serviceable market? If your market is growing, how quickly? What is your market share?

5. **Competitive Advantage.** Why do customers choose to do business with your company rather than with your competitors? More efficient processes? A vertically integrated supply chain? Proprietary technology? Better employees?

6. **Growth Strategy.** Here's your chance to crystallize your company's vision/mission. Include no more than three goals (e.g., expand into new markets, develop new products and grow through acquisition) that are attainable given the current state of your business, and outline the strategies you'll use to reach them.

7. **Key Facts.** Relevant statistics vary by industry but may include:
   a. Year the company was founded.
   b. City and state of headquarters.
   c. Number of locations.
   d. Number of customers.
   e. Number of employees.
   f. Average customer tenure/customer retention rate.
   g. Industry standard metrics/stats (For example, a SaaS company would include monthly recurring revenue, retention rate, usage figures, average contract value, customer acquisition cost, etc. An ecommerce company would include average order size, cart abandonment rate, conversion rate, customer lifetime value, etc.).

Consider communicating these facts in a timeline or chart. Figure 15.1 is an example of an executive summary (or "investment summary") that we would create for an audience of debt or equity providers.

Both your summary and pitch should be brief, data driven, easy to understand and compelling. If the response to your presentation isn't "I get it!" or in the case of a buyer isn't "I see why this business makes sense both today and in the future," you aren't there yet.

FIG. 15.1 Investment Summary

Market Leader in Widget Implementation

Overview: The company dominates the micro-widget market.

· It specializes in three major widget types that serve health care, insurance and finance customers.
· Its industry-leading products are differentiated by higher quality and longer usable life.
· The increase in same-customer sales year after year demonstrates strong customer appreciation for superior technology and customer service.
· Due to increased widget production capacity, the company is quickly moving into the automobile market.

WIDGET SALES BY QUARTER

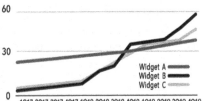

REVENUE BY QUARTER

INVESTMENT HIGHLIGHTS

Rapid Revenue Growth
· By rapidly increasing sales of Widget C, the company has achieved near 100% revenue CAGR over the past two years, as shown above.
· The company's flagship product (Widget A) provides a stable base for continued growth.

Large Addressable Market
· The company can further penetrate the three very large market segments it currently serves.
· The company is expanding its product line.
· The company has scaled its number of employees and its sales staff to maintain its growth trajectory in current and new markets.

Robust Technological Process and Product
· The company exhibits strong pricing power as the industry's quality leader and is able to effectively generate cash by operating at a higher margin than industry peers.
· The company's seamless widget development allows for quicker market entrance with new widget products.

I have only made this letter longer because I have not had the time to make it shorter.[45]

Blaise Pascal
Mathematician and physicist

Your Audience: Investors And Buyers

Once you have the content of your pitch and summary figured out, you're going to adapt it to various audiences: prospective customers and employees, bankers, potential investors or lenders, suppliers, strategic partners, and even friends or family members who want to understand what you do. For each group, consider the sophistication and interest level of your listeners and customize the words you use and the level of detail you provide.

Think of your executive summary as a resume. Do you follow up on ones that are vague, don't define the applicant's skill sets and expertise, and contain a typo or two? Do you waste time trying to figure out how a candidate might fit into your company?

You don't. And buyers don't.

Strategic buyers and private equity groups review hundreds, if not thousands, of investment opportunities each year. Yes, thousands. As my friend Bryce Youngren pointed out in Reason 5 (page 105) financial buyers typically review 1,000 companies before closing ONE.

> If the key aspects of an executive summary confuse me, that's a no. If my eyes glaze over halfway down the page, that's a no. If an owner can't deliver well-organized, relevant data in a memorable way, I'm not inclined to say yes.
>
> Senior Vice President
> of Corporate Development
> Business services company

If your executive summary doesn't tell them exactly what your business does, how it makes money and how you plan to execute your growth strategy, they don't call to ask questions. They move on to summaries that communicate how well a company aligns with the readers' investment mandates.

"A confused mind always says no." I don't know who first said this, but it is as true of two-year-olds as it is of institutional buyers reviewing executive summaries.

You May Be A Star, But You Are Not A Soloist.

Your executive summary not only keeps you on task, but it also focuses your team on its core competencies and constantly reminds all of you why your customers choose to do business with you. This summary should be a great communication tool and team unifier.

Your job as a leader is to make sure everyone on your team understands the summary and can, in turn, deliver a compelling elevator pitch. If you do not require this of your team…well, here's how that worked out for one owner.

Years ago, "Aurora," the owner of a company in the online advertising space, asked us to help her with some discussions she had started with a potential majority recapitalization investor. She did not want to run a full market process because she was convinced that she'd found her partner. We agreed to help her organize her data room and assist her team in building a financial model.

When my team reviewed the numbers, we found that most metrics indicated that her company was an excellent investment. The company was recognized as an industry leader, and her highly experienced management team had spearheaded annual revenue growth of over 55 percent for the past few years. Her company's EBITDA margins continued to expand along with growth. We found that the systems she put in place made the company scalable and her market was large enough to support substantial continued growth.

After we prepared high-level materials that highlighted her company's strengths, we talked to her about the next step: fielding a call with her interested buyer.

"We want to come out of the gate strong, so let's review an outline of an introductory management call," I suggested.

"Not necessary," Aurora assured me. *"I've been handling calls from potential investors for years. I don't need you hovering during this get-acquainted call. I promise I'll bring you in if something gets technical."*

Even after I made my best case for preparing for and practicing her team's presentation, Aurora blew me off. *"We know our company better than anyone,"* she said with confidence.

Against my better judgment, and after explaining to Aurora again how much was at stake, I agreed to her terms and authorized my team to schedule an initial management call with the potential buyer.

As promised, Aurora did ask me to follow up with the prospective buyer. When my team called the buyer, we ran headfirst into a remarkable lack of enthusiasm. In multiple ways, the buyer expressed confusion about the basic functions of Aurora's company. Here are just a few of the buyers' comments: *"We don't understand the revenue streams" "It isn't clear to us what makes the company unique" "We don't understand the growth strategy"* and *"We can't get comfortable with the business model."*

This seemingly great-fit buyer had been intrigued enough by the high-level information we had provided about Aurora's company to want to pursue the opportunity, but after a single management call was confused and unenthusiastic. What happened?

When we called Aurora and members of her team to ask some of the same questions that we knew the buyer had asked, the problem became immediately clear. Neither Aurora nor members of her management team could clearly communicate the most important functions of the business.

For example, when we asked, *"How do you make money?"* answers not only varied widely but were long-winded and highly technical. When we asked, *"Who is your target market?"* their answers were vague. When we asked, *"Where do you see opportunity for growth?"* managers sounded hesitant as they rambled on until they sputtered and gave up. Their *"explanations"* of the company's business model and prospects for growth left prospective buyers confused and completely unmotivated to continue the conversation.

Without a compelling story, Aurora and her team turned a potentially large offer into *"Thanks, but no thanks"* from their highly qualified investor.

Aurora and her team taught me two important lessons: Having an executive summary is one of the 17 characteristics of an investment-grade company, and NEVER let a client *"wing it"* with a serious investor!

But summaries have value beyond simply preparing for a buyer. Executive summaries provide everyone a single vision of who the company is and where it is going. Shared understanding has a powerful impact on future performance because it enables employees to "buy in" to achieving the company's goals and empowers them to act as ambassadors for the brand.

"Compelling" Defined

I've used one word over and over that should describe your pitch and summary: "compelling." If you finish this chapter and remember only one thing, let it be the importance of making our messages compelling. If your executive summary and elevator pitch are ho-hum, they are worthless. Forgettable stories don't cut it. (And as Brooke demonstrated to her colleagues, neither do unorganized presentations.)

Owners find their own stories to be thoroughly compelling. I do. You do. We're fascinated by what we do and how we do it. Perhaps you haven't realized it yet but—I'll try to break this news to you gently—the rest of the world is not fascinated by you or by me.

We *could be* fascinating if we communicated relevant information in a way that made people want to know more about why our companies have been, are, and will continue to be successful. People pay attention when we communicate in the way that our audience "really hears" and finds engaging. The burden is on us to be interesting to listen to. It is our job as leaders to evoke positive emotions from our listeners and readers. Properly packaging our message truly does create value.

Since packaging is part of our job, let's talk about the qualities that make a message compelling:

- **Relevant.** There's a place for "all the news that's fit to print." Neither your executive summary nor your elevator pitch is that place. Ruthlessly limit your story to its most interesting points.
- **Simple.** Present information in a logical way. In written presentations, make sure the layout is clean (e.g., use subheadings and bullet points).
- **Clear.** Use words that are unambiguous. In writing, use charts judiciously. You don't have to be a great orator or writer to attract and keep your audiences' attention. But it helps!
- **Succinct.** Readers and listeners are easily bored, so make your points quickly. Eliminate superfluous adjectives and adverbs, and stick to the facts. If you can't wield a bonsai shear to your pitch or summary, find a candid colleague or trusted mentor who will.

Winners Don't "Wing It."

Remember what my dad said about great speeches? The part about practice, practice and more practice? He could have been talking about what makes a great pianist, stunt person or quarterback. No winning quarterback takes the field on a Saturday or Sunday afternoon and "wings it." Winning and "winging it" are just not compatible.

If you have not learned by heart the compelling story of your business or have not "made it yours," you can't be creative, nimble or focused. You certainly can't tailor your pitch to the individual listener or to the reason you are asked to deliver it. That's just impossible when you are searching for the right words and concepts that will resonate with listeners.

I compare memorizing your story to having good manners or muscle memory. We teach our kids table manners because we don't want them so preoccupied with wondering which fork to use that they can't concentrate on the conversation. When premier athletes throw a pitch, hit a topspin shot, or shoot a free throw, they've done it tens of thousands of times. Their bodies and subconscious minds know exactly what to do. That's how your executive summary and elevator pitch should work.

One day I stopped to reflect on what knowledge, relationships and skills differentiated our business from its competitors. A teammate pointed out that I had overlooked the cornerstone of our practice's success: storytelling. All our know-how, deal experience and capital connections were critical to great outcomes, but all were irrelevant if we could not articulate a compelling story about a client's market position, growth potential and strategic value. Since that day, I have encouraged owners to put as much effort into crafting their stories as they do to identifying their core differentiators.

Sterling Smith
Managing Director
Founders Advisors

FIG. 15.2 **Strategic Plan Summary**

5-Year Vision	Current YE Goals

CORE VALUES
Treat customers with respect, fairness and honesty.

Provide the leading widgets in current markets and expand into promising adjacent markets.

Continually improve our people and processes.

BRAND PROMISE
Drive change one widget at a time.

STRATEGY STATEMENT
Drive innovation and change through our markets and create additional efficiencies through the implementation of our widgets.

CRITICAL NUMBERS
LTM Revenue:	$60MM
LTM Units:	456
LTM EBITDA:	$11.6MM

DUPONT ANALYSIS
LTM Net Income:	$10MM
Avg. Total Assets:	$18MM
Total Equity:	$32MM
Return on Equity:	31.2%

FINANCIAL TARGET
Widgets Sold:	1,500
Sales:	$150MM
Widget Products:	6
Markets Served:	5
Net Income:	22%
Total Assets:	$35MM
Total Equity:	$70MM
Return on Equity:	47.1%

WHAT IT LOOKS LIKE
We Lead the Industry in Quality:
· Proprietary Technology
· Continued Innovation
· Robust Processes
· Friendly Sales & Customer Service Staff

New Customers
· Leverage past relationships and experience to win new customers.
· Increase market share.
· Win business in new markets.
· Attend and sponsor industry conferences.

New Facilities
· Continued growth forces multiple locations.
· Potential international sales presence
· Select new cities for regional presence in North America.
· More efficient production

FINANCIAL TARGET
Widgets Sold:	600
Sales:	$72MM
Widget Products:	4
Markets Served:	3
Net Income:	18%
Total Assets:	$15MM
Total Equity:	$35MM

WHAT IT LOOKS LIKE
Development Leads the Way
· Widget D in production
· New price points to gain market share
· Widgets C & A profitability drives increase in net income.
· Purchase and finance assets for Widget D development.

New Employees
· Promote Eric to manager.
· Hire three new sales reps.
· Hire five developers for Widget D.
· Start quarterly employee events for morale.

Balance Sheet Initiatives
· Increase cash position and leverage short-term investments to increase return.
· Build buffer to invest in developing our fourth served market next year.
· Decrease payables to promote stronger working capital position.

Quarterly Plan		

KEY METRICS & INITIATIVES
Increase QoQ Widget Sales:	20%
Total Widget D Investment:	$4MM
Employee Count:	50
Additional Plant Capacity:	100 Units
Six Sigma Implementation:	40%
Widget B Gross Margin:	30%
Customer Count:	33

Q1/Q2 INITIATIVES
Drive Current Product Sales
· Reduce Inventory of Widgets A – C.
· Increase rack storage for Widget D.
· Increase sales rewards for Widget D pre-order and pipeline leads.
Employee Culture
· Company picnic in Q2
· Increase warehouse bonus.
· Treat sales team to dinner.
· New break room and employee amenities

Q3/Q4 INITIATIVES
Increase Industry Awareness
· Attend three trade shows for each key industry segment.
· Marketing campaigns for key industries
· Customer appreciation gifts and holiday cards
· Note key product changes and development process for refining/trimming in Year 2.
Banking & Finance Relationship
· Finalize previous year audit.
· Renegotiate current debt.
· Implement $3MM line of credit through current facility.

Memorizing also prevents you from leaving out key points and gives you confidence in your delivery. If you hesitate or grasp for your points, you may ruin your one opportunity to make a great connection for your business. You never know when or where you might meet a prospective client, employee or investor.

Laminate Your Executive Summary, And Keep It Up To Date.

I am a big fan of laminating an executive summary. A placemat-size, laminated document (or what I call a "Waffle House® menu") serves as a powerful discussion tool and communicates important ideas to your clients, recruits, employees, suppliers and investors. Laminating your executive summary does not mean that you do not revisit it on at least an annual basis and update it as necessary.

Invest the time and energy to design, create, update and deliver an A+ executive summary. You'll reap the benefits in every interaction with all stakeholders.

From The Summary And Pitch, A Strategic Plan Summary Is Born.

Once you create an executive summary, you should create a summary of your strategic plan. (For an example, please see Figure 15.2) It should communicate the tactical plan for improving your KPIs and summarize the main features of your growth strategy. Your strategic plan summary communicates your operational goals and vision to your leadership team and key advisors. Compare its level of detail to the information in an investment summary (Figure 15.1) that is used to raise capital or sell equity.

> ## You might not be able to attract investors or buyers if you can't articulate a compelling elevator pitch about your business and clearly present your business unit economics.

RECOMMENDATIONS

1. Know your own story.

Leaders of investment-grade companies can tell the story of their companies in a way that informs and intrigues listeners. A great pitch separates you from your competitors.

If I listened to your three-minute pitch, would I be able to answer these questions:

1. Who are you, and what's your reason for being in business?
2. How does your company make money?
3. How does your company invest money?
4. Where is your company going, or what is your growth strategy?

2. Put it on one page.

In both your elevator pitch and executive summary, limit yourself to the most relevant and compelling information.

- Is your executive summary well designed and pleasant to the eye?
- Does it include the most important elements?
  - Revenue model
  - Value proposition
  - Financial summary

> · TAM (Total Addressable Market)
> · Competitive advantage
> · Key facts/metrics
> · Growth strategy
>
> - Is it clean, simple and compelling?
> - Does it rely on provable data?

3. Relate to your audience.

Not all data is appropriate for all audiences, so you'll adjust your elevator pitch to your purpose and to the sophistication of your audience. The "standard" executive summary contains information you and your team will use to educate (in varying levels of detail) prospective customers and employees, vendors/suppliers and interested family members. Your investment summary covers the information you'll use to solicit equity investors or debt providers.

4. Take it to your team.

Once you've gathered the information you need to create your executive summary, plan an off-site meeting with your leadership team. If you let your team take the first crack at an executive summary, give them one of the examples in this chapter to use as a template. Oversee their work, but hold senior executives accountable for producing each part.

5. Solicit candid feedback.

A lot can get lost between what we say and what others hear.

- Have you asked other trusted owners or advisors/mentors to critique your pitch and executive summary?
- Have you used their input to improve?

6. Laminate and use your executive summary, and keep it relevant.

Once you and your team "finalize" your executive summary, don't let it collect dust in a drawer or disappear on your desktop. Give this document the attention it deserves.

- Do you continually refer to it?
- Do you carry it with you?
- Do you bring it to employee lunches, meetings with prospective clients and employees, investor presentations, etc.?
- Do you review it at least annually?

7. Practice and memorize your pitch.

In three minutes, can you tell me a clear, concise and compelling story that highlights your company's growth rate, scalable processes and reputation? No rambling, ad-lib, stream-of-consciousness tales are acceptable.

- Have you practiced your pitch until it is authentic and deeply felt?
- Does your pitch lead with and communicate your "big rock" elements?[43]

8. Preach it.

Share your elevator pitch and executive summary with all the members of your leadership team. Ask them to create their own pitches consistent with your company's summary, and make sure they can tell the story as well as you can. Then you and your leadership team should tell your company's story to employees, prospective customers and prospective employees, bankers/lenders and potential buyers/investors.

9. Update and refine it.

An executive summary is an evolving document, not a stone tablet. As your business grows and evolves, so should your executive summary. We laminate summaries; we don't deep-freeze them.

TAKEAWAYS

1. The ability to articulate your company's story in three minutes or in one page adds enterprise value to your company.

Packaging and presentation create value.

2. It is your job to organize your company's story in a manner that attracts stakeholders (prospective employees and customers, investors, vendors and family members).

It is also your job to make sure that your management team and employees can tell the same story.

3. Stellar executive summaries and elevator pitches don't just happen; they take intentional work and ongoing attention.

They involve: (1) understanding your business model, (2) organizing that information to tell a story, (3) delivering that story in a compelling way, and (4) continually refining the content as you gather feedback each time you deliver it.

4. Effective elevator pitches and executive summaries elicit "Tell me more!" responses (not yawns) from listeners.

Ideally, they create active evangelizers for your business.

REAS🔆n

You Are Unprepared To Reap A Return On Your Investment.

DEVELOP A REALISTIC EXIT STRATEGY AT EVERY BUSINESS STAGE TO OPTIMIZE RETURN.

Begin with the end in mind.

Steven Covey, Author

I know it's going to be a great day at the office when there's an early-stage entrepreneur on my calendar and our agenda includes reviewing business models, growth strategies and pitch decks. Typically missing from the agenda, however, is perhaps the most underrated of the 17 Reasons: a viable, well-thought-out, realistic, and flexible exit plan.

I'm no longer surprised by this omission, but, in a sense, I suppose I am. How can owners who are consumed with producing strong financial returns on a daily, quarterly and annual basis pay little to no attention to the return on their enormous investments of time, cash and sweat equity? Surely they've wondered, "How will I get my (and my investors') money back and when?" and "What must happen for my company to have viable exit options that produce outsized returns on my invested capital?"

Inevitably, I find that they have. Now, is their thinking thorough or realistic? That's another question entirely.

"Matt" was the college roommate of "Dustin," a client whose company I had helped sell to a private equity group. Both had started out as engineering students, but Matt became fascinated with biomedical engineering and had gone on to medical school. In addition, Matt had created a monitoring and intervention application for people with chronic high blood pressure. When speaking with Dustin, Matt shared that he'd been contacted by two interested parties (aka buyers) in the past few months. Dustin suggested to Matt that we meet.

When I met with Matt, he described his app and the results that health systems he'd partnered with were achieving. I asked him if he'd created a business plan for his company, BeatBeatBeat. I suspect that Dustin had warned Matt about this part of our meeting, because Matt reached into an oversized port-folio case and, with a flourish, dropped onto my desk a laminated, full-color, 12-by-18-inch executive summary.

At first glance, it contained all of the basics: revenue model, value proposition, addressable market, competitive advantages and a quick summary of the key facts about Matt's company. Those included the year of founding, number of employees and customers, average customer tenure and retention rate, monthly recurring revenue, and customer acquisition cost. Then I spotted it—tucked into the bottom corner was a small green box titled "Exit."

Since most entrepreneurs don't include an exit strategy in their executive summaries, I once again sus-pected that Dustin had a hand in preparing Matt for this meeting. What I read, however, convinced me that these were Matt's thoughts alone:

> **In 10 to 15 years, ownership will be ready to sell BeatBeatBeat to a global health care, cloud computing or giant software company (e.g., Microsoft, Oracle or IBM). Alternatively, man-agement will consider pursuing an IPO.**

So close, yet so far off the mark. With most of Matt's 17 Reasons in order, I decided to start this meeting with Reason 16 and work backward.

Matt had unknowingly violated two of the rules I ask entrepreneurs to remember when they consider how they'll ultimately reap the return on their investment:

1. Acquisition by a Microsoft, Amazon, Oracle, Google, McKesson or IBM is not an exit strategy. Being purchased by a technology behemoth—like winning the Powerball® jackpot—is a dream, a hope, a fantasy. Relying on a big-name acquirer or an IPO as your strategy to reap a return is not a strategy.

2. You are an investor, so be impatient with your capital. Your exit strategy shouldn't be on a horizon that's more than three to five years away. You and all of your stakeholders should have the option to "get off the train" every three years. Being stranded with no exit options is not good!

The five exit strategy topics that Matt and I talked about in my office that day are the same ones we'll discuss in this chapter:

1. Know why it pays to be "exit ready" at all times.

2. Know what your company must be in order for you to have viable exit options. (Hint: 17 characteristics come to mind.)

3. Know what you and your stakeholders need your exit to accomplish. (What are your specific needs, goals and nonnegotiables?)

4. Understand an exit planning process.

5. Understand the market process that will generate optimum control and results, mitigate your risk, and give you peace of mind throughout your exit. (That's the topic of Reason 17.)

But before I could help Matt develop a realistic exit strategy, I had to make my case for why an entrepreneur who considered himself to be years away from exiting his company should spend valuable time thinking about it.

"Matt, I've been doing deals for over 20 years. Never in all that time has even one founder/seller of a software or tech-enabled services company ever said to me, 'Zane, I sold or recapitalized my company

too early. I really wish I hadn't done that.' On the other hand, I can't tell you how many times I've heard, 'Why didn't I pursue the offer I had on the table two years ago?' or 'Why didn't I take growth capital from that value-added PEG? What was I thinking? Why wasn't I better prepared when I knew that day would come?'"

"Okay, Zane," Matt responded. "So owners have regrets, but I'm years away from anyone making me the kind of offer I'd even consider."

"Really?" I asked. "That's not what Dustin told me." I continued, "You are already at the 'pick-or-don't-pick' point . . . a choice home gardeners must make every summer about the tomatoes in their gardens."

I'm sure that Matt was now wondering why Dustin had suggested that we meet, so I quickly plowed on, "Do gardeners pick that almost-perfectly-ripe tomato now, possibly saving it from bad weather or rabbits, or do they leave it on the vine just one more day to sweeten? Some pick the tomato and put it in the kitchen window. Others leave it on the vine, only to find that a nasty nighttime critter dined on it before they had the chance to harvest it."

"So you're telling me that I need to know when to pick my tomatoes?" Matt asked with more than a little skepticism in his voice.

"Well, yes and no. Choosing the right time to exit your company is much more than a tomato-picking or regret-prevention exercise, but there are similarities." I went on to quickly explain what I meant. "The consequences of picking the right time to exit your company are far more significant than those of picking tomatoes at the right time. And the nighttime critters that threaten your business can damage it faster than a rabbit can ravage a whole bushel of tomatoes."

"Rabbits?" Matt's voice trailed off.

"Competitors dropping into your market space, tech obsolescence, macroeconomic risks," I clarified. "Those risks to your business are real, so you must be prepared to exit or recapitalize your company (or pick your tomatoes) before the rabbits . . . I mean, when market conditions are most favorable."

As the point I was trying to make became clear, Matt exhaled with relief and I resolved to improve my tomato-picking/rabbits analogy. Still, I wanted to make one more argument. "In addition to making sure that you and your company are prepared to sell when the time is right, the preparation process has other really critical benefits." I paused before ticking off the following list.

Thinking about and taking steps toward preparing your business and yourself for exit:

- Gives you the opportunity to operate a better business before you exit and have more fun along the way.
- Positions your company to recruit top talent, attract great customers and use your company's equity as a currency in acquisitions.
- Positions your company to raise capital if your growth strategy calls for it.
- Makes it possible for you to adjust or exit quickly when change affects your products or services. Unprepared owners risk becoming marooned in an obsolescent segment of the market.
- Creates an investment-grade company with the foundation for growth that financial buyers demand.
- Makes you the master of, instead of the servant to, your business.

Matt looked both relieved and amused. "Zane, at first the whole tomato thing made me think you were telling me to forget about building a company that I love running and instead concentrate on building one for someone else to eat."

"Maybe the rabbit idea needs to go," I agreed, "but I don't want you to take your exit strategy and its timing any less seriously than you've taken all of the other issues on your executive summary."

Of course, the "other issues" on Matt's executive summary were 16 of the Reasons that make a company investment grade.

The point I tried to make to Matt (and in this chapter) is not to ignore Reason 16: a viable exit strategy. Don't take your business exit opportunities lightly. Think through and plan for them.

WHY IT PAYS TO BE EXIT READY AT ALL TIMES

Intentional Owners Keep An Eye On Their Tomatoes...Er, Exits.

Smart owners share a characteristic with Navy SEALs and Mafia dons: They keep one eye on the exit at all times and in all settings. They know that response time matters, and they situate themselves to retain maximum control. Intentional owners are self-aware enough to have defined what they want and need from their businesses. Then they set about reaching that goal.

Healthy owners are those who think about their companies in terms of return. We have defined what we want and need from our businesses in terms of financial security for ourselves, our families, the generations that follow and our valued employees. We see our companies as the vehicles that will carry us to our goals. Because of that mindset, healthy owners enjoy balanced relationships with their companies. Our businesses work for us instead of the other way around. In balanced relationships, we aren't so focused on the day-to-day that we ignore the horizon. We continually scan it to see which buyers are out there, what they look for (and whether we've got what they want), and when the timing is right to pursue them.

Do you remember Gil from the Introduction? I put his story up front to illustrate what happens when owners fail to make their companies investment grade. Gil's company had all the necessary tools to: (1) build the branded intellectual property or products that could have generated healthy recurring income streams, (2) erect strong barriers to entry, (3) develop sales and marketing systems, and (4) sustain high margins. If he had done so, numerous buyers would have been interested in his business. Because he had not, Gil had no good option but to close the doors.

The M&A market in his niche was healthy and active, but Gil had never responded to even one of the many PEG outreach emails he'd received over the years. Instead, ignorance—and a failure to think about how he'd eventually reap the investment he'd made in his company—cost him, his family and his team dearly. Fortunately, Gil had invested a significant amount of his income in commercial real estate. Not all owners are so lucky.

> Owners of investment-grade companies are always looking ahead to the horizon. Understanding current trends in the M&A marketplace and how those trends influence their exit options is part of being proactive. Owners who meet regularly with investment bankers also gain insights that help them refine their competitive strategies. The most successful market processes that I have ever led involved owners who understood and had prepared for the market process.
>
> Michael White
> Managing Director
> Founders Advisors

I recommend that every year you take a few calls from private equity groups just to find out what size, margin and growth rate excites buyers in your space. These conversations are a treasure trove of firsthand knowledge about your industry, competitors and trends. If you are not yet prepared to engage with a PEG, contact an investment banker with experience in your industry to ask about active buyers and recent sales.

If you have a sense that your relationship with your business may look a lot like Gil's—not smart, intentional or healthy—and you have not been looking ahead to how you will get a return for the hard work you have poured into your company, how do you go from knowing you need to change to actually making the change?

First, know that you are not alone. Estimates are hard to come by, but perhaps only 12 percent of owners have created formal exit plans.[44] Keep in mind that for most owners, 80 to 90 percent of their wealth is tied up in their companies. Second, know that you don't have to reinvent the wheel. There are as many approaches to exit planning as there are to getting fit, but the most successful involve accountability and an advisor (personal trainer). As for the particular planning process, beginning on page 216 I outline the one we use in our firm.

If I've persuaded you that having an exit plan is an important element of an investment-grade company, let's tackle the next deliverable: knowing what your company must be in order for you to have viable exit options.

WHAT YOUR COMPANY MUST BE IN ORDER FOR YOU TO HAVE VIABLE EXIT OPTIONS

Let's look at the characteristics that make an exit plan practical and worthwhile.

A viable exit plan:

- Clearly outlines the path you've charted to secure a return on your capital.
- Lays out the rational reasons why specific acquirers would be idiots not to acquire your company once you reach scale.
- Is not a theoretical exercise. Instead, it is the result of real research on potential acquisition partners. I encouraged Matt to have "feeler conversations" with multiple targeted strategic buyers years in advance of his exit because doing so is a great way to get on their radar screens, learn what qualities they find highly attractive, and form pre-acquisition partnerships.
- Indicates to sophisticated investors that you and your management team are focused on making sure that their money won't be marooned in a small, illiquid company.

What then are realistic exit options?

1. Once a company is highly profitable, distribute profits to generate a return on your investment.
2. Sell to a strategic buyer.
3. Sell to a financial buyer.
4. Recapitalize with a financial buyer or debt provider, and offer shareholders a return on their capital.
5. Create an Initial Public Offering. I know, I said it wasn't a realistic option, and for most of us it is not. In fact, IPOs are rare these days. The only companies that qualify have: (1) substantial revenue (think hundreds of millions of dollars), (2) a multibillion dollar TAM, and (3) a justifiable reason to pay the almost prohibitive costs and put up with endless regulations. If this exit option is in your company's business plan and/or pitch deck and you can't justify including it, expect to be considered borderline delusional.

Again, if your company provides a lot of exit options, it can be a great company for you and your stakeholders to continue to own—*if you choose to do so*. But choosing is an active decision. Owners who passively go with the flow rather than plan for their exits don't just fail to create investment-grade companies; their companies end up running them.

So what must your company be to have realistic exit options? Simple: It must be investment grade. And what makes a company investment grade?

1. Recurring revenue that comes from the continual addition of new customers or selling more to the same customers
2. Company growth rate and scale that merit buyer attention
3. Success in an attractive market
4. Leadership in a market niche
5. Having what it takes to scale (systems that are constantly improved, delegated, automated and documented)
6. A culture that attracts and keeps the best people
7. Competitive advantages that protect and grow market share
8. Owner-independent sales and marketing processes
9. A customer base that is diverse
10. A brand that translates into client acquisition
11. Innovation that relies on process (not just inspiration) and drives scalability because it is embedded in the culture and technology
12. Customers who are Net Promoters®
13. Financials that are buttoned-up, and owners who can relate them to their business models
14. Pristine legal housekeeping
15. An owner whose executive summary and compelling elevator pitch demonstrate a holistic understanding of the company and reasons for its existence
16. A realistic exit strategy—deployable at all times—that optimizes return on the owner's investment
17. An owner who understands how the market process works and how it maximizes return

Yes, building an investment-grade company—one that has value to buyers or investors—is how I view exit planning. But exit planning is more than just positioning your company to sell. It is about options; options that may better achieve your goals, e.g., continue to own the business but remove yourself from its operations, transition your company to younger family members or set up an ESOP.

Consider for a moment the triple-threat position in basketball that one of my coaches drilled into me as a fundamental. This attack stance and ball positioning give a player three immediate choices: pass, shoot or dribble. A good exit plan gives owners three options as well:

Option 1. Stay actively engaged in running your life-giving (and highly profitable) business.

Option 2. Be ready (and prepared) to sell or recapitalize when an exceptional offer presents itself or you decide to solicit one.

Option 3. Take weeks, even months, away from your business to do other things while your business continues to grow, throw off cash and thrive culturally. Enjoy owning a "17 Reasons company!"

Exit Planning And Risk

One purpose of this book is to show you how to minimize the risk that buyers and investors hate. If you fail to minimize their risk in any of the first 15 Reasons, buyers will not pay their highest and best prices. In the best-case scenario, buyers will structure a deal in their favor, but more than likely, they will lose interest in purchasing your company altogether. But in the case of Reasons 16 and 17—having an exit strategy at all times and using the market process to optimize value—you minimize *your own* risk.

When you plan for a great exit outcome, if the perfect buyer shows up, you are prepared to accept or reject its offer based on your terms—terms you identified well in advance. Your house is in the "show ready" condition that motivates interested parties to make their offers. Because you put in place what they look for in a quality investment, you've given buyers the confidence to pay up.

If that perfect buyer doesn't show up, you are running a great company and can decide whether to go out looking for a perfect buyer or simply take more time away from your company to pursue the activities you enjoy.

You Are Not Alone.

Planning an exit is not a job for one person, especially one who is busy running a growing company. Good, comprehensive exit plans require input from a number of professionals and nonprofessionals including:

- A certified public accountant with experience in tax issues related to ownership sales.
- An attorney with significant experience in M&A transactions from a multidisciplinary law firm who can quarterback tax and estate planning attorneys.
- A financial advisor, wealth manager and insurance professional who have worked extensively with business owners.
- An investment banker who can educate you on market valuations and how to maximize exit value while alleviating common risks of selling.
- A coach who has helped owners balance priorities and plan for life after a business sale.
- Personal advisors and peer groups.
- The owner's spouse (and other affected family members).
- A spiritual mentor. This person knows your blind spots and cares deeply about your personal and spiritual growth. This is a person you respect, who knows you well, and whom you listen to when he or she holds up a mirror to you or doles out healthy doses of as-needed reality therapy, confidence or clarity. By reacting well, you allow this person to speak the truth to you with persistence.

Board Of Advisors

I'm a huge fan of setting up a board of advisors, because what you know is important, but whom you know is critical. Your advisors' perspective on your exit, their ability to help you prepare for it, and their understanding of optimal timing can be priceless.

The right advisory board members offer your company:

- Experience.
- Accountability.
- Contacts.
- Strategic thinking.
- Access to partnerships, investors, customers and advisors.
- Credibility.

Other than experience, the most important characteristic that all of your advisors must possess is that you trust and respect them. Without trust, it is incredibly difficult for them to do their job, which, in addition to giving you the best possible advice, is to help you avoid frustration and failure.

Know Your Goals.

It's not where you start, it's where you finish.

Dorothy Fields and Cy Coleman

Unless owners establish a North Star, they don't know in which direction the decisions they make move them, and they can't measure progress. I don't understand how these owners choose between investing in growth or making cash distributions. What I do understand is that if you are not crystal clear on the return you need from your business, you cannot maintain a healthy relationship with it.

Every owner has different goals—personal and financial—but the one we'll focus on later in this chapter is the financial goal, or the "Enough Number." (See pages 220-221.)

One Exit Planning Process

There are consultants and exit planners across the U.S. who use a variety of techniques to help owners plan business exits. I've worked with several of them and in this chapter I will describe only the highlights of a process that my firm has crystallized from the many exit planning processes out there.

To organize the exit planning process into bite-size pieces, I typically use five questions:

1. When do you want to leave your company?
2. Whom do you want to succeed you?
3. What is your Enough Number?
4. What might threaten your ability to reach your Enough Number?
5. What will you do after you leave your business?

Let's examine each.

Question 1. When do you want to leave your company?

I have argued that you should be exit ready at all times, but now I want you to think about your ideal time to exit. Do you want to leave when you are young enough to enjoy "retirement"? (At my first software start-up, I always told my team and partners that I wanted to exit while I was still young enough to ski moguls.) Or does your ideal departure relate to an event such as the day after your youngest child graduates from college, the year you turn 50, the quarter your company's sales exceed $20 million, or the moment your children can run the company without you? Is your ideal departure date the day your company's market share equals X percent or is No. 2 in the international market?

The date you select is a very personal choice that only you can make, but the date isn't as critical as picking one is. If it helps, know that owners frequently revise their exit dates either because of internal events (e.g., an illness or simply changing their minds) or external events (e.g., a buyer makes an offer or the marketplace changes dramatically). Most of us will revise our departure dates based on how quickly (or slowly) our companies' value can support our Enough Number. More on that number in a moment.

Question 2. Whom do you want to succeed you?

Owners can pick from a menu of possible successors.

- A third party:
  - · Financial buyer
  - · Strategic buyer
  - · Recapitalization/partial sale to a financial buyer
- Employees or partners
- Key employee(s) or co-owner(s)
- Employee Stock Ownership Plan
- Family member(s)
- Planned liquidation

Not surprisingly, there are pros and cons to each choice, as well as myths that surround each one. I'm not going to explain each possible successor in detail, but I will describe some of the highlights of each choice.

- ■ *Sales To Third Parties*

    There are three broad types of third-party sales: a sale to a financial buyer, a sale to a strategic buyer, and a partial sale to a financial buyer via a recapitalization. If you are to build a company that third-party buyers want and will pay up for, it is critical that you understand their goals, concerns and investment criteria. You'll find detailed descriptions of various types of buyers in Reason 2, but in this chapter we discuss how buyers' wants relate to your goals.

    Financial buyers that invest capital in companies with "good bones," for the purpose of realizing a desired rate of return include venture capital funds, search funds, private equity groups and family offices. With the exception of family offices, these buyers don't plan to run and own companies forever. Instead, they work to supercharge and sell them at the end of their prede-termined hold periods (typically between four and six years).

    Both financial buyers and strategic buyers evaluate a potential acquisition based on their par-ticular goals. For example, a strategic buyer will look for ways to integrate your operation into its own to achieve better, long-term value. A financial buyer, on the other hand, will evaluate your company as a self-sufficient business.

    Generally, only financial buyers are interested in any form of recapitalization. Recaps are an option worth examining if you need or wish to sell some equity and diversify your wealth. Many entrepreneurs have way too much (upwards of 80 percent as I mentioned before) of their wealth tied up in their private companies.

    Strategic buyers often understand your industry better than financial buyers because they are part of it. They typically aren't as interested in a company's back-office infrastructure because they have duplicate functions in their much larger companies. They will often eliminate much of it to achieve even greater cost synergies. On the other hand, financial buyers will want to invest in your infrastructure to promote faster growth and scale.

    In a sale to a third party, you must consider whether you wish to make a clean break from your business at closing or if you are willing to work for a new owner, and, if so, for how long. Financial buyers typically do not want the keys to your business, because they are investors, not operators. They gladly provide valuable support and resources, but they do not want to take over operations. In their optimal scenario, you and your proven team maintain operational control and execute on the growth strategy. If they are suddenly forced to become operators, they have invested in the wrong company and team. Something bad has typically occurred.

The Second Bite—How Sweet It Is!

Would you be surprised to learn that many of my clients, after selling a portion of their equity to financial partners, happily do it all over again?

After owners take what I call the "first bite of the apple" (or take a few chips off the table to diversify their wealth), their financial partners use their expertise and resources to help take those companies to the next level. Four to six years later, when the new investors sell the company for a much higher price, the now-minority (or majority owner if the initial deal was a minority recap versus a majority recap) the founding owner gets the second, and often much larger, bite of the apple.

In our firm, we regularly see these second bites yield more cash to the founder than the often much larger first-bite percentage. Recently, we orchestrated a deal between a business services company founder and a private equity group. The founder sold (recapped) 60 percent of his equity for $17 million cash. (The implied company valuation for this initial bite was approximately $28.3 million.) He rolled the other 40 percent of his equity into the new partnership. Less than three years later, this business sold to a strategic buyer for $70 million. That created a second liquidity event for the founder and made the remaining 40 percent stake he owned in the business worth $28 million.

It is worth noting that this company's 17 Reasons Assessment Score continued to move north rapidly as the new private equity group invested aggressively in the platform company in anticipation of the second bite.

In majority recapitalizations, owners generally stay on for the duration of the financial backer's hold period. Some private equity buyers maintain a stable of experienced CEOs that they bring in to run the businesses they acquire. This can be great for sellers who are ready to move on to the next stage or opportunity in life.

Once you sell either your business or majority control of your business to a third party, you will have less input about how your company will run. How much less depends on whether you've created an investment-grade company. Owners who have done so and sell a majority interest to a financial buyer retain more control than those who have not. The loss of control does not bother many owners, but others don't want to lose any control of the culture they've worked so hard to create. For that reason, they view transfers to employees or family members as better options.

The highlights of the three major types of third-party transactions are summarized in Figure 16.1. Strategic buyers fund the first scenario: sales and corporate mergers. Financial buyers fund the second and third scenarios: leveraged buyouts/recapitalizations and management buyouts.

- *Employees (Or Co-owners)*
  Selling a business to employees gives owners the opportunity to handpick and train their successors. On the other hand, there can be considerable risk in transferring to employees unless:
  - Owners design and implement a plan well in advance of their departure.
  - Owners transfer ownership incrementally (based on employees' success in meeting performance standards tied to increases in business cash flow or value).
  - The plan keeps the owner in control of the business until employees bring the entire purchase price, in cash, from whatever source.

FIG. 16.1 Third-Party Transaction Scenarios

SCENARIO	DESCRIPTION	ADVANTAGES	KEY CONSIDERATIONS
Sale of Company/ Corporate Merger	➤ Sale to or combination with a strategic operating company	➤ Shareholders realize full liquidity ➤ Minimizes shareholders' future liabilities	➤ Loss of post-sale upside ➤ Value is maximized through the sale of entire equity interest ➤ Typically two- to five-year noncompete agreement
Leveraged Buyout/ Recapitalization	➤ Acquisition by a financial sponsor	➤ Greatest potential for optimal valuation ➤ Provides a "second bite of the apple"	➤ Liquidity and pro forma ownership depends on deal structure ➤ PEGs typically retain management
Management Buyout	➤ Management team (with a financial sponsor) purchases company from current ownership	➤ Provides full liquidity to owner and transfers ownership to key management/employees	➤ May not generate the highest possible valuation due to absence of competitive process

If handpicking your successor or rewarding loyal employees attracts you to this type of sale and your employees are not able to buy you out all at once, you and your advisors have much work to do to set up a transfer that protects you and tests your employees' ability to run the company and their willingness to commit to its success.

Private equity groups look for management buyouts in which a solid current management team needs the capital to buy out an owner. Don't assume that the only ways to get paid in an employee transition are long-term seller notes or incremental stock purchases over several years. PEGs will write sizable checks if you bring to the table a strong company whose management team has demonstrated its ability to operate and grow the company and is committed to continuing its efforts under new ownership. PEGs value and pay handsomely for management teams that are highly adept, motivated and have plenty of "gas in the tank" to execute the growth strategy of a business.

- *Employee Stock Ownership Plan (ESOP)*
  Selling to an ESOP is only worth considering if:
  - Your business is people intensive.
  - Your company has reached a high level of sophistication and substantial size.
  - You want to see your company remain in your community.
  - You have created a culture of employee initiative and leadership.
  - You want to reward all (not just your senior) employees.

If you can check all of those boxes, talk to your advisors about the advantages and disadvantages of selling your company to an ESOP. Owners who sell to ESOPs reap huge tax advantages but, in return, are subject to intense scrutiny by both the IRS and Department of Labor. For that reason, owners must work with highly specialized professionals who are experts in this area.

- *Family Members*

  If your goal is to create a family business as your legacy, and you have family members who are willing and able to run the company successfully, you may have the opportunity to act with both your heart and your wallet. To toil for years without the reward of financial security at the end of the road is not an outcome many owners find acceptable, so you must find advisors who know how to help you secure compensation from nonbusiness as well as business assets. Private equity groups are standing by to provide the capital for qualified family members to provide departing parent/owners with immediate liquidity.

- *Planned Liquidation*

  Before you skip this option because you think it is not one that could possibly apply to your company, please consider that planned liquidations are often the best, or perhaps only, feasible conclusion for businesses (usually retail or service) that are dependent on their owners. If a planned liquidation makes sense in your case, you are not off the exit planning hook. In fact, you need to pay special attention to building wealth outside of your business; creating post-liquidation plans for your customers and employees; implementing tax-minimizing strategies; planning to terminate contracts in an orderly way; liquidating retirement and benefit plans; and adhering to any applicable state, local or federal regulations that might apply.

Question 3. What Is Your Enough Number?

Of all the questions to ask yourself during the exit planning process, this one is the most personal. Only you can decide how much money you need when you leave your business.

For example, young tech founders sometimes simply want a base hit or a double. That means they are satisfied with an exit that generates a nice return for themselves and their investors and builds credibility. From there, they go to the next venture. Other owners want their exits to be their Big Finish. They want to walk away with the war chests that allow them to enjoy the lifestyle they desire for the rest of their lives.

Your Enough Number may be anywhere along the continuum between a nice return and a Big Finish. Determining it is your job. Calculating it requires input from your advisors.

Let's begin with this simple calculation:

The Value of Assets You Need Upon Exit
− The Value of Assets Outside Your Business
Your Enough Number

Unless you plan to start or work in another business after you leave the one you own now, the assets you'll need when you exit will have to support you (and perhaps a spouse and family) in the lifestyle you desire until you die. The data that go into calculating that amount of assets are:

- The likely (realistic rather than optimistic) rate of return on your investments.
- Your life expectancy (and that of a spouse), which is likely longer than you think.

Many wealth managers suggest that business owners should calculate what they desire in an annual income and multiply that number by 30. This simple calculation will help you determine your Enough Number. If you need $250,000 in annual income, your net proceeds number is $7.5 million.

• A realistic projection of what it will cost to maintain your lifestyle.

A skilled wealth manager can help you with these estimates and assess the value and future performance of your nonbusiness assets.

Once you do the math (subtracting the value of your nonbusiness assets from the total asset value you need at your exit), you've defined your Enough Number. With that number in mind, you know the net proceeds you'll need from the sale or transfer of your business.

In a mathematical sense, calculating your Enough Number involves solving a simple equation. But determining how much is truly enough for you involves more variables, such as your upbringing, personality, spiritual outlook, values and goals. Your Enough Number is influenced by how you feel about the resources you had, or didn't have, growing up. If you are an early adopter or social animal, you may need the latest and greatest gadget, vehicle or experience to feel satisfied/happy. If giving generously or living simply is part of who you are, those attributes also affect your Enough Number.

There is huge value to you (and to those who love you) in taking time to sit down by yourself (and then with your spouse) to determine your Enough Number. That number provides the peace of mind that often eludes owners who, by and large, are competitive by nature. Without our Enough Number, we are like sharks—insatiable eating machines—that can't stop hunting and consuming. Once we know our Enough Number, peace and purpose can settle in. We give ourselves permission to pause, enjoy a time of rest/Sabbath, attend a child's Bring A Parent To School Day, and not think once about what's going on back at the office.

Question 4. What might threaten your ability to reach your Enough Number?

Owners are quite familiar with external threats to their businesses: changes in legislation; the emergence of a very creative, large and tenacious competitor; a reversal in the broader capital markets; and unfortunate timing come to mind. But what about the risks that arise from a business's dependence on you? What would happen to your business if you were absent, either for an extended period of time (due to an accident or illness) or permanently (due to death or disability)? These are not questions that we like to think about, but they are ones we can't afford to ignore.

As owners, we also have to consider how the absence of key employees or key customers would affect our companies' success. What would happen if the person working on your Next Big Thing disappeared into a Tibetan ashram or if your biggest customer decided to shop elsewhere? If you read the chapters on culture and customer concentration (Reasons 6 and 9), you are already working to eliminate these single points of failure, thus averting these two doomsday scenarios. But how do you minimize the risk that your absence presents to both your business's future and your family's financial security?

Question 5. What will you do after you leave your business?

If you have the drive and talent of 99 percent of the owners I've met who run successful companies, the answer to this question is simple: Anything you want. Figuring out exactly what "anything" is, presents the challenge. Do you want to start another business or finish an IRONMAN triathlon?

The life we will live after we exit our companies is an expression of why we started our businesses in the first place.

Do you want to build water wells in the Sudan or an incubator for young innovators? Would you like to spend more time on your favorite hobby or head off to the mission field?

I don't know what your post-exit goals are, but I know from experience that owners who exit their businesses *toward something* (no matter what that something is) are healthier and happier than those who wait until they burn out and only exit to *get away from something*. My point is you should know your purpose and then live on purpose.

I also know that buyers are adept at sensing sellers' exit motivations, although some sellers try to hide them. When buyers detect the "getting away" scent (whether caused by burnout, illness, greed or divorce), the financial outcome is generally not as good as it is for owners going toward another goal. In any area of your life, you want to plan your exits.

You might not be able to attract investors or buyers if you are unprepared for an exit and don't have an exit plan that clearly states your goals and maps out how you plan to achieve them.

RECOMMENDATIONS

1. **Conduct due diligence on your company by using the 17 Reasons Assessment™ to assess your company's strengths and weaknesses in each of the 17 Reasons. (See page 243 or *17-reasons.com* for details.)**
   How does your company measure up to each Reason?

2. **Set up a meeting with your advisors in the next few weeks.**
   Tell them that you want to talk about your endgame.
   • Do you have realistic exit options?

3. **Make a list of individuals you would like to pursue as advisory board members, and develop a plan to recruit them.**
   I recommend paying a small board fee as soon as your company can afford this. It professionalizes your advisory board and forces you to treat your advisory board as a valuable asset.

4. **Review and answer the five exit planning questions in this chapter.**
   Be realistic about your most probable exit paths. Prioritize the options you prefer.

TAKEAWAYS

1. **If your only documented exit strategy involves being acquired by an industry behemoth or IPO, sophisticated investors assume you are not a serious thinker.**

2. **Your business works for you.**
   Too many owners sacrifice their personal time, lives and relationships at the altar of their businesses. That is tragic. Your business is your life's work. As you exit, your business should work for you and support your purpose.

3. **Creating a strategy to recoup your investment of time and money in your company is as important as the other 16 Reasons.**

   Having an exit strategy decreases the risk that you and your stakeholders won't reap a maximum return in the form of a premium value.

4. **Being exit ready at all times is critical because unplanned exits are rarely good exits.**

   Intentional value creation is always wise and positions your company for multiple options as your industry, markets and competitive environments continually change. Having an exit plan also positions you to stay, sell, or become an owner who can take months away from the business to do other things.

5. **It is never too early to begin building your exit advisory team.**

   Your exit team should include an M&A attorney, CPA, wealth advisor, insurance professional and investment banker. Members of this team must work well together, meaning no big egos, no games of good cop/bad cop, and no problems talking candidly and transparently.

6. **If you don't have a plan, you will be a part of someone else's plan.**

REAS⚙n

The Market Process Is Not In Your Plan.

UNDERSTAND THE EXIT METHOD THAT MAXIMIZES RETURN ON INVESTMENT-GRADE COMPANIES.

I've argued throughout this book that selling equity is not the only reason to create an investment-grade company, but it is a solid one.

I'll admit that, technically, running a confidential market process to sell a company is not a characteristic of an investment-grade company. Yes, some brokers and investment bankers will run the market process on less than-investment-grade companies, but that's like putting low-grade gasoline in a Ferrari. It takes an investment-grade company to truly recap the benefits of the market process. For many owners, it is the prospect of maximum return on the blood, sweat and tears that they've invested in their companies that motivates them to do the work necessary to create investment-grade companies. Therefore, for its role in maximizing return—whether for the purpose of selling equity or raising capital—the market process earns a spot on the list of 17 Reasons.

Do you remember my meeting with Matt in the previous chapter? His friend Dustin had recommended that Matt meet with me, not because Matt was ready to sell his company, but because it was likely that he would be one day. Dustin knew from experience that putting ducks in a row (aka building an investment-grade company) is an intentional, years-long process. Let's pretend now that Matt returned to my office after creating an investment-grade company and that his ideal departure date (keyed to an event) had arrived.

I've had the opportunity to experience this market process twice as a founder/owner, and over 80 times as an M&A advisor. I can heartily attest to its incredible effectiveness in driving outsized outcomes.

"Zane, the national rollout of BeatBeatBeat's app is complete," Matt began. "Half of the top 20 nonprofit hospital systems have deployed it with their physicians and so have about half of the top 20 for-profit systems. I said that when we reached 50 percent market saturation of the leading hospitals I'd look for a buyer, and, quite frankly, I've got another idea in mind that I'd like to develop."

"Congratulations, Matt," I said, "not only on your success, but for your discipline: You made a plan, and you're sticking to it."

"Maybe," Matt hedged. "I seem to remember you saying something about departure dates being flexible."

"I did. What are you thinking?" I asked.

"Well, I've reached the goal I set, but what about the market for companies like mine?"

"A great question," I responded. "So great, in fact, that it's the one we have to answer before we put your company on the market."

PRESALE PROCESS ASSESSMENTS

Timing

The consequences of diving into the M&A market at the wrong time or in an emotionally unprepared state are hugely negative for sellers, so we assess a number of factors before readying owners for the plunge. Figure 17.1 identifies the timing elements, both external (e.g., market cycles) and internal (e.g., an owner's mindset).

FIG. 17.1 Transaction Timing

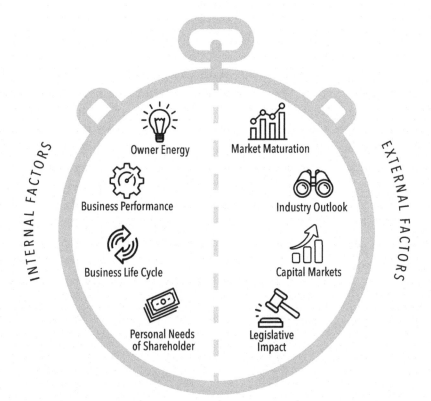

In Matt's case, timing was right when it came to internal factors.

- He had the energy to orchestrate a sale or stay in ownership. There would be no scent of burnout for buyers to detect, because there simply wasn't any.
- Matt's company was going gangbusters. Performance was on a steady and steep upward trajectory.
- The app that Matt's company was producing had been tested and rolled out successfully. It was the first of its kind, and users, in their first year of deployment, were Net Promoters.* The business was out of the start-up stage but still had plenty of meat on the bone to attract buyers. It had achieved the sweet spot in the business life cycle.
- The income that Matt had already generated from his company enabled him to live far beyond his expectations. A sale would ensure his financial security for a lifetime and allow him to diversify his wealth.

With all of the internal timing boxes checked, Matt and I turned our attention to the external issues.

- The market for Matt's application at the early adopter stage was exciting, and all signals pointed realistically to a $300 million initial niche market size within the next seven years. It was also evident that Matt could grow his initial TAM by moving into other chronic disease categories/markets.
- Health care payers and providers across the globe were eager to find better (and cheaper) protocols to help type 2 diabetics and other high-risk patients control their blood pressure.
- Capital markets were teeming with financial buyers (especially ones that focused on the health care segment) holding more cash to invest than they could find qualified investment vehicles. Strategic buyers had extremely strong balance sheets and were acquiring for growth.
- There were no legislative risks on the horizon, and some innovative insurers/payers appeared to be on track to approve the app for reimbursement in the near future.

If Matt had had business partners, we would have walked them through this exercise as well because it is critical that all partners be on the same page when assessing these factors. We often encounter partners who are at very different seasons in their lives and find consensus on their personal goals difficult to reach. We can navigate these differences, but only if we bring them to the surface.

With our examination of Matt, his company and the marketplace complete, it was time to take a deep dive into the market cycle.

Market Cycle

Matt was considering a sale at the best possible time from the market's perspective: private company valuations were at a 20-year high, and the U.S. economy was nearing its longest monthly expansion cycle in history.

NOTE: Matt was considering a sale at a great point in the market cycle, but not all owners have that luxury. In every cycle, there are high points, low points and all points in between. When a poor economy suppresses private company valuations, there's no reason to lose heart. Owners who take action to build an investment-grade company can accelerate value creation. They can leverage their operational strengths to gain ground on their competitors. Also, companies with healthy balance sheets can take advantage of down markets to acquire less-prepared companies for low valuations. Many emerge stronger than their competitors when the market shifts. Even better, the momentum and efficiencies generated during the market's low points can drive valuable increases in market share when good times return.

Owner Mindset

When I pulled out Figure 17.2 and asked Matt to tell me where he was in the Owner Mindset cycle, he pointed to "excitement," "thrill" and "euphoria" and said, "Pick one."

FIG. 17.2 **Owner Mindset**

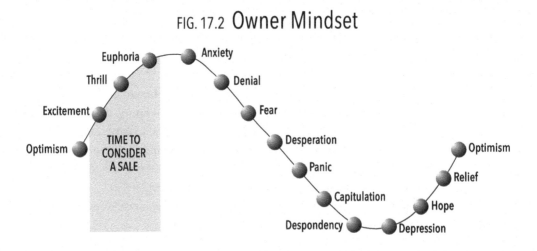

Not all owners are so enthusiastic. I remember asking "Carson," the CEO/founder of a very fast-growing AdTech company, to show me where he was on the chart.

Pointing to "anxiety" on the Owner Mindset roller coaster, Carson said, "This is where I feel we are as a company. We've ridden this incredible wave of growth and success, but I see huge headwinds ahead."

"Tell me what you mean by 'headwinds,'" I asked.

"Well, 'headwind' may be too tame a term for what I see ahead for my industry in general and for the regulations and several up-and-coming competitors that could completely derail us."

Carson was acutely aware that the current macro business cycle we were in at the time could not last forever. His anxiety was compounded by his expectation that a market correction was overdue. His position on the Owner Mindset cycle prompted him to seriously consider options that would allow him to: (1) de-risk his business, (2) take some chips off the table, and (3) find a partner to provide the ballast necessary (in the form of additional capital) to navigate the turbulent waters ahead.

I can identify with Carson. I distinctly remember the nights, as an entrepreneur, I woke up in fear bordering on panic. I also remember the hope, relief and optimism I felt as I made the emotional trip back up the cycle's curve.

It can be difficult to recognize that the Owner Mindset cycle is normal (as are all the emotions along the way) and be realistic in our assessments of where we are in that cycle. A board of directors or trusted mentor can help us see things more clearly. Denial doesn't help us make decisions—especially about whether to continue growing our business on our own, pursue a growth strategy with the help of debt or growth equity, or exit our companies by selling to a new owner.

THE MARKET PROCESS

The most sophisticated private company owners in the world are private equity groups. I've yet to see even one of these talented investors and operators exit a holding without relying on a seasoned, industry-focused intermediary to deploy a market process of some type. The most sophisticated owners in the world understand that the market process drives investment return.

With our discussions about the internal and external factors and market cycle complete, I began to explain to Matt the sale method that provides owners the greatest return and best protects them from risk: the market process. It is a variation on what others refer to as the competitive, confidential or controlled auction process.

The market process is designed to efficiently and confidentially attract as many qualified buyers to the table as possible. It gives owners the assurance that the "market has spoken" to the company's real value.

The market process is the best possible way for owners of investment-grade companies to:

• Maximize the return on their huge investments of time, effort and capital.
• Bring transactions to a successful and efficient close.
• Satisfy all of the goals they have set for their exits.

I base these bold claims on experience. Over the past 20 years, in both hot and cold markets, our firm has used a finely tuned version of the market process over 150 times to achieve optimal results for owners of energy, industrial, technology, health care, consumer, manufacturing and distribution, and business services companies.

To show Matt the power of the market process, I brought out Figure 17.3. I find that there's nothing like a picture (or a lame tomato metaphor) to make a point memorable.

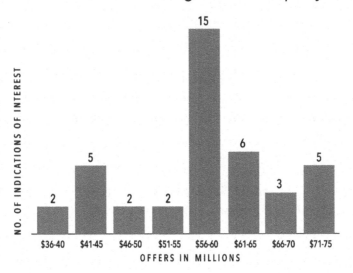

FIG. 17.3 **Valuation Ranges For Company X**

I could have shown Matt dozens of charts similar to this one, but I chose this one and told him this story.

Late one Saturday, as my wife and I drove back into town from our family lake house, my cell phone alerted me to a message. During a gap in cell coverage, "Bob," a buddy (and wealth manager) had called to talk to me about one of his clients. "Zane, I've got a client who owns a tech-enabled services business in the insurance space. If you can manage to pull yourself away from that puddle you call a lake, call me back. I think this could be interesting."

I was just about to call him back when my wife suggested that Bob might not appreciate a call from me at 10:30 p.m. She'd remembered that Bob's oldest daughter had brought home his first (and nearly newborn) grandchild earlier that week. She reminded me that after we brought our youngest child home, none of us slept through the night for six months. That I remembered.

It took us a day or two to connect—I suspect (but cannot confirm) because Bob was turning off his phone to nap at the office. I was anxious to talk because calls like his often lead to nice sell-side opportunities for our deal team.

When we finally connected, Bob proceeded to tell me that "Phil" and "Bill" were a father and son who owned a novel software and services business that they started from scratch.

"They're doing well and not really looking to sell," explained Bob. "But Phil called me last week to ask a few questions. He wanted to know if I knew anything about a strategic buyer who had been calling them persistently over the past eight or nine months to discuss selling their business."

Bob told me the name of the caller, but it meant nothing to me. Before I could promise Bob that I'd do some research, he continued, "Phil finally agreed to share some high-level financials in return for a confidentiality agreement, mostly because he was curious about how a strategic buyer might value his company." I held my breath out of habit I suppose, since rarely does sharing information directly with one possible buyer end well.

"Zane, Phil figured that the benefit of a 'real-life' value estimate outweighed the risk since this buyer isn't currently in their marketplace," Bob said.

"The buyer isn't in that market right now..." I began.

But Bob continued. "Zane, it's fine. This buyer came back with an indication of interest (IOI) for $32 million. Cash."

Since I knew zero about the business, the total dollar amount was meaningless. But an all-cash offer? That could mean a number of things—most of them very good for these owners.

"Phil is very happy because he thought that the company was in the $25 million range," explained Bob.

"Based on what?" I asked.

"Just his gut and the company's numbers," Bob responded. "Since Bill and Phil had no plans to sell, they'd never pursued a formal valuation."

In chugging along with a "gut valuation," Bob's clients were like most owners: Unless they have an interest in selling, they typically have no interest in paying for a market valuation.

"Where do things stand now?" I asked.

"Well, that brings me to the rest of Phil's questions," Bob said. "He wants to know what I think of the offer and asked what the risks were in trusting this buyer. He also wants to know whether he has any other options."

"Bob, have they agreed to the IOI?" I asked.

"Nope. I told them that I'd call a guy I know who may not be able to tell the difference between a sardine and a lake trout, but who matches buyers and sellers so well that when it's over both sides think the whole thing was their idea."

"Shoot, Bob," I replied. *"Let's set up a meeting before you run out of heartfelt compliments."*

"I've got plenty more, Zane, but I would like to set you up to meet with both owners sooner rather than later. My daughter and grandbaby leave on Wednesday. How does Thursday look?" Bob asked.

Bob slept during our flight to the Midwest to see Phil and Bill and during the entire drive to a small town two hours from the airport. But he was wide awake as we listened to father and son tell the story of their company and describe their goals and the market in which they operated.

Given what the two had accomplished, we helped them understand their transaction options using a chart similar to Figure 17.4.

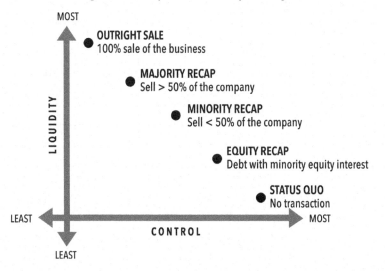

FIG. 17.4 **Ranges Of Options: Liquidity vs. Control**

After reviewing their options, father and son decided that it made sense to prepare for a confidential market process. They expected it to tell them how a broader slice of the market valued their company, and they were right.

Within 60 days we completed extensive buyer research, created a Confidential Information Memorandum (CIM), set up a virtual data room (VDR), and kicked off our marketing campaign.

Figure 17.5 on the following page shows the initial indications of interest (IOIs) that we received on the date we gave interested buyers as a deadline.

By the way, as part of the market process, the original strategic buyer submitted an initial bid that was $10 million higher than its unsolicited IOI. The market process was working exactly as we intended: It was attracting more buyers and persuading them to bring their best offers to the table.

Ultimately, Phil and Bill chose a minority recap with a PEG that had deep experience in their space. Father and son sold 40 percent of their business (valued at $60 million) for $24 million. Of course, they had to pay transaction fees and taxes, but they walked away from the closing table with enough cash to set them up for life.

FIG. 17.5 Indications Of Interest

The market process delivered as promised: the right option and right structure at the right value. The transaction proved to the owners that they had received the best transaction terms that the market had to offer.

Three years after closing, father, son and the PEG had grown the business substantially. Four years out, the private equity partner paid for a mark-to-market valuation, which showed that the company's value was now $120 million.

There are no typos here. These owners took millions of dollars in cash at closing; continued to run their company; and three years later, their 60-percent stake had an estimated value of $72 million.

The only people more thrilled with the outcome than their wealth advisor (Bob) are a father and son from a small town in the Midwest.

FOUNDERS ADVISORS' MARKET PROCESS

Figure 17.6 illustrates the market process that our deal teams deploy. It consists of four major phases, each consisting of several tasks.

Phase 1. Preparation: The Key To Standing Out In A Crowded Market

When there are numerous quality targets for buyers to choose from, as there usually are, it can be difficult for a company to stand out. A disciplined market process differentiates your company from others. That means that your transaction team knows how to speak in a language that investors understand and appreciate. Your team should be able to tell the past, present and future story of your company, using compelling words and financial models that the right investors understand and respond to.

Your company's marketing materials must demonstrate persuasively to investors that your company has the management expertise necessary to drive value, add complementary products and services, and/or facilitate the investor's expansion into new markets. Making your company stand out from others has to happen if your company is to garner a higher valuation, you are to receive the ideal deal structure your company attract and the optimal post-acquisition partner.

FIG. 17.6 Founders Advisors' Market Process

Our Market Process has created valuation outcomes that far outpace client expectations and accomplish objectives such as minimal disturbance to ongoing business operations.

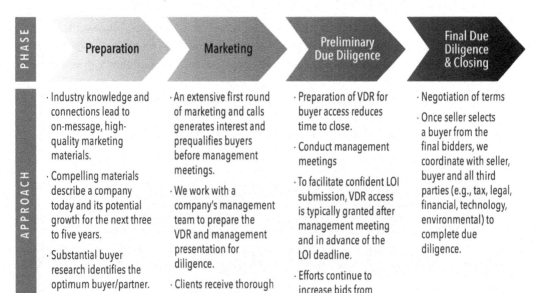

PHASE	Preparation	Marketing	Preliminary Due Diligence	Final Due Diligence & Closing
APPROACH	· Industry knowledge and connections lead to on-message, high-quality marketing materials. · Compelling materials describe a company today and its potential growth for the next three to five years. · Substantial buyer research identifies the optimum buyer/partner.	· An extensive first round of marketing and calls generates interest and prequalifies buyers before management meetings. · We work with a company's management team to prepare the VDR and management presentation for diligence. · Clients receive thorough weekly marketing updates.	· Preparation of VDR for buyer access reduces time to close. · Conduct management meetings · To facilitate confident LOI submission, VDR access is typically granted after management meeting and in advance of the LOI deadline. · Efforts continue to increase bids from IOI to LOI. · Analysis of all options before seller selects buyer/partner	· Negotiation of terms · Once seller selects a buyer from the final bidders, we coordinate with seller, buyer and all third parties (e.g., tax, legal, financial, technology, environmental) to complete due diligence.

Your company deserves a well-run process to highlight its value to global investors/buyers. Consequently, you must find an experienced M&A advisor (or "market maker") who has a successful track record in developing and executing a confidential market process like the one outlined in Figure 17.6.

- **Reaching The Right Buyers**

Typically, company owners don't have a good grasp of the number or variety of players in the universe of potential buyers. They think way too narrowly and limit their mental list of possible buyers to competitors, employees, family members, regional investors and suppliers.

In addition to each of those categories, there are domestic and international companies, both private and public. Add to that group private equity firms and family offices. As we discussed in Reason 2, each type of buyer has its own list of characteristics it looks for in a target acquisition and its own way of assessing value. As a result, the chances of finding the right buyer increase exponentially when your transaction advisor uses a system to cull the list to the absolute best buyers.

The screening system that our team uses relies on analysis of the company for sale (or that is looking for growth equity), continual research into prospective buyers who are (or want to be) active in various markets, and past experiences with specific buyers. We include past experiences in our considerations because we know that a buyer's track record of success is a good indicator of future success. Through research and ongoing contact, we know the capabilities and ideal target profiles of numerous investors of all types. Our goal is to cast a wide enough net to include the best buyers, but not one so wide that it catches unqualified candidates.

Figure 17.7 highlights how we set up a screening process to separate desirable from undesirable buyers as we perform comprehensive buyer research. Out of all the buyers in the universe, you only need one to achieve a great outcome. But to find that one, you must methodically conduct wide-ranging and deep research.

FIG. 17.7 Finding The Optimal Partner & Unlocking Premium Market Valuation

BUYER CLASSIFICATIONS

FINANCIAL Private Equity Groups	STRATEGIC Operating Companies	HYBRID PE-Backed Strategic Buyers

Leverage Market Conversations & Knowledge

· Our team maintains relationships and open lines of communication with the most acquisitive strategic and financial groups in various segments regarding the targets that interest them.

· We leverage our internal CRM to track and analyze these buyer conversations in order to quickly derive which groups could be a fit for specific investment opportunities.

Perform In-Depth Buyer Research

· Because new buyers are constantly entering the marketplace, we supplement our market knowledge with thorough buyer research, utilizing several tools and proprietary data sets.

· To identify viable buyers, we analyze recent and historical M&A activity, explore industry conference attendees, screen PE portfolio companies, and digest reports from public companies.

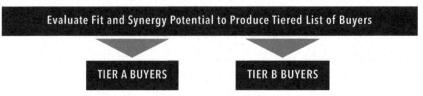

Evaluate Fit and Synergy Potential to Produce Tiered List of Buyers

TIER A BUYERS   **TIER B BUYERS**

Phase 2. Marketing: High-Impact Materials Create Value.

Wall Street investment banks drive up the IPO value of a company during the "go public" sequence by preparing a compelling company prospectus. Your investment banking team must do the same for your company when orchestrating a capital raise or liquidity event. To accomplish that, we customize a company's marketing materials based on what we learn about the targeted buyers' strategies and growth plans during our Preparation phase. We highlight those areas of a business that we know are of particular interest to a target buyer. If our target buyer is a PEG, for example, our marketing materials focus more on our client's current team and growth plan. If the target is a strategic buyer, we focus on potential synergies.

Remember that your company is worth what it is worth on a strategic buyer's platform, and the range of value is wide. By building a great case for attractive synergies, you can direct buyers to the high end of their range.

Professional packaging and customized management presentations play important roles in telling your company's story. Sophisticated and clear materials are not window dressing. Instead, they create value. We call on skilled financial storytellers to architect gripping, data-driven materials that demonstrate to investors: (1) why your company is valuable, and (2) how and why it is going to continue to grow rapidly and produce predictable risk-adjusted future cash flows far into the future.

We work with our clients' management teams to collect the data and to organize how it is presented in both the confidential information memoranda and in-person management meetings.

Phase 3. Preliminary Due Diligence

Your M&A advisors prepare for preliminary due diligence by updating the virtual data room (VDR) several weeks before holding management meetings. The major sections of the VDR are:

- Financials and Sales Pipeline.
- Customer-Level Data Analysis.
- Technology/IP/Product.
- Legal Documentation.

VDR access is typically granted to prospective buyers after we hold management meetings and in advance of the deadline we set for their letters of intent (LOIs). In a strong auction, bidders increase their offers between submitting their indications of interest and their final LOIs, as they become more confident in the deal and their fear of losing out on it heightens.

During the preliminary diligence phase, your advisors negotiate multiple key business points in the LOI, including:

- Consideration sources and structure (especially details related to any proposed earnouts or seller notes).
- Rollover equity components (and any associated rights).
- Working capital methods for calculation.
- Deferred revenue positions.
- Scope of due diligence.
- Exclusivity period.
- Indemnification terms.
- Buyer's post-closing expectations of seller and key employees.

Buyers require detailed and accurate information to put forth their best LOIs with conviction. They need to feel confident that they fully understand the business so they can consummate the deal based on their original acquisition models.

Phase 4. Final Due Diligence & Closing

The execution of a letter of intent with the chosen buyer kicks off the final due diligence and closing phase. Our deal team quarterbacks this stage by coordinating all of the activities that involve the client, buyer, legal, and all third-party diligence organizations (those retained to review financial, legal, and technology/IP issues and even conduct customer interviews).

While every transaction is different, the confirmatory diligence required in this phase is very information-centric and includes all details the acquirer/investor needs about a company. The depth of diligence that buyers require usually depends on their unique approach to diligence and the number of third parties involved. The final due diligence and closing phase is the most trying part of the market process for owner/sellers because it requires significant time, energy, resources and patience.

One absolutely no-exception lesson I've learned over the years is that due diligence is much more difficult and taxing than any owner expects. No owner—no matter how sophisticated, book-smart, street-smart or experienced—appreciates in advance how much homework buyers do before laying out the big bucks. Preparing owners for the effort, pain and surprises that are so typical of this phase of the process is one of my greatest challenges.

In my never-ending attempt to address this challenge, I use several analogies. The first is to compare diligence to the most detailed physical examination you can imagine: one that takes all of your time for 45 to 60 days, requires countless blood draws, and involves hours of lying stark naked on a cold metal table while scopes and cameras invade every one of your orifices.

Or how about Navy SEALs' Hell Week? Think fasting, sleep deprivation and extreme environmental and physical challenges until your body quits. I once worked with a CEO (and former Green Beret) who told me that his military training was nothing compared to his diligence experience with his company. Of course, whether due diligence is a 60-day physical or Hell Week, you have to remain laser focused on your company and its growth for as long as it takes—without blinking. No days off, no reboots and no operational hiccups are allowed.

Before attempting to survive diligence, you must be well-prepared, and your company tightly buttoned up. The purpose of Phase 1 of our Market Process is to uncover any issues you need to shore up. If they can't be fixed, we will develop strategies to mitigate them. What we will not do is hope a buyer will fail to discover them.

Entering the diligence phase with a buyer without going through the proper preparation sequence is like walking onstage on opening night without having seen the script, much less rehearsed your part.

- *Purchase Price Is Not The Only Measure Of Success.*

    Before owners choose the winning buyer, we work with them to understand the structure of all of the offers on the table. It's not just how much you get paid for your company that counts; it's how much you keep. That's why, as the following two options demonstrate, deal structure is critical.

    ### Option 1. Total purchase price: $40MM

    $25.0MM - Cash at closing
    $ 7.5MM - Restricted stock with a lockup period
    $ 5.0MM - Seller note
    $ 2.5MM - Earnout

    ### Option 2. Total purchase price $33MM

    $33.0MM - Cash at closing
    Three-year employment/consulting agreement

    At first glance, Option 1 looks like the way to go. After all, not only does $40 million beat $33 million, but it also comes with bigger bragging rights. But if the acquiring company's stock price plummets and it suspends payment on your note to preserve cash (because its lines of credit are drying up), and internal accounting transfers have caused an operating loss—thus eliminating your earnout since it was tied to profit versus revenue—then Option 2 looks very, very good. Of course, it could go the other way: The acquiring company's stock could appreciate in value (providing tax benefits because gains are taxed at the capital gains rate), and the interest rate on your seller note could exceed what you could earn from an investment in fixed income securities. Your buyer could gladly pay the earnout because the acquisition of your company surpassed its revenue targets, and you could receive a nice stream of monthly income.

Purchase price numbers are the beginning of a buyer's story, not the end. Deal structure, risk, future upside, the buyer's ability to complete the transaction as promised, and your goals and tolerance for risk play significant roles in the choice of the best or right offer.

THE VALUE OF THE MARKET PROCESS

The market process is designed to achieve maximum value for sellers, while limiting disruptions and optimizing the probability of success.

Maximizes Return By Letting The Market Speak

The Founders Advisors' Market Process puts the investment opportunity (your company) in front of the widest range of qualified buyers and presents it in the best possible light. By tightly structuring the Process, we aim to capture every available ounce (or dollar) of financial, synergistic and opportunistic value.

When multiple bidders submit indications of interest (IOIs) simultaneously, we create a bidding environment that drives valuations up—often way up. Of course, multiple offers allow you as a seller to choose the one that fits best, and the auction environment also provides good back-up buyers should the first-choice buyer not be able to consummate the deal. These stalking horses apply the pressure that your preferred suitor may need to close the deal.

If well executed, the process keeps all interested parties marching toward closing at the same cadence. To facilitate that synchronization, we describe every step and deadline involved in a formal letter to interested buyers and regulate the release of information. If some buyers are allowed to move ahead of others, it can be very difficult (if not impossible) to build a competitive auction environment.

Limits Disruptions

Once you enter into the market process, please understand that time is not your friend. My clients hear me repeatedly say, "Time kills deals." In the deal business, speed is your friend and time is your enemy. If your deal slows down, the probability of failure increases dramatically.

Typically, if your M&A team rigorously manages the market process, the process will require 1,500 to 1,700 hours over a period of months from your advisory team alone. To stay on its timeline, your deal team must push the market process and insulate your management team from the distractions of the market process so it can continue to perform well until the transaction closes.

Optimize The Probability Of Success

In any transaction, leverage improves negotiating position, and the sale of a company is no exception. Great preparation and careful execution of a disciplined and highly organized market process give sellers control and leverage. Even if you have only one great buyer (although that buyer doesn't know it), the process allows you to bring leverage to bear and be confident that the buyer makes its best offer.

WHAT CAN GO WRONG?

There are several mistakes that I see far too often during an owner's sale of equity that significantly damage outcomes. Some mistakes are the responsibility of owners who try to "go it alone," but we can blame out-of-their-depth transaction advisors for many of the others.

On the sellers' list of mistakes are those that occur when they are not prepared to complete a transaction, usually because they simply don't understand what it means to be prepared to close a deal or survive due diligence. Some owners don't understand how a well-orchestrated market process protects and maximizes their investments in their companies. Some don't appreciate that when they "save money" by representing themselves in the marketplace, they forfeit any confidentiality and alert everyone (competitors, customers and employees) to their desire to sell. Other owners underestimate the complexity of the sale process or the sophistication and experience of professional buyers and investors. (The professional or institutional buyers make their living doing deals and, with rare exception, are very, very good at it.) Finally, some so want to believe everything a suitor promises that they forget that buyers look out for themselves—not owners.

As Figure 17.8 illustrates, the mistakes that owners or "C-Grade" transaction advisors can make typically fall into four categories.

FIG. 17.8 Common Mistakes In The Market Process

MISTAKE	RESULTS
Failure to Be Process Driven	• Allows buyers to control the sales process • Slows momentum • Sellers lose negotiating leverage. • Erodes value
Failure to Appropriately Position a Company	• Leads to poor preparation and unproductive discussions with potential buyers • Spoils credibility with buyers and other market players • Limits potential deal leverage
Limiting and/or Taking for Granted the Potential Buyer Universe	• Unnecessarily and inappropriately limits the number of prospective buyers • Creates a stale investment thesis built on broad-based assumptions that reduces the likelihood of a premium value
Mismanaging the Advisor/Seller Relationship	• Failure to appreciate all of a seller's emotions and goals produces an outcome that does not accomplish all of the seller's objectives. • Poor communication prevents sellers from making timely and fully educated decisions necessary to ensure a smooth transition.

Avoiding these mistakes is critical because institutional buyers/investors rarely make mistakes! They buy and sell companies/divisions all day every day, and you may do this only once in your career. I mean no disrespect, but you are no match for these seasoned dealmakers. Put an experienced team on your side of the table. There is simply too much value at stake.

Top Four Deal Killers

When deals go wrong and fail to close—even after a great buyer executes a letter of intent—we can usually blame one of four deal killers:

1. **Poor Business Performance.** Nothing is more lethal to a deal than a missed forecast, loss of a major customer or a downward turn in gross margins.

2. **Egos.** Sophisticated buyers rarely do deals with immature sellers, and when deal fatigue sets in, sellers can become frustrated. Some grow increasingly apprehensive about giving up total post-acquisition control and react negatively.

3. **External Factors.** In this category are factors outside of the buyer's and seller's control. For example, imagine how a change in a Google algorithm might cause website traffic to plummet or how a 20 percent one-month decrease in the price of oil might affect the value of an oil field services company.

4. **The Diligence And Pre-Diligence Stories Are Inconsistent.** When buyers uncover negative items that sellers do not disclose early in the discussions (typically due to a lack of appreciation for the value a piece of information has to a buyer rather than a lack of integrity on the seller's part), deals die a quick death.

The Investment Banking Team

Typically, a project team includes four investment banking professionals—an analyst, associate, vice president and managing director—and administrative support personnel. Roles and responsibilities vary among investment banking firms, but here's a summary of the primary roles of the professionals on a Founders Advisors' project team.

Managing Director

- Spearheads transaction marketing efforts
- Leads overall process strategy, management meetings and deal negotiations
- Troubleshoots and acts as a resource to team and clients, as needed
- Typically has 15 to 20+ years of deal-making experience

Vice President (the true Project Manager)

- Manages all parties (i.e., client, prospective buyers, lenders and deal team)
- Oversees associates and gives strategic direction to the underwriting team
- Typically has eight to ten years of transaction experience

Associate

- Leads financial modeling, preparation of marketing materials and buyer research
- Works as the liaison with client's team during data collection and information gathering
- Directs the customization of marketing materials for individual buyers
- Typically has four to eight years of transaction experience

Analyst

- Gathers information for market research and industry analysis
- Assists in the merger, financial and forecast models
- Generates models for valuation metrics
- Provides detailed market, competitive and buyer research
- Maintains CRM/system related to buyer intelligence and conversations
- Documents all calls, meeting summaries and buyer conversations

NOTE: To pursue all available securities deal structures for a company, M&A advisors must be security licensed and under the supervision of a FINRA-regulated broker-dealer. In the U.S., private companies that sell under structures other than asset sales are considered security sales.

A well-run market process uses rationalized models and materials, a masterfully told story and a comprehensive search of the worldwide buyer pool to create a competitive bid environment that ultimately proves the true value of a business. This process gives owners/sellers confidence that they have achieved the best outcome the market has to offer and efficiently closed on the optimum deal with the right partner. The value created by this process is remarkable.

You might not be able to attract investors or buyers if you don't run the structured market process that sophisticated owners use to maximize enterprise value.

RECOMMENDATIONS

1. **Timing is critical when putting your company on the market.**
   - Have you reviewed and analyzed all of the external timing factors?
   - Have you reviewed all of the personal/internal timing factors?
   - Do you know where the M&A market is in its cycle and how that affects your company's valuation?

2. **Realistically assess your readiness, and that of your company, for the demands of a market process.**
   - Are you prepared to provide all of the data buyers will need to complete their diligence, including financial data and sales-pipeline data; customer-level data; documentation of your technology and key processes; and legal data?
   - Is your business running smoothly enough to continue to execute while you and your team work double time to keep up with buyer diligence requests?
   - Are you and your team prepared and stable enough for this emotional roller coaster?

3. **If you are ready to exit and your company has achieved investment-grade status, leverage your investment of time and effort by deploying a confidential market process to maximize the value of your business.**
   - Have you had a market valuation completed for your company?
   - Have you invested time and energy to hire the right investment banking team?

4. **Even if you are not ready to enter the market, you should regularly schedule conversations with investment bankers who have expertise in your industry.**
   Have you created a list of topics to discuss that includes market trends, timing considerations, current valuation drivers and competitive insight?

5. **To survive, prepare early and cultivate the virtue of patience.**

TAKEAWAYS

1. **Buyers know more about dealmaking than you do.**

2. **Begin regular discussions with industry investment banks long before you're ready to embark on a process to sell your company.**

3. **Leverage doesn't just happen.**

   Leverage is created through great preparation and careful execution of a disciplined and highly organized market process. Private equity groups use the process to exit their companies, and they are the most advanced owners on the planet. Why not follow their lead?

4. **The buyer research phase of a market process can drive enormous value by finding that one "best" buyer that has to have your company.**

   Don't leave out international buyers.

5. **Time kills deals.**

6. **If well executed, the market process lets the market speak and assigns the "true value" to your company.**

7. **Purchase price isn't the only measure of the deal.**

8. **Be prepared for diligence.**

   It is worse than you think.

17 Reasons Assessment™

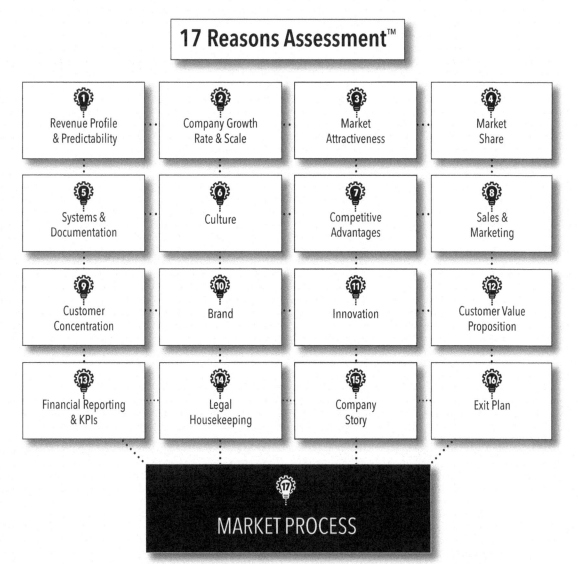

How does *your* company measure up to investment-grade standards?

Designed For Owners:
- Looking for an objective, market-based valuation
- Considering a market process and interested in understanding how investment professionals will view their companies

Purpose:
- Identify specific areas that warrant attention
- Assign a score to each of the 17 Reasons

Takeaway:
A market valuation report and specific recommendations to increase enterprise value

Acknowledgments

I hate being a quitter at anything, and writing a book almost earned me the label. Only innate stubbornness; the encouragement of my wife, dad, friends, clients and colleagues; and a well-timed message from my uncle, Dr. Floyd Oscar Parker, kept me on track. I'm so thankful for their support.

First, I thank my beautiful bride of 31 years, Jamie, and my amazing three daughters, Anne Ellison, Mary Judson and Emma Barksdale. Your patience with my many inconvenient disappearances to write gave me energy to keep working toward my goal. I'm smitten with each of you and cannot tell you how much joy I find in spending time with "my sorority."

To my parents, Paul T. and Elaine (Mimi) Tarence, and my sister, Twyla Tarence Jones: I'm grateful for your constant encouragement and your prayers for me to be a faithful steward. What a blessed man I am to have you three in my corner.

To Epes Robertson, the neighbor who took a chance on the preacher's kid next door: I'm so grateful that you recognized the young man who was hungry to learn, grow and succeed. You put your professional reputation on the line when you convinced IBM to hire me as a college intern. You never stopped believing in me throughout all my ventures, and I can still hear you say, "Go get 'em, Z-Man" as I left for sales calls.

To Roy W. Gilbert Jr., who gathered up six of his best friends and provided the seed funding for my first SaaS company, Virtual Learning Technologies: I'm forever grateful to you for believing in our vision and writing those checks.

To my past partners in that software venture and others—Roy Gilbert III, Alan Ritchie, Kevin Hendrix, Lee Ross, Mary McSpadden, Frank Dixon and David Hobbs: Your steadfast support through the wins and the losses demonstrated your relentless focus, amazing leadership and clear vision.

To my uncles Rex and Beau (Dr. Rex Turner Jr. and Beau Greer): I thank you for making me believe I was a valuable contributor to your businesses. Uncle Rex taught me the incredible power of single-mindedness: to pursue opportunities with dogged determination. He took the time and energy to teach and model for me what it takes to succeed as an entrepreneur. Uncle Beau: You instilled in me the joy and fulfillment of hard work. I remember well the many summers I spent on your farm cleaning fence lines, working in the hayfields and pulling up gourds from acre after acre of soybeans. Today I recognize your well-orchestrated plans to mentor a young man in the "ways he should go."

I'm forever indebted to Kathryn Bolinske, my editor and writing partner. She patiently labored away to organize my multiple streams of consciousness and make them readable. Her editorial help, keen insights, storytelling skills and persistent support got us to the finish line.

Without support from my peers and team at Founders Advisors, I could not have written this book.

- Duane P. Donner II and J. Wesley Legg, my business partners and friends, encouraged me to develop these 17 Reasons and a workshop to share them with business owners. I'm so grateful for our partnership.
- Brad Johnson, Chris Weingartner and Billy Pritchard are the leaders of our technology practice and are exceptional at what they do. Not only did they contribute significantly to this book's content, but they also lived many of the stories with me. I respect them as men, friends and M&A advisors.

· The Founders Advisors' technology practice team—William Short, Matt Stanford and Rebecca Askew—provided insightful guidance, unsparing reviews and candid feedback.

· My colleagues—Mike McCraw, Gene Bazemore, Michael White, John Sinders, Sterling Smith, John Sullivan, Nathan Kelly, Kimberly Boackle, Vaughn McCrary, Jack Houtz, Evan Klisares, Tripp Salem, Katie Burns, Kendrick Vinar, David Szell, Miller Williams, Scott David, Randy Freeman, Hayes Musser, Nick Pope, JP Sloan and Cassie Cole—keep me on my toes and make it a joy to come to work every day.

But the heart of this book comes from the business owners who placed their trust and confidence in my team and me to help them navigate the capital markets, and those in multiple Vistage® and Convene® CEO peer groups who provided invaluable feedback. (Thank you to Frank Day for sponsoring me as a Vistage® speaker.)

No less valuable are those on the other side of the table: the buyers and investors. Without exception, their professionalism and deep understanding of business brought out the best in all of us. The rides we've experienced getting to the closing table have been both fun and memorable, but the relationships are priceless to me.

Finally and always, my gratitude to my Lord and Savior, Jesus Christ. May I be a faithful servant and grow in my desire to live a life worthy of my high calling in You.

Zane Tarence

About The Author

Zane Tarence is an expert in the "business of technology." He is an experienced investment banker, dealmaker and serial technology entrepreneur. He sold his first software company to a publicly traded company in May of 2000 and his second in June of 2007. Ten years later, he sold two additional start-up companies to public companies after acting as the lead investor, hiring CEOs and serving on both boards.

Since 2007 Zane has served as a partner and managing director of the Birmingham-based investment banking firm Founders Advisors, LLC. He holds FINRA Series 24, 63 and 79 licenses. Zane has worked with hundreds of owners to position their growing companies to attract both investors and strategic buyers, and he has orchestrated over 82 transactions, primarily for technology and tech-enabled service businesses.

Zane is a dynamic speaker, dedicated mentor to numerous entrepreneurs and an active investor and board member in lower middle market businesses. He serves on several nonprofit boards, is a husband and is a father to three daughters.

List Of Figures

Footnotes

Introduction

1   You can learn more about The 17 Reasons Assessment™ at *17-reasons.com*.

Reason 1

2   *http://siliconyall.com*

Reason 2

3   GF Data M&A Report, November 2019, page 2

4   EBITDA is an indicator of a company's financial performance.

5   An acquisition is accretive when the price-earnings ratio of the firm making the acquisition is greater than that of the company being purchased. The acquiring firm expects this type of acquisition to increase its own share price.

6   In finance, carried interest, or carry, is a share of the profits that is issued to the general partners of a private equity or hedge fund if the fund performs at or above a designated threshold.

Reason 3

7   Andreessen, Marc. (2007, June 25) *Product Market Fit, EE204: Business Management for Engineers and Computer Scientists, http://web.stanford.edu/class/ee204/ProductMarketFit.html*

8   Andreessen, Marc. (2007, June 25) *Product Market Fit, EE204: Business Management for Engineers and Computer Scientists, http://web.stanford.edu/class/ee204/ProductMarketFit.html*

9   Nascent unproven markets can provide huge upside for the pioneering entrepreneur, but with opportunity comes risk. Pioneers who blaze trails into these markets often get shot while future settlers learn from the pioneers' mistakes and succeed.

10 Hey, fans of *The Lean Startup*: please don't confuse this with the abbreviation for Minimum Viable Product.

Reason 5

11 Kelly, Gary, (2016, May) *The Ultimate Team Sport*, Southwest The Magazine, page 14, *http://issuu. com/southwestmag/docs/may_digital_edition*

12 Kirchmer, Mathias. (2017) *High Performance Through Business Process Management: Strategy Execution in a Digital World*, Third Edition, Springer

13 Gawande, Atul. (2009) *The Checklist Manifesto: How To Get Things Right*, Metropolitan Books

14 Paton, Mike. (2018, August) "Systemizing The Predictable" May Be The Key To Achieving Your Vision, *EOS Worldwide Blog*, August 2018, *https://blog.eosworldwide.com/blog/systemizing-the-predictable-may-be-the-key-to-achieving-your-vision*

15 Ibid.

16 Ibid.

17 My memory serves me well because Gino is quoted as saying something similar in "Systemizing The Predictable" May Be The Key To Achieving Your Vision, EOS Worldwide Blog, August 2018, *https://blog.eosworldwide.com/blog/systemizing-the-predictable-may-be-the-key-to-achieving-your-vision*

18   Elmasry, Talal. (2018, January 31) *Alabama coach Nick Saban explains 'The Process' and where it all started*, Dayton Daily News. *https://www.daytondailynews.com/sports/college/alabama-coach-nick-saban-explains-the-process-and-where-all-started/xNc5RETMHdwaL9PaE42IvN/*

19   *How to know if your business will scale.* (2011, June 1), Fortune. *http://fortune.com/2011/06/01/how-to-know-if-your-business-will-scale/*

Reason 6

20   U.S. Department of Labor as cited by Nixon, W. Barry. (2017, July) *Right Hiring: Best practices for background screening provider selection,* Talent Acquisition Excellence, Vol. 2, Issue 7, p. 22

21   Galbreath, R. (2000) *Employee Turnover hurts small and large organization profitability* [SHRM white paper] as cited by Gusdorf, MBA, SPHR, Myrna L. (2008) *Recruitment and Selection: Hiring the Right Person,* Society for Human Resource Management. *https://cdn.ymaws.com/ise.org.uk/resource/resmgr/files/knowledge_reports/Recruitment_and_Selection_IM.pdf*

22   CareerBuilder. (2018, May 8) *More Than Half of Companies in the Top Ten World Economies Have Been Affected By a Bad Hire, According to CareerBuilder.* http://www.careerbuilder.com/share/aboutus/pressreleasesdetail.aspx?sd=5/8/2013&siteid=cbpr&sc_cmp1=cb_pr757_&id=pr757&ed=12/31/2013

23   Weiss, Donna as cited by Tuggle, Kathryn. (2014, January 17) *The Real Cost of a Bad Hire,* The Street *https://www.thestreet.com/story/12243638/1/the-real-cost-of-a-bad-hire.html*

Reason 7

24   Porter, Michael E. (1985) *Competitive Advantage,* The Free Press, page 3

25   Porter, Michael E. (1985) *Competitive Advantage,* The Free Press, page xxii

26   Porter, Michael E. (1985) *Competitive Advantage,* The Free Press, page 11

27   Berkshire Hathaway 2008 Annual Report, p. 4 *http://www.berkshirehathaway.com/letters/2008ltr.pdf*

28   Berkshire Hathaway 2007 Annual Report, p. 3 *http://www.berkshirehathaway.com/letters/2007ltr.pdf*

29   *http://siliconyall.com*

Reason 8

30   Cespedes, Frank V., and Bova, Tiffani (2015, August 5) *What Salespeople Need to Know About the New B2B Landscape,* Harvard Business Review *https://hbr.org/2015/08/what-salespeople-need-to-know-about-the-new-b2b-landscape*

Reason 9

31   I define "early stage" generally as Year 2 to Year 5: those years during which your company is breaking even or becomes profitable, but before it experiences healthy profits and rapid growth.

32   A product road map is your service or product portfolio. It contains those products/services that your company already offers and its plan for future product development.

Reason 10

33   *The Picture of Dorian Gray,* Chapter 1, 1890

Reason 11

34   Moving the chains refers to a football team's forward progress. Every time the team on offense makes a first down the chains are reset for another 10 yards. Sorry readers, I'm from the South and football metaphors just roll off my tongue.

35 Richard Simmons argues that Sam Walton's intellectual humility separated Walmart from its equally successful competitors. Simmons III, Richard E. (2017, August 3) *The Walmart Story*. The Center For Executive Leadership. *https://thecenterbham.org/2018/08/03/the-walmart-story/?mc_cid=035e228b2f&mc_eid=1bb8c02161*

36 Catmull, Edward. (2014, March) *Inside the Pixar Braintrust,* Fast Company *https://www.fastcompany.com/3027135/inside-the-pixar-braintrust*

37 As quoted in *https://www.complex.com/pop-culture/2012/10/steve-jobs-quotes/its-about-the-people-you-have*

38 Personal protective equipment (PPE) is the protective equipment workers wear to minimize exposure to hazards that cause serious workplace injuries and illnesses. Examples include gloves, safety glasses and shoes, earplugs, muffs, hard hats, respirators, coveralls, vests, and full body suits.

39 Singh, Shelley. (2010, June 30) *Innovation is about delivering real-world value to customers: Steve Ballmer,* The Times of India. *https://economictimes.indiatimes.com/opinion/interviews/innovation-is-about-delivering-real-world-value-to-customers-steve-ballmer/articleshow/6108420.cms*

40 *http://www.wipo.int/about-ip/en/*

Reason 12

41 How the Net Promoter Score[*] Relates to Growth *http://netpromotersystem.com/about/how-is-nps-related-to-growth.aspx*

Reason 15

42 The Provincial Letters, Letter 16, 1657

43 Covey, Stephen R., First Things First, *The Big Rocks of Life. http://www.appleseeds.org/Big-Rocks_Covey.htm*

Reason 16

44 According to Exit Planning Institute as quoted in *Study Shows Why Many Business Owner Can't Sell When They Want To,* (2017, February 5) Forbes *https://www.forbes.com/sites/sageworks/2017/02/05/these-8-stats-show-why-many-business-owners-cant-sell-when-they-want-to/#1444c7cb44bd*

Notes

Notes

Made in USA - North Chelmsford, MA
1164622_9781734673203
08.19.2021 1150